Portrait of
OXFORDSHIRE

by

Christine G. Bloxham

ILLUSTRATED
AND WITH MAP

ROBERT HALE · LONDON

ISBN 0 7091 9448 X

Robert Hale Limited
Clerkenwell House
Clerkenwell Green
London EC1R 0HT

Photoset by Rowland Phototypesetting Limited
Printed in Great Britain by
St Edmundsbury Press, Bury St Edmunds, Suffolk
Bound by Weatherby Bookbinding Limited

Contents

Illustrations

Credits

Illustrations in this book are reproduced by permission of the following: Ashmolean Museum, 5, 6, 7; Blinkhorns, 39; Christine Bloxham, 8, 18, 38; John Bloxham, 14, 15, 16, 37, 42; Christopher Burnell Photography, Wallingford, 41; Andrew Esson, 4, 10, 12, 20, 22, 24, 26, 28, 29, 30, 31, 36, 43, 44, 45, 46; Jon Hall, 40; Oxfordshire County Museum, 1, 2, 9, 11, 13, 17, 19, 21, 25; Oxfordshire County Museum (photo John Steane), 3, 23, 27, 32, 33, 34, 35; His Grace the Duke of Marlborough, 47.

Dedication

To my parents,
Peggy and John Bloxham

Acknowledgements

This book is the product of ten years' work in Oxfordshire, during which time I have consulted many books and been helped by many people. Above all I must thank my mother, who has patiently deciphered and typed my manuscript, in addition to giving moral support, and my father, who has criticized chapters and taken photographs. My colleague James Bond has given me much help and advice, and other colleagues from the Oxfordshire County Museum, John Campbell, Daniel Chadwick, Christopher Page and John Steane, have also read chapters, saving me from foolish mistakes. I would also like to thank Norman Blanks, Jeffrey and Julie Bloxham, Dianne Coles, Jeremy Gibson, Diana Keay, Roger Jacobi, David Miles, Crispin Paine, Mary Prior, Mary Tame, Martin Welch, the Ministry of Agriculture, Fisheries and Food, and not least my agent, Christine Green. Many of the photographs have been specially taken by Andrew Esson. The book would not have been written at all without the suggestion from Lydia Lenthall of Blenheim Books, Woodstock.

Introduction

Portraying the character of a county is as difficult as describing a personality—everyone perceives different facets and lays emphasis on different aspects. This book gives my personal view of Oxfordshire, a county which has been my home and my place of work for a decade.

Oxfordshire is a fascinating county. It may not have the rugged beauty of the Yorkshire Dales and Moors or the rocky cliffs of Cornwall, but it radiates its own quiet beauty and has a wide variety of scenery—driving along the M40 from London, there is a marvellous panoramic view from the top of the hill over the low-lying countryside of the Thames Valley, with Didcot power-station and the city of Oxford in the background. The River Thames, meandering through the countryside, creates many beautiful vistas, contrasting with the dry heathland areas around Stoke Row. The upland areas of the wooded Chiltern Hills contrast with the bleaker wind-swept Downs of the Vale. West Oxfordshire is on the fringes of the Cotswold Hills, with grey stone villages, while the hummocky hills of north Oxfordshire are distinguished by their red ironstone and many traces of ridge and furrow, indicating earlier farming-methods. Despite the introduction of modern industries such as British Leyland, Oxfordshire is a rich rural county, relying heavily on its agriculture.

The differences between its regions give little homogeneity. Banbury has a long-standing rivalry with Oxford; Henley has far stronger links with Reading and London, and the people of west Oxfordshire tend to shop in Cheltenham. However, the most distinct area is without doubt the Vale, which has very much its own identity and appearance, and even its own dialect, retaining more loyalty to its old county, Berkshire, from which it was snatched against its will during the local government re-organization of 1974.

The local government changes which brought the Vale into Oxfordshire are merely the latest in a long process, although they can claim to be the most drastic. The county of Oxfordshire, together with its neighbours, was first laid out by King Edward the Elder in AD 911–12. Most changes have merely affected the boundary areas between counties—Shenington and Widford on the north and western fringes have been acquired from Gloucestershire; Mollington was in Warwickshire until 1895; Grimsbury, now a suburb of Banbury, was a haven for malefactors fleeing from the Banbury constables who had no jurisdiction in Northamptonshire, until 1889, when it joined Oxfordshire; Horton-cum-Studley, Caversfield, Thomley, Towersey, Draycott and Tythrop have been transferred from Buckinghamshire at varying times since the early nineteenth century, while in return Buckinghamshire has gained Kingsey, Stokenchurch, Cadmore End and Lewknor Uphill. Other logical changes have included the loss of outlying islands of Oxfordshire in the heart of Buckinghamshire such as Lillingstone Lovell and Boycott in 1805. Caversham became part of Berkshire in 1911.

It is not only in its boundaries that Oxfordshire has changed —one of the themes of this portrait is the development and change of the county. No book of this size can hope to cover every nook and cranny, and many beautiful and delightful places have been sorely neglected, but I hope that people will be stimulated to discover more about this kaleidoscopic county.

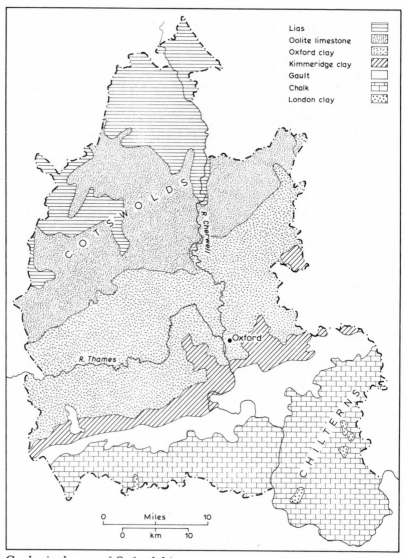

Legend:
- Lias
- Oolite limestone
- Oxford clay
- Kimmeridge clay
- Gault
- Chalk
- London clay

Geological map of Oxfordshire

1

Geology, Archaeological Sites and their Folklore

The rolling landscape of Oxfordshire which we see today is a complex collage, formed over many million years, under many different climatic conditions. It is still evolving and eroding, the surface-changes today being hastened by the action of man who builds towns and villages, canals, roads and railways, clearing woodland, farming, mining and quarrying.

It is meaningless to talk about the geographical unit of 'Oxfordshire' in geological terms, as it has formed part of islands, continents and the sea bed in the different geological eras, all of which have contributed to its structure and appearance. Much research is needed on the deep rock structure, to reveal its history, but deep bore-holes have revealed rocks up to 440 million years old, including coal-measures, laid down when the land was roughly on the latitude of the equator.

The oldest surface rocks in the county are Jurassic (155–136 million years old), laid down during a time when the area was alternately deep and shallow sea. The Corallian, a sub-division of the Jurassic, is represented by fossil remains of a massive coral reef around Cumnor. The Jurassic and Cretaceous (136–64 million years old) rocks have eroded so that they outcrop in diagonal stripes stretching across the county from north-east to south-west. These alternate hard and soft rocks form a tilted plateau creating the structure of hills and valleys, the hard rocks exposed to form steep north-west facing ridges and escarpments, where the soft rock has been eroded away.

The Middle Lias rock of north Oxfordshire contains iron ore. The Clypeus Grit, part of the Inferior Oolite rubble limestone which occurs further south is much used for hardcore, while the Great Oolite limestone, colloquially known as 'Cotswold Stone', is good for building. The fissile Stonesfield Slate, which is easily split by frost action to form roofing-slates, was formed when the area was a lagoon, with islands or lands nearby, as revealed by fossils of insects such as dragonflies found embedded in the slates. William Smith, the canal-builder and geologist from Churchill, who is regarded as the father of British geology, named the Forest Marble (which is used for stone-flagged floors) after Wychwood Forest, the area in which he found it. Corn-brash, a rubble-like limestone, forms the eastern edge of the Cotswold Hills, with calcite throughout formed by water passing through the rocks. Oxford Clay, which underlies the Thames Valley above Oxford, was once extensively used for brick-making, as at Wolvercote, but none is now exposed. In places the clay bed is up to 400 feet deep, reflecting the length of time the area was sea-covered. Corallian deposits outcrop from the Swindon area towards Wytham, Cumnor, Headington and the Oxford heights. Corallian sands are extracted for commercial use, but the stone, once in great demand as building stone, is now scarcely quarried.

Kimmeridge Clay, laid down under deep water, forms a band across the centre of the county, most of which is now covered by river gravels. The hills around Wheatley are capped with Portland limestone. Cretaceous Wealden Clay is found only in the south-east of the county—Shotover Hill is capped by such sand and gravel deposits. The Lower Greensand, deceptively named as it is seldom green, is called 'Sponge Gravel' in the Faringdon area because of the number of fossils, particularly those of sponges found in it. Gault Clays too are now largely gravel-covered. The Upper Greensand of the Vale of White Horse provides fertile land for arable and fruit farming. The Downs and Chiltern Hills are of chalk, once laid down under water. The Upper Chalk contains bands of flint, used for building and, from Palaeolithic times, for flint tools. Chalk, being a pure limestone, was burned to make lime and is now quarried for cement around Chinnor. The Tertiary Eocene Period is represented only by the Reading Beds and London Clay in south Oxfordshire, scattered areas of clay mixed with pebbles found on the dip slopes of the chalk hills.

More recently the landscape has been affected by the Quaternary Ice Age, of which we may be a part, the warm climate of today being merely the latest interglacial period. The Quaternary started 1,800,000 years ago, the last ten thousand years being termed 'Holocene'. The climatic changes between the glacials and interglacials was enormous, supporting very different flora and fauna. Fossilized bones of elephant and hippopotamus have been found locally, dating from the warm interglacials, plus those of fallow and giant deer, hyena and rhinoceros. During the last cold glaciation these were replaced by animals better adapted to the cold, such as the woolly rhinoceros, mammoth, horse, artic fox and cave lion.

Only the Anglian Ice Age reached Oxfordshire, flowing down to Cumnor and Wytham. Although the amount of ice was not large, it has left distinct traces behind it, such as the Boulder Clay in the Evenlode Valley near Kingham, a gorge at Stonesfield, abandoned river-meanders between Asthall and Swinbrook and glacial erratic stones from East Anglia, the Midlands, Devon and Cornwall. The retreating ice left unbedded Glacial Drift consisting of clay, sands and gravels, with small areas of acidic soil. Over the millennia natural forces such as rain, wind and frost have eroded the rocks, creating gravels which formed terraces, particularly over the clays of the Thames Valley. These gravels are being extensively extracted commercially, in the process destroying many important archaeological sites, so it is fortunate that the companies involved realize the implications of the extraction and give money towards exploratory archaeology under the auspices of the Oxfordshire Archaeological Unit, to investigate and survey sites before they are destroyed.

Small groups of Palaeolithic hunter-gatherers first reached Britain during the Ice Age, about 400,000 years ago, living on meat, berries, fruit and roots and following the movement of the herds of animals, such as deer. A small number of their scattered stone tools survive, such as hand-axes, found principally in the Thames Valley gravels, together with the bones of the animals they hunted. The first visitors to the area have been termed 'Clactonians' after the Essex site where their tools were first identified. Their flint chopping-tools and flakes have been discovered in river gravels near Henley. They were followed by the 'Acheulians', whose culture was widespread in southern Europe, the Middle East and India, identified by their oval, pear-shaped or pointed stone hand-axes. Their flint-knapping was more elaborate, and they produced beautiful, extremely sharp tools for skinning their prey. Examples have been found in the Ice Age layers of a brick-pit at Wolvercote, at Radley,

Cholsey, Wallingford and South Hinksey and in south Oxford-shire from Mapledurham.

Traces of Upper Palaeolithic man in Oxfordshire are almost non-existent, apart from a very rolled flint spearhead dredged up from Osney Lock. These men were *homo sapiens*, whose culture began thirty to forty thousand years ago, and they would have hunted prey such as mammoths, woolly rhinoceros and cave lion.

As the climate became warmer, such animals became extinct, and the post-glacial tundra became increasingly forested, inter-spersed with marshes, lakes and fens. Early woodland was light birch and pine; then hazel and alder became established, and gradually after 7,000 BC the forests became dense, with oak, ash, beach, lime, elm and hornbeam. The changed environment brought red and roe deer, wild ox and pig, which were more elusive, so Mesolithic man evolved new hunting techniques, making lances, spears and bows and arrows, using wooden or bone hafts with points and barbs of 'microliths', small pieces of delicately chipped geometric flints. Flint axes and adzes were manufactured for felling trees and working wood, and these, plus fire, were used to clear areas within the forest, perhaps for settlements or for herding the deer during hunting. Evidence of Mesolithic man has been found throughout the county, but particularly in south Oxfordshire between Dorchester and Henley and among the Chiltern Hills, where heavier tools found suggest woodworking. Evidence of several occupations by Mesolithic hunter groups was found beneath the Neolithic long barrow at Ascott-under-Wychwood, when the environment consisted of a pine and birch forest. Most other finds are small surface scatters of flint tools. Britain was in the early period the further limit of the European continent exploited by the hunters, some of whom remained after the sea level rose in about 6,000 BC to make Britain an island.

Neolithic people, the first farmers, made a significant impact on the landscape, coming to Britain in about 4,000 BC, by boat, bringing their seed-corn and their livestock with them. They cleared and burned areas of forest for their fields, planted their primitive cereals, emmer, eincorn and barley, and tended their livestock, sheep and cattle. Their mattocks and primitive ploughs were suitable only for light soils such as the gravels of the Thames Valley, which were extensively occupied. They had not discovered how to make metal, and their sickles were of flint, attached to wooden or bone handles. Grain may have been parched before being stored in pits to prevent it from going mouldy—traces of what may have been a parching-oven have been found at Stanton Harcourt, and storage pits abounded in the Neolithic settlement at Sutton Courtenay. The animals, in addition to providing food, supplied wool and skins which could be cured to make leather. Their manure fertilized the fields, and their grazing prevented the land from reverting to forest. Quantities of animal bones have been found in the causewayed camps or enclosures the Neolithic farmers built, such as that excavated at Abingdon.

In addition to their farming, Neolithic men hunted, and their exquisite, finely chipped flint leaf-shaped and transverse arrowheads have been found in large numbers in the Vale and the Chilterns and on the upland area between Woodstock and Churchill.

Because they led more settled lives, Neolithic people were able to develop a more complex society, acquiring new techniques. They introduced the use of pottery for cooking and storage, developing regional styles such as the crude Abingdon Ware found at the Abingdon causewayed enclosure. Later Neolithic pottery, c.2,500–200 BC, is decorated with fingernail marks, bird bones and twisted cord. Other wares known as 'Grooved Ware' may have been influenced by the pattern of woven baskets.

The best evidence for trade comes from polished stone axes. Through 'sectioning' Neolithic axes, to remove minute portions for analysis, it has been discovered that the stone came from axe factories at Great Langdale in Cumbria, Graig Lwyd in North Wales, Cornwall and Northern Ireland.

The increasing sophistication is shown by their funeral customs and religious monuments. Neolithic long barrows, usually found on high ground, are still important features of the landscape, although many have been robbed and the stone re-used over the centuries. Large chambered tombs, such as those at Wayland's Smithy in the Vale and Ascott-under-Wychwood, were used for collective burials over a long period of time. It has been estimated that one could build a parish church from the stone used in the construction of a single long barrow and that five hundred man-hours would be required to quarry the stone, shape it and construct the chambers, which were then covered with a turf mound. The Oxfordshire County Museum's excavation of the long barrow at Ascott-under-Wychwood, a portion of which has now been reconstructed in the museum, revealed much about the people—fifty or so bodies were buried in the low stone-lined chambers, with an age ranging from under a year to fifty years. The majority of adults died in their twenties; they were mainly between 5 feet 4 inches and 5 feet 6 inches in height, and the bones revealed diseases such as spina bifida. One unfortunate woman was born with spina bifida, had a very severe throat infection which dislocated her neck and died after a flint arrowhead pierced her vertebra—the offending arrowhead, still embedded in the vertebra, forms part of the museum display.

Many archaeological sites have become the focus of folklore, as later civilizations attempted to explain the strange monuments left by their predecessors. Wayland's Smithy is an excellent example of this. It began as a small earthen long barrow constructed over a timber burial chamber containing about fourteen bodies laid out on sarsen stones, with a ditch and kerb of upright stones round it. Later generations in the Neolithic period covered this with a larger trapezoid barrow, again ditched and kerbed, with three chambers approached by a passageway, built of massive stones, in which eight people, including a child, were buried. A Saxon boundary charter dated AD 955 calls the site 'Welandes Smidthan'. Wayland is a mythical blacksmith who was, according to Anglo-Saxon tradition, the son of the sailor hero Wade and a mermaid, and married a Valkyrie, eventually going to live with the immortals, making impenetrable armour for the gods. The sagas noted mysteriously that his bones were never laid in any earthly grave. The legend of the Smithy on the Downs was first written down by Francis Wise, under keeper of the Bodleian Library in 1738: "At this place lived formerly an invisible Smith; and if a traveller's horse had lost a shoe upon the road, he had no more to do than to bring the horse to this place, with a piece of money, and leaving both there for some time, he might come again and find the money gone, but the horse new shod."[1] The discovery of two iron bars, originally thought to be Iron Age currency bars, seemed to lend a little weight to this legend, but these have subsequently been identified as eighteenth-century door-hinges!

Until about 1940 there was a standing stone at 'Snivelling Corner', Ashbury, said to have been hurled by the angry smith at his assistant Flibbertigibbet who had idled his time away bird's-nesting when sent to get some nails which Wayland needed urgently. A golden coffin is said to be buried on the Ridgeway somewhere between Wayland's Smithy and the Uffington White Horse.

Many long barrows have disappeared, leaving perhaps a single standing stone, such as the Hoar Stone at Enstone, which gave its name to the village. This stone is said to go down to the brook to drink on Midsummer Eve and is said to resemble a man mounted on horseback, because a squire of Ditchley, out riding with his dog, was turned to stone by a local witch, or alternatively to have been erected in memory of a general named Hoar who was killed during the Civil War, or to be the 'War Stone' marking the site of a battle.

A single stone at Spelsbury is called 'The Hawk Stone'—the slit in its top is attributed to the friction of a chain attached to it when witches were chained up and burned. As with so many of these legends, there is no evidence to support them. Thor's Stone at Taston was said to be so wicked that a cross had to be erected nearby to counteract its evil power.

We know little about Neolithic religion, but there are a number of ritual sites in Oxfordshire, several of the *cursus* type, consisting of long parallel ditches running in a straight line. Some have been discovered through aerial photography, particularly in the south and west at Dorchester, Abingdon, Crowmarsh, North Stoke, Drayton, Buscot and Clanfield. The purpose of these ditches is a mystery. 'Henge' monuments with a circular ditch and bank, some of which originally contained timber uprights, were begun in the Neolithic period and extended during the Bronze Age. Several have been found at Dorchester-on-Thames, which has been an important religious centre from a very early date.

The Rollright Stones have captured the imagination of countless generations, acquiring more folklore than any other site in Britain. They consist of the 'Whispering Knights', a Neolithic long barrow which has lost its earth mound, the outlying 'King Stone' (which may have been used as a marker, being clearly visible against the horizon) and the stone circle itself. The circle originated in the late Neolithic period, owing its present form to

the Beaker People who emigrated to Britain around 2,500 BC
and adopted Neolithic religious sites, aggrandizing them by
adding standing stones. According to legend, a certain king (in
one version a Danish general fighting the Saxons) was on his
way into battle with his army when he encountered the local
witch—sometimes called Mother Shipton—and asked her what
his fate would be in the coming affray. She replied:

> "Seven long strides thou shalt take, and
> If Long Compton thou canst see,
> King of England shalt thou be."

The King was jubilant on hearing this prediction, as he was
near the top of the hill and confident that he would be able to see
over it after taking seven strides. At the seventh stride, to his
horror a long mound appeared before him, obscuring his view,
and he heard the witch cackling with glee:

> "As Long Compton thou canst not see,
> King of England thou shalt not be.
> Rise up, stick, and stand still, stone,
> For King of England thou shalt be none.
> Thou and thy men hoar stones shall be,
> And I myself an eldern tree."[2]

True to her word, the witch turned the King and his men to
stone—the King was left standing alone at the top of the hill, the
Whispering Knights being a group of dissidents plotting
against him, and the stone circle his army. The army is said to
be under a spell which will, when the country is in dire need, be
broken and the men restored to flesh and blood, and the King
will at last achieve his ambition to rule England.

A legend which seems to apply to every stone circle, not least
to the Rollright Stones, is that one cannot count the number of
stones—one man, a baker, tried to disprove this legend by plac-
ing a loaf on each stone as he counted it, but either he did not
have enough loaves or they were mysteriously spirited away,
perhaps by the fairies, who were regularly seen near the stones
until the early twentieth century. Anyone who succeeds in
counting the same number of stones three times will have his
wish granted.

Any attempt to move one of the stones was unlucky and even

dangerous—two men were killed carting two stones down the hill on a wagon drawn by four horses, and when the farmer decided that the stones had caused this ill-luck and should be returned to their rightful places, it took only one horse to haul them back.

The site has been connected with rituals and ceremonies. On Midsummer Eve people stood round in a circle partaking of cakes and ale, the eldern tree would be cut, allegedly bleeding real blood, and the King Stone would bow his head. The stones were thought to bring fertility if a woman visited them at midnight and pressed the tips of her breasts against them. A dowser who visited the site recently felt a distinct change in the atmosphere after dark which made her light-headed and made the thread of her pendulum so taut and stiff that it stood up on its own. The stones are now very eroded, the King Stone in particular, because pieces were chipped off; they were sold for as much as £1 each at Faringdon Fair to bring luck and were greatly prized by drovers and soldiers.

Stones from the circle at Stanton Harcourt were removed, apparently without harming those who moved them, to make an airfield during the Second World War. They were known as 'The Devil's Quoits', because it is said the Devil was caught playing quoits on a Sunday and, on being told it was wrong, threw his three quoits in his fury, and they became the stone circle.

The Bronze Age saw many developments and changes: perhaps the most important was the use of metal for the first time in Britain. Bronze was valuable, so flint continued to be used for barbed and tanged arrowheads, scrapers, knives and sickles. Weapons of war—swords and spearheads—were made of bronze, as were axes and ornaments. Bronze was made from a mixture of copper from Ireland, Wales and Scotland and tin from Cornwall. Travelling smiths collected old scrap and melted it down to make new items, and hoards of scrap which belonged to such smiths have been found in Oxford. Because the sources of metal were so widespread, trade both within Britain and with the Continent increased, and early routeways such as the Ridgeway became increasingly important.

In Bronze Age society for the first time we find traces of important chieftains such as those whose rich burials have been found at Stanton Harcourt and Radley in the wealthy Wessex province. Instead of communal burials in long barrows, there were single inhumation or cremation burials in round barrows, often accompanied by grave-goods such as beakers and weapons. A large number of the ring ditches in the upper Thames Valley surround burials. Fieldwork has revealed many previously unknown barrows, particularly around the 'Lambourn Seven Barrows'—the mystical number seven is very misleading, as there are at least forty-six barrows, with another scattered group at nearby Nutwood Down. The Lambourn valley was obviously focusing a sacrosanct area with its linear barrow cemetery on Rams Hill with its Bronze Age hill-top settlement site, a pallisaded enclosure housing timber buildings and pits, and an extensive field system. The enclosure was altered in the late Bronze Age, and a ritual dog-burial, a rare instance of dogs during this period, dates from this phase. The enclosure does not appear to have been occupied at that time and may have acted as a gathering-point for men and their livestock. Other groups of barrows have been found near the Bronze Age ceremonial complex of the Big Rings at Dorchester and around the Devil's Quoits at Stanton Harcourt. The ring ditches at Brighthampton near Standlake have been almost ploughed out, but when the corn is young, they are distinguished by dark crop-marks, which the local inhabitants have described as 'fairy rings'.

As the climate gradually worsened, woodland again encroached, and in about 1400 BC Bronze Age society changed—the immensely powerful lord appeared, although the warrior class remained important.

Despite all this archaeological information, we know considerably less about life in the Bronze Age than about the Iron Age people who invaded England in about 500 BC. Their society was based on tribal patterns and the use of a new metal—iron, which was stronger and more adaptable than bronze. The hill forts set on the crests of hills serve as a tangible reminder of their warlike nature, although the large number is misleading, as they were not all in use at the same time. In periods of political instability and danger the local communities and their livestock could take refuge inside them. Many date from the first century BC when the upper Thames became the frontier between the strong Belgic Dobunni and Catuvellauni tribes. A series of hill forts straddles the Ridgeway: Alfred's Castle (Ashbury) is an irregular hexagonal shape and has a single ditch and rampart reinforced with sarsen stone. Ram's Hill (Kingston Lisle) was also univallate, but its use as a hill fort was short-lived, and its defensive role may have been taken over by Uffington, which is actually built astride a boundary ditch. Segsbury Camp (Letcombe Regis), a large D-shaped enclosure, has settlements clustered around it—pottery found there suggests it was occupied in the fourth century BC. Blewbury Hill (Blewbury) was fortified in about 400 BC to dominate the area overlooking the Goring Gap and the Downs. Four complete horse-burials and fragments of others were found in the entrance passage, perhaps the remains of ritual sacrifices. The camp was abandoned, possibly after a fire, in the mid-first century AD.

A little to the north of the Ridgeway, in Charney Bassett parish, is Cherbury Camp—the only multivallate hill fort in the county—situated in an easily defensible position bounded by two brooks and marshland. Other hill forts in south Oxfordshire are Bozedown at Whitchurch and Wittenham Clumps, also known as 'Sinodun Hills', and the double rampart of the Dyke Hills, both near Dorchester, which defended the Iron Age town of 46 hectares established in the first century BC, defended on the other three sides by rivers. The Vale hill forts are accompanied by extensive field systems—this may have applied to the other hill forts, but the evidence has not been preserved. The most prominent boundaries are those known as 'Grim's Ditches', or 'the Devil's Ditch', generally thought to be Iron Age ditches enclosing pastureland from marauders. One stretches right along the top of the Downs—the section near Blewbury was marked on a Saxon charter as 'Dragon's Ridge', and legend says that the Devil ploughed it during a single night, two barrows in the vicinity of the ditch being his plough-scrapings, and a small mound the clod he hurled at his imp as a punishment for driving the plough crooked. More areas of Grim's Ditch, apparently dug in the first century BC by the Catuvellauni as they moved westwards, are found in the Blenheim, Glympton, Kiddington and Charlbury area.

Further hill forts are found in west and north Oxfordshire—Chastleton and Lyneham hill forts appear to have been used sporadically from the early Iron Age, perhaps as cattle-ranches. Ploughing has destroyed much of Madmarston, near Swalcliffe, which was occupied again by farmers in the fourth century AD, after a lengthy desertion. Another hill fort is found at Tad-marton Heath.

The warlike nature of Iron Age people is also shown by finds of weapons, such as swords, and horse-equipment, exemplified by a hoard of metalwork found at Hagbourne Hill, which included horse-bits and chariot-fittings. Finds of horse skeletons at Blew-burton and at Ashville near Abingdon suggest their special significance, but little is known of Iron Age religion. Isolated burials have been found at Cassington, Stanton Harcourt and Standlake, and a few cremations are known.

Iron Age settlements at first occupied much the same areas as their predecessors, but as the population increased they were forced on to less easily cultivated soils, such as the area around Farmoor, which flooded regularly, being suitable only for summer grazing. Extensive settlement took place in the Wind-rush and Evenlode Valleys and in the vicinity of Dorchester. The people lived in round houses, sometimes built in groups, such as the group of eighteen of varying dates at Ashville. The community was self-sufficient in food, obtaining meat from sheep, their most important livestock, cattle, pigs and goats, growing corn, peas and beans, making their own beer, cheese and bread.

Finds from villages like Ashville of spindle-whorls, clay loom-weights and bone weaving-combs indicate spinning and weav-ing, and other crafts including leatherworking, bronze- and iron-smelting and pottery. Four or five families lived there, excavations indicating that their most important crops were barley and spelt, supplemented by two varieties of wheat—emmer and club-wheat. The fields attached to the settlement were small regular plots covering an area of 80–100 acres. An iron reaping-hook has been found, and threshed grain was stored in pits, while seed-corn was kept in granaries.

The life in the countryside was not disrupted by the Roman invasion in AD 43, which after the initial arrival of the legions under Claudius was a largely political one. The Dobunni and Catuvellauni tribes who controlled the area from Corinium (Cirencester) and Verulamium (St Albans) rapidly accepted their new overlords. The Romans imposed their more ordered civilization, building roads (Akeman Street connecting London, Verulamium and Corinium; another road from Silchester to Towcester, together with a network of smaller roads) and setting up military posts beside them—Alchester and Dorchester, the only two Roman towns in Oxfordshire, began in this way. The remains of Alchester are situated south of Bicester, at the junction of Akeman Street and the Silchester-Dorchester Road. It was founded shortly after the Roman Conquest, possibly as a fort. As it lies on low ground which floods frequently, the level was raised towards the end of the first century, and the stone defensive walls with corner towers were constructed enclosing an area of 10.5 hectares. It was laid out internally in the Roman fashion on a grid system, with metalled streets. Most of the buildings were small rectangular structures with at least one larger porticoed building which possibly served a public function. The walls enclosed only part of the settlement, which covered approximately 43 hectares. The town did not survive the Saxon invasion—little remains above ground as the local inhabitants used it for generations as a stone-quarry.

Dorchester, unlike Alchester, had been the centre of an important area before the arrival of the Romans, with Neolithic and Bronze Age ceremonial structures and the Iron Age hill fort of Sinodun Hill. A Roman fort appears to have been established shortly after the conquest, and during the first and second centuries AD the settlement extended outside the walled area towards Dyke Hills promontory fort. The early earth-bank was extended and strengthened with a stone wall in the third century, and the ditch re-cut during the fourth century. The present town layout hides the Roman grid system, portions of which have been discovered during excavations, which have also revealed first- and second-century timber buildings, some decorated with painted wall-plaster.

The most spectacular find, now alas lost, was that of an altar, discovered in 1731, which had been erected in the late second or early third century by a tax-gatherer, or 'beneficarius consularis', by the name of Marcus Varius Severus, inscribed: "I[ovi] O[ptimus] M[aximo] et Numinib[us] Aug[ustis] M[arcus] Var[ius] Severus B[eneficarius] Co[nsulari]s Aram Cum Cancellis d[e] S[uo] P[osuit]."

Marcus had at his own expense given the altar and railings to Jupiter Optimus Maximus and the deity of the Emperor. This is indicative of Dorchester's importance as a regional centre, which is corroborated by the relatively large amount of Theodosian coinage which may reflect the payment of local Roman troops from here. The town was still occupied in the fifth century, and the presence of German mercenaries and their families is postulated by early pagan Saxon burials with late-Roman fittings. It remained an important centre under the Saxons.

Although Alchester and Dorchester were the only defended towns, there are a number of important settlements in the county—Swalcliffe Lea, alongside the Roman road known as 'Salt Way', was larger in size than either town, covering 50 acres, with extensive buildings, and the site of a possible furnace for extracting iron from the local ironstone. Other Roman settlements were established at Bloxham Grove, Chesterton and Oxford, and there was a group in West Oxfordshire at Yelford, Stanton Harcourt, Eynsham, Cassington, Yarnton, Wilcote, Asthall and Stonesfield and in the Vale at Abingdon, Wantage, Little and Long Wittenham and Wallingford. There are remains of a number of wealthy villas, some of which perhaps served as country houses for the upper classes from Corinium. The mosaic pavements of North Leigh were executed by Corinium paviours. Some of the grandest villas are at Fawler, Stonesfield and North Leigh. The latter is in the custody of the Department of the Environment and is open to the public. It is situated near Akeman Street, on the bank of the River Evenlode, on the site of a Belgic farm. The earliest Roman building, a modest farmhouse with separate bath-house, was erected around the late first century AD. The buildings were extended gradually until they formed, in the fourth century, a complex courtyard house with underfloor heating and elaborate tessellated pavements and painted wall-plaster, probably belonging to a member of the British governing class. The villa at Ditchley was on a more modest scale, yet it had slave-quarters; the size of its granary suggests that 1,000 acres of land attached to it were under plough, and a circular threshing-floor indicates the use of oxen. A black and white mosaic was found in the Woolstone villa in the Vale.

In some areas Iron Age settlements continued into the Roman era, as at Barton Court near Abingdon and at East Challow. An enclosed settlement at Lowbury Hill, Aston Upthorpe appears to have been walled in about AD 200. The site was occupied in the Iron Age, the Roman buildings being wooden structures with tiled roofs variously interpreted as a farm or a temple.

Many smaller villas and farmsteads existed throughout the county, and excavations such as those at Wigginton and Shakenoak are revealing more about Roman life. It has proved more difficult to reconstruct Roman field systems, but farming was evidently extensive on the gravels. The fertile north and west of the county—the Redlands—were ideal for large scale crop-growing, whereas, when re-occupied, the Farmoor area was evidently used for pastoral grazing.

The new road system encouraged trade and industry, particularly the flourishing Roman pottery industry. Thirty or so kiln sites are known, on the Oxford clays and along Akeman Street. Excavation of those on the site of the Churchill Hospital, Headington, have revealed workshops, pot-drying ovens, kilns and pottery tips. One kiln has been reconstructed in the Museum of Oxford, and another in the County Museum at Woodstock. Roman pottery was made in Oxfordshire from the late first century AD, and the kilns at Headington began their operations towards the end of the third century, producing more ambitious products such as *mortaria* (vessels with gritted bases for grinding food), flagons, bowls and copies of Samian forms. At the end of the third century the potters branched out in new directions to produce parchment ware, white and colour-coated wares and new types of *mortaria*. The decline in imports of Samian ware in the third century encouraged the popularity of such Oxford wares. The rapid expansion of the industry suggests some external influence such as the immigration of potters from the Rhineland, perhaps brought over by a far-sighted *entrepreneur*. Local products were extensively traded throughout Britain.

The Romans worshipped the spirit of the Emperor and a panoply of gods headed by Jupiter, Juno and Minerva, and in Britain they took over the native gods. Two shrines have been excavated locally—that at Frilford began as a small henge-shaped Iron Age shrine, and the Romans subsequently erected a round stone building and a double-square temple. The Roman temple at Woodeaton, a small square building in a rectangular walled enclosure, took over an Iron Age site. Excavations revealed a number of votive offerings. Romans both buried and cremated their dead—the latter being the earlier practice. A conical Roman barrow exists at Kingston Lisle, but this is unusual. A large cemetery containing up to seven hundred graves has been partially excavated at Queensford Mill near Dorchester where the townspeople were buried.

Roman rule came to an end in the late fourth century when, despite the Saxon raids, the Roman legions were withdrawn. Much Saxon colonization took place in the sixth century, in a second burst of immigration. With the loss of Roman rule, organized society declined—roads and towns decayed, villas were deserted, and the pattern of life was distorted. However, there was a certain amount of continuity—some settlements continued without a break, such as Shakenoak Farm, near North Leigh, which was inhabited from the first to the eighth century. It is inconceivable that all the native inhabitants disappeared in the wake of the Saxon immigration, so the two cultures must have become integrated, with the Saxons dominating. The Thames, Cherwell, Windrush and Evenlode valleys again proved popular areas for settlement, as did the rich redland area of north Oxfordshire. Early Saxon settlement is distinguished by pagan burials such as those at Soudern, Hornton and Berinsfield. The latter cemetery was used in the fifth and sixth centuries. Warriors were buried with spears and shields (only the aristocracy carried swords, and none of these were found at Berinsfield). The women's graves contained brooches and glass and amber necklaces. Most of those buried in the cemetery died aged about thirty, many of them having suffered from arthritis.

A particularly rich grave contained several gold objects excavated at Cuddesdon in 1847 may be that of a sub-king of Wessex, as Oxfordshire was absorbed into that kingdom by King Ceawlin during the sixth century, the Thames becoming a boundary between Wessex and Mercia. One of his allies by the name of Cutha may be buried at Cutteslowe.

The hamlets at Purwell Farm, Cassington, and New Wintles Farm, Eynsham, date from Ceawlin's time. At New Wintles, situated on the gravel terrace of the Evenlode, twenty sunken huts, four post-hole structures and a staked enclosure, possibly a sheep-pen, were found, together with a trackway and several isolated pits and hearths. The inhabitants had a pastoral economy, but their livestock was poor, perhaps due to overstocking. Most of the meat eaten was beef, the sheep being kept to maturity, probably because of the value of their wool and hides—weaving took place in some of the huts. The settlement died out in the eighth century.

Dorchester remained an important settlement—it was chosen as the centre for the first see of Wessex by St Birinus who in 635 launched his mission to convert the area to Christianity, culminating in the baptism of King Cynegils of Wessex. Troubles between Wessex and Mercia resulted in the see being moved to Winchester by the 660s, but Dorchester became a Mercian bishopric in the ninth century. Abingdon Abbey, which became one of the richest and most powerful ecclesiastical foundations—its landholdings in Berkshire second only to the king's —is said by twelfth-century chroniclers to have been founded as a religious establishment for men and women in AD 675 by a nobleman, Hean, and his sister, Cilla, on lands given by Cissa, a Wessex sub-king. The first attempt to build it, in the Boars Hill area, were fraught with difficulties, and in 695 Hean himself took vows, becoming the first abbot of the new foundation on the present site between the Rivers Thames and Stert in Abingdon. The nunnery did not long outlast Cilla, but the monastery went from strength to strength, receiving gifts from King Ine and St Adhelm. It was ravaged by the conflicts between Wessex and Mercia, and in 944 the church was in ruins and its lands restored to royal ownership, being refounded by King Edred who in 955 made the Benedictine St Ethelwold the new abbot. During this golden age, its monks were sent to help other foundations at Thorney, Winchester, Ely and Peterborough.

Eynsham Abbey was founded around AD 1004–5, its first abbot being Aelfric; St Frideswide founded her monastery in Oxford in the eighth century, and there may have been a religious house at Islip at about the same time, both the latter being destroyed during the Danish raids. Many of the Saxon villages had churches, and traces of Saxon workmanship can be seen in the churches of Aston Tirrold, Cholsey and Wallingford, in the tower of North Leigh church and the chancel at Swalcliffe.

Being on the boundaries of Wessex and Mercia, the county was in a parlous position in disputes between the two, suffering such ravages as the destruction of Benson by the Mercian King Offa in the late eighth century, in his successful bid to gain political ascendancy over Wessex. Squabbles between the rival kingdoms proved paltry in comparison with the dangers offered by the Viking raids. The Thames was an ideal route for lightning strikes by Viking longships, and it took a strong ruler like King Alfred to deal with the situation. He was born in the royal *vill* of Wantage in 849, the fourth son of Ethelwulf, King of Wessex. His brother, King Aethelred I, fought the Vikings at the battle of Ashdown in the Vale of White Horse—they successfully routed their enemy, and the battle was hailed as a great triumph, although a few weeks later Alfred and his brother were on the run. A tale says that the Iron Age hill fort at Ashbury was built by Alfred and that the Lambourn barrows contain the remains of five Danish princes killed in the battle. The Blowing Stone at Kingston Lisle is said to have been used by Alfred to summon his troops in time of danger. Alfred became king in 871 and pursued his attempt to stem the progress of the Viking raiders. In 878 he converted the Danish King, Guthrum, to Christianity and made a treaty with him keeping the Danes north of the River Lea and Watling Street and out of London. He strengthened his defences at fords across the River Thames, creating fortified *burhs* at Wallingford and Oxford. Wallingford was laid out on a rectilinear street pattern surrounded by a rampart, which can still be seen. It and Winchester, the capital of Wessex, had 2,400 hides (each of 120 acres) of land allotted to it which had to provide a man each in time of need, indicating its defensive importance. Oxford was allotted only 1,500 hides and was probably first fortified in 912 by Edward the Elder, who may also have laid out part of the regular street pattern.

Wantage has always been proud of its connection with King Alfred, and in 1849, the millenary of his birth, there were three days of celebration: a committee was formed to produce a jubilee edition of all his works and essays on his life, which was published in two volumes in 1851; Count Gleichen erected a statue in the market-place, using Lord Wantage's features for those of Alfred, with the inscription:

> Alfred found learning dead, and he restored it:
> Education neglected, and he revived it:
> The laws powerless, and he gave them force:
> The Church debased, and he raised it:
> The land ravaged by a fearful enemy, from which he delivered it.

Oxfordshire had further connections with royalty. The Viking Cnut held an assembly at Oxford shortly after he became King of England in 1016. He probably had a palace at Cherbury and is said to have granted the manor of Pusey to Wyllyam Pewse on 'horn tenure'—meaning that Pewse had to blow a horn for his lord. A horn, 2 feet 6 inches long, said to be the actual one granted by King Cnut, was produced in the Court of Chancery in 1681 and accepted as genuine. Edward the Confessor, the last Saxon king, was born at Islip.

That tantalizing hill figure the Uffington White Horse is a subject of much controversy among archaeologists as to whether it is Iron Age or Saxon in origin. Popular tradition says that it was carved to commemorate Alfred's victory at the battle of Ashdown, and the scales are beginning to weigh in favour of the Saxon school of thought. The main argument for the horse's dating from the Iron Age is its segmented and stylized shape, resembling horses depicted on Iron Age coins, but a detailed examination of the horse reveals apparent changes in shape which have taken place over the centuries. Rain (and tourists) cause the turf to crumble and be washed down to the bottom of the cutting, and the hill-wash formed is gradually turfed over. This weathering is evident on the horse, and traces of earlier outlines are visible. There was plenty of time for erosion between scourings, and it might not have been possible to determine the shape that should be re-cut. A multiple survey is now being conducted, recording hachures, contours and resistivity, to determine whether, and how much, the shape has changed. If, as appears probable, the horse was not originally segmented, the argument in favour of its being Saxon is strengthened. It is said to be lucky to stand in the eye of the horse and make a wish, but this is discouraged by its guardians, the Department of the Environment, because of the perils of erosion if thousands of tourists tramp over it.

The scouring of the horse was a customary duty of the villages from Ashbury to Sparsholt, which together formed the Hundred of Hildeslow, and in later years it became a memorable event, the occasion for a fair and games. About thirty thousand people flocked to the Scouring in 1780, participating in cheese-rolling, competing for a silver cup in the 3-mile pony race, the women racing for smocks. The prize for the asses' race was a side of bacon, that for 'grinning through a horse collar' 5 shillings, and men indulged in wrestling and backswording. Perhaps the most famous description is that by Thomas Hughes in *The Scouring of the White Horse* describing a revival of it in 1857, when the revels included cheese-rolling down the 'Manger', as the hill below the horse is called, a carthorse race and a pig race.

The White Horse is commonly thought to be St George's steed, and the flat-topped hill below it is known as 'Dragon Hill', said to be where St George killed the dragon—the bare patch on the top of the hill, where nothing will grow, being where the dragon's blood was shed.

Oxfordshire once had another hill figure—that of a giant with a bow or a staff in his hand—at Shotover, referred to by Aubrey in his *Monumenta Britannica* written in the seventeenth century. Large spherical nodules found in the Shotover quarries are nicknamed 'the Giant's marbles'; a large stone shaped like a cottage loaf was 'the Giant's loaf', and a low bank 60 feet long, 5 feet wide and 18 inches high was 'the Giant's Grave', so although all trace of the hill figure had entirely disappeared by the early nineteenth century, the memory of it remains. Colourful legends have grown up over the origins of the name 'Shotover', one version ascribing the name to Cromwell firing his muskets over the hill.

2

Agriculture

Even today Oxfordshire has a predominantly rural character, with vast expanses of green and gold land, interspersed with towns and villages, so agricultural changes have had a great impact on its appearance.

Traces of ridge and furrow, the open field system used from medieval times until enclosure, are still seen, particularly in the north around Shenington and South Newington. At Shenington the hilly landscape required the building of lynchets which gave a stepped appearance, allowing a larger area for tillage and lessening the slipping of soil downhill.

The medieval manorial system gradually changed as the Black Death reduced the number of agricultural labourers, encouraging lords to let more land to tenants. Much land was acquired by Oxford colleges and wealthy men at the dissolution of the monasteries in the sixteenth century. Early enclosures took place, particularly in the Chiltern and Cotswold districts, usually to increase sheep flocks. Although most land was enclosed between 1758 and 1882, land use was improved within the open field system. The number of livestock increased in the eighteenth century, and the cultivation of rye, barley and oats decreased in favour of wheat—one indication of the richer harvests was the adoption of four-wheeled wagons instead of two-wheeled carts. Enclosure, although it benefited tenant farmers and landowners, could be disastrous for labourers, many of whom relied on common land for pasture. Flora Thompson commented wryly on their decline in fortune:

Country people had not been so poor when Sally was a girl, or their prospects so hopeless. Sally's father had kept a cow, geese, poultry, pigs and a donkey-cart to carry his produce to the market town. He could do this because he had commoners' rights and could turn his

animals out to graze, and cut furze for firing and even turf to make a
lawn for one of his customers. Her mother made butter, for themselves and to sell, baked their own bread and made candles for
lighting . . . Sometimes her father would do a day's work for wages,
thatching a rick, cutting and laying a hedge or helping with the
shearing or the harvest.[1]

Some labourers could not find jobs to employ them full-time
locally, so they went in groups round the neighbouring counties.
Nineteenth-century mowers from Filkins illustrate this:

They used to go to London mowing the parks and fields with the
scythe; then helped to make the hay and put it into ricks. When the
haymaking was done they worked their way back by doing hoeing
for market gardeners. After working a week in one place, they
walked on Sunday a few miles nearer home, and by the time they got
to Wantage the harvesting was ready as it was earlier on the downs.
After cutting the corn with their fagging-hooks, the harvest at
Filkins itself was ready; then they would go on to Northleach where
the harvest was later still.[2]

Yarnton is one of the last villages to have lot-meadow mowing, a relic of the open field system. Irish labourers were employed to mow the meadows by scythes in one day, until the
havoc they caused encouraged the vicar to ban them. However,
the custom itself continues. The three lot meadows are Pixey,
the largest, Oxhay and Westmead. The rights to mowing the
meadows were originally divided between thirteen people, each
one represented by a little wooden ball, kept by the Meadsman.
Each ball has a name written on it: Freeman, Gilbert, Dunn,
Harry, William, Water Molley, Water Jeoffrey, Perry, Boulton,
Green, Boat, Rothe and White. These balls were taken into the
fields in a small bag, the Meadsman drew out each in turn, and
the strip assigned was then marked by stamping down the grass
around its boundary. Pixey is divided into twenty-six lots,
Oxhay thirty-nine and Westmead sixty-five. The owners do not
always require their rights, so there is frequently an auction at
the Grapes Inn at Yarnton. Unfortunately for the last few years
all the rights have been purchased by one person, so the elaborate division of the strips has not been necessary. As Yarnton
meadows are never artificially fertilized, they are rich in wild
flowers.

Agriculture at the beginning of the nineteenth century was on the verge of an important period of change, which continues today. The Napoleonic Wars and ensuing trade blockades encouraged the country to be more self-sufficient in food, particularly in corn, although the period after the wars was one of agricultural depression. The first Oxfordshire Agricultural Show took place in 1811 "to promote the well-being of agriculture and stock-breeding" and country life in general. Oxford was the venue of the first Royal Show in 1839. Such competitions encouraged farmers and stock-breeders.

With enclosure it was easier for the different areas to develop their specialities to greater advantage. The Chiltern area includes woodland, and the soils on the hills are thin, but in the late nineteenth century the growing demand for milk from Reading, much of which went to the biscuit-factory, encouraged milk-production. In 1879 corn and milk were the main products, and sheep, once considered an essential part of Chiltern farming, as their manure consolidated the soil, were in decline.

The area between the Chilterns and Oxford contains a wide variety of landscape, with the hills between Chinnor and Watlington, and the heathland between Goring and Ipsden with its large fields and few fences, hedges or trees, then hills and woodland around Cuddesdon and Shotover. Sheep and cattle were the chief products near the Chilterns and around Forest Hill. The high land around Chinnor and Watlington had a rotation of wheat, barley, roots, oats and a short fallow and clover. Around Goring and Ewelme the farming was considered some of the best in the county, with some 1,000-acre farms, growing wheat, roots, green crops, oats, barley, beans and clover. Much of the milk from the Thames Valley was sent to London, and butter was made and bullocks fattened. The Littlemore and Horspath area had market gardens supplying Oxford.

The Vale of White Horse was famed for its dairying—most farms consisted of long strips of land containing part vale and part downland, and one complemented the other. Jethro Tull, the Berkshire gentleman farmer, invented a nine-share plough and a seed-drill in the eighteenth century which eased cultivation on the downs, some of which had not been ploughed since the Roman era. Despite the high quality of the land, its poor drainage was a major obstacle to increasing the arable area, but the larger landowners, such as Edward Loveden who ran Buscot Park as a model estate in the early nineteenth century, experimented successfully with a mole plough. He was an 'improving farmer', turning his meadows into water-meadows to support more cattle. He made the best use of his estate, using the upland for willow, alder and ash coppices, the products from which provided local and London markets with the raw material for basket-making. This trade was large enough to merit having a private wharf on the Wiltshire and Berkshire Canal for despatching the bundles of wood to London. He revolutionized his fishery to trap trout, perch, pike, carp and eels from the River Thames. However the downland squires were dismissed by the novelist Thomas Hughes as "bloated aristocrats, who by the time they were thirty had drunk out all the little brains they ever had, and spent their time in preserving and killing game and foxes at the expense of the farmers, and sending every good man in their village either to the Bastille (as we called the workhouse) as a pauper, or to the county gaol as a poachers".[3]

South-west Oxfordshire had a dual system of cropping and pasture for dairying, but the heavy clays which required three or four horses for cultivation were, in the nineteenth century, left as grazing. Stock-breeding, particularly of Oxford Down sheep and cattle, was concentrated in the Kelmscott area. In north-west Oxfordshire less than a quarter of the total area was kept under corn, and the west bank of the Cherwell provided good meadow land. The rich ironstone soils of the northern area, being fertile, commanded high rents, but the remoteness of villages such as Epwell, Shutford, Shenington and Hornton provided transport difficulties for fragile products, so much butter was made and sent to Birmingham.

Arable farming was greatly changed by the rapid invention of new machinery. The wealthier farmers were often go-ahead, such as Sir Henry Dashwood of Kirtlington, Viscount Dillon of Ditchley and the Hon. J.H. Langston of Sarsden, who were three of the first people in the county to have reaping-machines. Yet even in the 1880s heavy machinery such as steam-ploughs and harvesting machines were considered impractical toys by the labourers of Juniper Hill, who did most farmwork without the aid of machines. 1840–75 was a golden age for the farmer, with new technology, mechanization, new manures and better breeds, but with the 1870s this prosperity came to an abrupt end, particularly for arable farmers threatened by free trade, easier transportation, imports of cheap grain from North America and the general world trade depression. This encouraged many farmers to concentrate on stock, but wheat remained the most important corn crop in Oxfordshire. Barley decreased in popularity after 1879 and was grown most extensively west of the Cherwell and at Bladon and Begbroke on stonebrash, and on gravels at Kelmscott and Black Bourton and the redlands between Banbury and Claydon.

The most popular breed of cattle in the early nineteenth century was the Longhorn, Robert Fowler of Little Rollright having an excellent herd, but later in the century they were superseded by Dairy Shorthorn. A herd of Holstein Friesians was kept at Blenheim. The only remaining Oxfordshire Longhorns are kept at Rousham, while old English Wild White Cattle are raised at Wilcote. Robert Hobbs' pedigree herd of Shorthorns at Kelmscott in the mid nineteenth century and that at Albury contributed to the improvement of the breed.

Nineteenth-century milk-production in the Vale led to the stretch of the Great Western Railway running through it being nicknamed 'Milky Way'. Vale milk too went to the Huntley & Palmers biscuit-factory at Reading. Butter and cheese, although of secondary importance, were far from negligible. Arthur Young wrote of wagons travelling from Bicester to London with 10 tons of butter per week, chiefly loaded between Bicester and Wheatley. Banbury cheese was an acceptable gift in the fifteenth century, when, in 1430, fourteen Banbury cheeses were among the provisions sent to France for the Duke of Bedford, and William Bulleyn claimed a special excellence for them in his *Book of Compounds*. During the sixteenth century two different types of cheese were made—Thomas Cromwell was given both hard and soft. Burton, who was so derogatory about Banbury cakes in his *Anatomy of Melancholy* (1586), obviously preferred its cheese: "Of all cheese, I take that kind which we call Banbury Cheese to be the best." Shakespeare was familiar with the thin cheese, as in *The Merry Wives of Windsor* when Bardolph slightingly calls Slender a 'Banbury cheese' to emphasize his thinness, and the same sentiment is echoed in *Jack Dunn's Entertainment* of 1601: "Put off your clothes and you are like a Banbury cheese. Nothing but paring." Beesley considered it important enough to merit a detailed description:

> A very rich kind of Cheese is yet made in the neighbourhood of Banbury, at a late season of the year, on some very rich pasture land; and this may possibly be the kind for which the town was formerly so highly celebrated. It is almost white, about one inch in thickness, and resembles in appearance the soft cream-cheese which is made in many parts; but it is of far more delicious taste and bears the high price of 1s.6d per pound when new, or about 1s.9d when ripe. It is generally called in the neighbourhood 'latter-made cheese', as it can only be made after Michaelmas. A considerable quantity of this Cheese is yet sent to distant parts, each cheese packed in its separate basket.[4]

Banbury Cheese has now disappeared, and when the Banbury Historical Society had some made a few years ago, they must have had the wrong recipe, as it was exceedingly tasteless.

The Vale of White Horse was famed for its butter and cheeses. The best butter was said to come from the Wytham and Radley area. A special wharf was built by Edward Loveden of Buscot on the Wiltshire and Berkshire Canal, rented to London cheesemongers, which stored the 2–3,000 tons of cheese transported each year to London from the Vale to the neighbouring region. The main cheese was similar to a single Gloucester, but there were several variants. A 'pineapple' cheese, famed for its rich delicate flavour, was made in the first half of the nineteenth century at Mr Pike's Snowswick Farm, near Buscot. The entire Pike family co-operated in making the cheeses, working the curds by hand, then putting them into flowerpot-shaped wooden moulds. When the 5-pound cheeses were removed from their moulds, they were rubbed in salt or steeped in brine, then put into nets and suspended from a beam to mature. They were called 'pineapple' because the meshes of the net made diamond-shaped indentations on the cheese. In the Stanford-in-the-Vale area, the speciality was sage-flavoured cheese moulded into the shape of a hare. Many Vale farms had cheese-presses in the kitchen or the dairy. Some cheese was made in other parts of the county.

In the nineteenth century South Down sheep were mixed with Cotswolds and Hampshire Downs, and the new breed, christened 'Oxford Down', was considered "the most cosmo-

politan brand of sheep". The breed was concentrated in the
Adderbury/Cheltenham/Faringdon area. In 1862 it was recog-
nized by the Royal Agricultural Society of England, and by 1870
its type and quality were much praised. One of the most famous
flocks was that of Robert Hobbs of Kelmscott, who greatly improved the breed. Other varieties in Oxfordshire included slow-
maturing Berkshires, South Downs, Leicesters and Cotswold
sheep. Despite the success of the Oxford Down, the number of
sheep in the county was reduced drastically in the second half of
the century and has never recovered its former position.

Shepherds were important farm labourers and received
special treatment from the farmers, who always gave them
lamb pancakes when the first lamb of the year was dropped;
when the lambs' tails were docked, one of the men's perks was to
keep the tails to make lambs' tail pie. Sheep-shearing feasts
were sometimes held, and at the feast at Chilsworth, near
Cuddesdon, the shepherds wore posies in their hats and had a
celebratory supper once shearing was over.

Pigs play a far smaller role than in the past. The day when
the farm labourer's pig was nourished on all the scraps from the
house until it became fat, then killed to provide the staple diet of
the family, is long over. Arthur Young observed that many pigs
were fed specially to make brawn, which was very popular in the
Oxford area. The Berkshire breed was most popular at the
beginning of the century.

Faringdon had a flourishing trade in smoked bacon, organized by two families, sending about eight thousand sides to
Oxford and London each year. Although Wantage bacon was
considered superior by some people, it was not produced in such
large quantities. In addition to Berkshires, a few Tamworth
pigs could be found in the Banbury area, and some white pigs.
Oxfordshire black-and-sandy pigs were a cross between Tamworth and Berkshire breeds—a profitable, reliable and hardy
breed, with a mottled black, brown and sandy coat.

The nineteenth century saw unrest among agricultural
labourers, who feared that new machines would deprive them of
jobs and were in some cases suffering from the impact of enclosure. They rioted at Banbury in 1830, and labourers burned a
threshing-machine belonging to Mr Bernard of Deddington;
other labourers from towns and villages as far apart as Little
Milton, Broadwell, Blenheim, Woodstock, Chipping Norton and

Abingdon were arrested and transported for machine-breaking, and an Abingdon man was arrested and convicted for merely "collecting the mob by sounding a horn".

Dissatisfied labourers joined the National Agricultural Labourers' Union founded by Warwickshire-born Joseph Arch, which aimed to raise labourers' wages to 14 shillings a week. In May 1873 some union men working for Robert Hambridge of Ascott-under-Wychwood went on strike in support of their claim. When Hambridge retaliated by bringing in two non-union men, thirty or forty local women marched to the farm to intimidate Hambridge and the blacklegs. Hambridge took out a summons against seventeen of the women, alleging threats, violence and molestation. The magistrates released one woman, but seven were sentenced to ten days' and nine to seven days' imprisonment with hard labour. The women were nicknamed 'the Ascott Martyrs', and the populace rioted in their favour. Despite this, they were imprisoned in Oxford Castle, but questions were asked in the House of Commons, leading to the remittance of hard labour for those who were still in prison. Their release was an occasion of public celebration, and a collection raised £3 for each woman.

Labourers eventually managed to raise their wages, but they were not highly regarded. Clare Sewell Read commented wryly:

> Perhaps in no county of England is the love of beer among the labouring poor so general or so extravagant as in Oxfordshire. If anything out of the common routine on a farm is to be done, 'a drop of beer' is wanted to make it all go off pleasantly. It is a usual thing for men at some early job by the day to club together for beer, and so spend twopence or threepence of their wages before they have earned it.[5]

The county has a few 'special' crops which, although not grown in any quantity, are an integral part of its economy. Market gardening flourishes in south Oxfordshire and the Vale, and many apples and pears grown in Vale orchards once found their way to London by barge and wagon. Milton boasted one of the largest orchards in Oxfordshire, with over 540 apple trees, while Edward Lovedon, at Buscot, devised canvas awnings to protect his trees from frost and blight. Most Vale villages had orchards in the nineteenth century, and in the 1860s the orchards of North and South Moreton, East and West Hagbourne, Blewbury, Upton Harwell and East and West Hendred were famed for apples, pears, damsons and cherries. Cherry feasts were held at Kingston Lisle on the first Sunday after 6th July, when cherries from the Vale orchards were sold in the streets and at Wantage. Cherry orchards abounded around Stoke Row in south Oxfordshire, and cherry-picking became an annual village activity. Today many soft fruits are grown under glass, and much is sold on a 'pick your own' basis.

Other special crops include woad, grown for its dye properties, in Wantage in the south and Broughton in the north. Flax formed part of the rotation at Eynsham, Blenheim, Water Eaton, Hempton and Yarnton—sometimes used for making linen, sometimes to make a jelly for fattening bullocks. The women of Baldon made their own linen from hemp cultivated in the parish until the beginning of the nineteenth century.

At Milton Hill and Watlington hops were grown, those from Watlington being used as a strong manure rather than for brewing. Manor Farm, East Hagbourne, once had three hop-kilns, but only one oast-house can be seen today. Faringdon had a 10-acre hop-garden, and some came from Kingston Bagpuize. Wallingford brew-houses took many local hops.

Ewelme and several Vale villages—the Letcombes, Ashbury, Childrey, Ginge, West Hendred and Blewbury—have for many years grown watercress. When Thomas Hardy christened 'Cresscombe' in *Jude the Obscure*, he was referring to Letcombe Bassett, the best-known watercress village. Ewelme watercress goes mainly to the north of England—to Manchester, Warrington and Wolverhampton. The watercress beds at Ewelme were prepared entirely by hand, and water came from springs near the village. At the end of the picking-season the plants were cut down to water level with a sickle, and the root stock was pulled out on to the bank while the beds were limed to kill insects and pests, then replanted. The water level had to be sufficient to protect the plants from frost, which could kill them. Two sorts of cress are still grown—green and brown—the latter having a hotter flavour. The original strains of green cress came from the Thames. Cress is cut (mostly on Thursday and Friday for week-end markets) with a knife and packed into strong osier hampers with cane lids made by Fleets of Thame, each taking 56 pounds of cress. Workers at the watercress beds believed in the magic of

watercress, which they thought imparted fertility to their
wives. They sang while working:

> While strolling out one evening
> Down by the running stream,
> Where water-lilies were growing,
> It was a lovely scene.
>
> The sight I saw was better,
> A damsel like a Queen.
> She was gathering watercress
> Down by the old mill stream.
>
> Her hair hung down in tresses
> As gently flowed the stream.
> She was gathering watercresses,
> Was that fair Watercress Queen.
>
> I asked her if she was lonely.
> She answered with a smile,
> "Oh sir, I am not lonely,
> For this is my daily toil.
>
> "I have to be up so early
> To gather my cresses green."
> She told me her name was —
> Better known as the Watercress Queen."

In the Vale, in downland villages such as Aston Upthorpe and
Aston Tirold, racehorses are trained and exercised, incidentally
improving the quality of the land:

Gentlemen of the Turf find the invigorating gallop over the downs so
beneficial to the training of their horses, that they have located
themselves at East Ilsley, Compton, Chilton, Letcombe, Lambourne,
etc., and by these means have much benefited a large tract of light
soil (much shut out from the convenience of railway transit), by the
quantities of horse provender of the best description which has
consequently been consumed and the large amount of manure restored to the adjacent farms in return for a supply of straw.[6]

An unsuccessful attempt at model farming took place at
Charterville. The Chartists were horrified by the poverty in
industrial slums and wanted to purchase land for small hold-

ings, build cottages and buy stock so that some of their supporters from the towns could be given the opportunity to become self-sufficient in the country. On 24th June 1874 Feargus O'Connor purchased 300 acres near Minster Lovell, consisting of upland meadows and pasture, with freestone and limestone quarries, bounded by the River Windrush with its resources of eels, crayfish and trout, and nearby was Wychwood Forest, which provided grazing for cattle. He paid £10,878 for this land, but an unfortunate slip was made over the contract, which made the subsequent dissolution of the venture almost inevitable. O'Connor and his colleague Christopher Doyle marked out the allotments, and within ten months almost eighty single-storey cottages had been built, of a far higher standard than those of most labourers, with water-tanks to provide water inside the house, cupboards, bookshelves, dresser and kitchen grate, wells and outbuildings plus a meeting-house and school. There was a great demand for allotments, but the Company failed to raise enough money to pay off the mortgage and were dispossessed. Some tenants remained, and others moved in. It was not easy to make a living on their 2-4 acre allotments, but they concentrated on potatoes which were not otherwise widely grown locally, until they were almost ruined in 1881-2 by potato disease. Later many became successful market gardeners. From 1877 to 1919 barley and potatoes were the chief crops.

The twentieth century has been a period of rapid and far-reaching changes in agriculture, but despite this the local agricultural economy still revolves around the basic elements of cereals, with approximately half the land used for arable, half for grass. Wheat remains the most profitable cereal, a twentieth-century development being autumn sowing. New machines and fertilizers have enabled rotations to be discarded, so that wheat can now be grown several years in succession. Barley needs a less fertile soil and can be grown successfully on the lighter calcareous soils in the west of the county—winter barley, sown in September, is increasingly important for animal feed and malting. Varieties of cereals change far more rapidly than in the past. The increasing use of chemicals has lessened the dangers from disease and pests—barley mildew used to be dreaded but can now be kept under control. As new chemicals are developed in quantity, production costs are reduced, so it is more economical for farmers to use them. Use of such weed-

killers as Paraquat has allowed the use of direct-drilling techniques which mean that the next crop can be planted straight
away, avoiding the necessity for cultivating in between, thus
saving labour, machines and oil. This technique is likely to be of
further use in the future.

A small proportion of crops other than cereals are grown.
Oil-seed rape, with its distinctive yellow flowers, is often seen,
particularly in the Cherwell area. Lupins, legumes related to
clover, which do not need nitrogen and which produce protein,
oil and linseed, are also found. Experiments with grain maize,
sunflowers, groundnuts and soya beans have not been a great
success.

An examination of the Oxfordshire Show catalogues reveals
changes in breeds: Oxford Down sheep and Berkshire pigs are
rare, and white-faced Hereford beef cattle are declining in
favour of South Devon and Charolais. Milk-production remains
more important than beef. Friesians have replaced Dairy Shorthorns to form the majority of dairy cattle, augmented by Jersey
and Guernsey cows. Machine milking has been the norm since
the Second World War: farmers experimented with bucket
milking-plants in which the milk was siphoned along pipes from
the cows to a central unit, and with breast parlours containing
double milking-units with tandem parlours where cows stood
head to tail; in the 1960s herringbone parlours came into
vogue—here the cows stand at angles with heads towards the
walls where feeding-troughs are situated. These accommodate
larger herds of up to two hundred more quickly and easily.
Cheese is no longer made commercially.

An important twentieth-century development is the stock
market in Banbury. Cattle were sold in the centre of town, in
Bridge Street and Broad Street, until in 1925 Midland Marts
began to organize cattle auctions in Grimsbury. Banbury's
central position, with good railway and road communications,
had encouraged the growth of the auctions. The cattle market
has now been taken over by Dalgetty's and is one of the largest
and most important in Europe.

Pigs' popularity fluctuates, as the financial margins are
narrow—their feed is expensive, and profits are small, so they
have been adversely affected recently by Britain's joining the
European Economic Community. Hybrid stock have replaced
the traditional breeds. The tendency is therefore towards larger

and fewer specialized units—one large unit is that of the Pig Improvement Company of Fyfield Wick.

Oxford Down and Cotswold sheep are no longer considered a commercial proposition, and sheep play only a small part in the local economy. Some sheep are still found in the Cotswolds, Chilterns and Berkshire Downs where, if they are folded on the root crops, they still provide good fertilizer. Experiments have been tried with Dorset Horn Sheep which can breed twice a year.

Poultry are widely kept but not on a large scale—many are kept in battery cages in specialized units.

Modern building techniques have partially succeeded in changing the appearance of the traditional farmyard. Most new buildings tend to be general-purpose, often with much use of corrugated iron. Silage towers abound, mechanical ones dating from 1960 onwards. The current trend is away from silage and haylage for feeding cattle towards 'complete-diet feeding' linked to a mixer-wagon.

Machinery has changed almost beyond recognition, the trend being towards bigger and better. Combine harvesters became popular after the Second World War. Balers have graduated from producing loaf-shaped bales to the immense coils to be seen in so many fields. The 'round' bales reduce the amount of handling required and shed water better, whereas traditional bales are more suitable if manual handling is required, but even the square balers have been improved with 'auto sledges', to take eight bales at once, and a pronged tractor attachment to stack them onto trailers.

Joining the European Economic Community has caused some headaches, and there are problems to be ironed out. Over-production in EEC countries has tightened profit-margins, and tariffs have had a detrimental effect on some aspects such as pig-production. It is likely that rapidly increasing oil and machinery prices will encourage more interest in direct drilling. The ubiquitous silicon chip will simplify the mechanization of direct feeders and milking-parlours, so larger dairy herds will become a more practical proposition, and less labour will be required. New chemicals are constantly being developed to cope with new diseases. Low-volume sprays which require smaller amounts of chemical—and therefore oil—will be used.

Farming has changed drastically and is likely to continue to do so at a fast rate in the future. Although basic elements remain the same, the techniques change. It seems unlikely that Oxfordshire will cease to be basically agricultural in character, as there is an insistent demand from government that we should concentrate more resources on our agriculture and become more self-sufficient in food so that we can reduce expensive imports.

3

Crafts and Industries

Witney blankets and British Leyland cars—two products of Oxfordshire industries which are household names and which reflect the radical changes between the old-established industries and those recently introduced.

The geological and geographical structure of Oxfordshire provided the raw materials for the traditional crafts and industries, such as those of stone and building, for ironworking and for possible coal-mining in the future. The Chiltern woodland has been managed to provide raw materials for the woodland crafts. Sheep provided raw materials for the woollen industry, glove-making and parchment-making. The demands of agriculture encouraged development of agricultural machinery manufacture. Oxford University stimulated the demand for parchment- and paper-making, printing and publishing.

Industries were closely woven into the life and requirements of the community, as, until canals and railways eased transport problems in the eighteenth and nineteenth centuries, country people were largely reliant on their own resources. Since the nineteenth century new industries have developed which no longer rely on the local raw materials and could have been set up anywhere—such as William Morris's motor industry, which has had such far-reaching consequences for the town of Oxford, and Alcan Aluminium (UK) Ltd, producing aluminium in Banbury, and General Foods, both part of international companies. The Atomic Energy Research Establishment at Harwell and the JET Nuclear Fission project reflect the concern about future energy resources. Although some of the traditional industries still flourish, they have less economic importance in the county than the new ones which have in large measure supplanted them and subtly changed the character of the county.

The most important traditional industry is woollen

manufacture, which has played a major role since the Middle Ages. Blankets are still made in Witney, and it is only just over thirty years since the Shutford plush industry, which provided livery plush for Courts from Russia to South America, ceased production. Medieval Cistercian monks at Bruern and Thame had great flocks of sheep, and woollen manufacture was encour-aged by the proximity of the Cotswolds, which provided ideal grazing—the wool from Cotswold sheep was famed for its high quality. The Thames, Windrush and Cherwell rivers provided power to operate fulling-mills, and the Thames highway brought additional wool from other areas and took the finished products to London, augmenting the inadequate road system. Armed with these advantages, the woollen manufacturers had established craft guilds of weavers and merchant guilds in towns such as Oxford, Witney, Burford and Chipping Norton by the twelfth century, and, as the industry expanded, these towns and Banbury acquired their own specializations.

Dr Robert Plot, the first curator of the Ashmolean Museum and author of the first book on the county, *The Natural History of Oxfordshire*, in 1677, wrote of Witney:

'Tis certain that the Blanketing Trade of Witney is advanced to that height that no place comes near to it: some I know attribute a great part of the excellency of these Blankets to the abstersive nitrous waters of the River Windrush, wherewith they are scoured . . . but others again that rather think they owe it to a peculiar way of loose spinning . . . However . . . 'tis plain they are esteemed so far beyond all others that this place has engrossed the whole trade.[1]

The local sheep were large, woolly beasts, nicknamed 'Cots-wold lions' because of their size and magnificence, and provided superb wool. However, even by the seventeenth century de-mand for wool was so great that it was brought to Oxfordshire from many parts of the country. A wide variety of fabrics was made, including 'duffields', alternatively known as 'shag' or 'trucking cloth', which was woven into pieces 30 yards long and 1¾ yards broad, then dyed red and blue, since those

are the colours that best please the Indians of Virginia and New England, with whom the Merchants truck them for Bever, and other Furrs of several Beasts, etc, the use they have for them is to apparel themselves with them, their manner being to tear them into Gowns

Beechwoods near Nettlebed.

A view of the landscape near Banbury.

Grim's Ditch, near Ginge, Vale of White Horse.

The Rollright stones

Uffington White Horse, with Dragon Hill immediately below and the Iron Age hill fort of Uffington Castle.

Madmarston Iron Age hill fort.

Lynchets in fields at Shenington.

Hook Norton Brewery

A brick-kiln at Nettlebed.

Bliss's tweed-mill, Chipping Norton.

Punts at the foot of Magdalen Bridge, Oxford.

The Oxford Canal at Cropredy

Turnpike house, Charlbury.

Railway housing, Didcot.

A May garland on the rood-screen of Charlton-on-Otmoor church.

Charlton-on-Otmoor.

View over Otmoor.

of about two yards long, thrusting their Arms through two Holes made for that Purpose, and so wrapping the rest about them as we our loose-coats.[2]

A special 'point' system was devised for trading duffields with the American Indians, the number of coloured stripes woven into each blanket indicating to the Indians the number of furs or skins which had to be exchanged for it. Other Witney products in the eighteenth century included hammocks for sailors, woven from the best tail wool; stuffing or 'Wednel' for collar-makers which utilized the worst wool; wrappers for blankets, and 'tilt cloths', coarse cloths used to cover the loads on barges, from poor wool.

The Early family of Witney has been associated with the woollen-industry since 1669, when Richard Early, a 'man-mercer' in Corn Street, who sold leather breeches and woollen stockings, apprenticed his son Thomas to a blanketmaker. Thomas inherited his master's business, and himself became a thriving blanketmaker. It is said that, when James II visited the town in 1688, Thomas was involved in the presentation of a pair of magnificent gold-fringed blankets on behalf of Witney traders. Maintaining the family tradition of meeting royalty, his son John at the age of eighty presented George III and Queen Charlotte with a pair of blankets and had the honour of kissing the Queen's hand.

During this period woollen manufacture was run on a 'cottage industry' basis, so people in many villages near woollen towns were closely involved. Wool was graded, then distributed to be carded by the men and boys and spun by women and girls. Handloom weaving could also be done at home, but the apprentices had to undergo a rigid training for seven years, as John Early (1801-76) reflected:

> The apprentices were bound generally at fourteen years of age and served six years with shooting the shuttle with the left hand and the last year they were moved to the right hand, which was done by the ceremony of a drinking holiday. The lads during their apprenticeship were rigidly kept from indulgences and [had] nothing to drink but small beer and water. Their usual breakfast was thick oatmeal porridge.

Apprentices were village lads "chosen for their strength and good conduct and their early habit of rising and temperate mode

of living, by the time they reached manhood they were pro-
digious strong. But when they became their own masters they
generally fell into drinking habits which in the eighteenth
century was carried on to a fearful and ruinous pitch".[3]

About 1800 the flying-shuttle loom was introduced, enabling
each loom to be worked by one man instead of two, and eighteen
years later John Early purchased spinning machines.

Although many woollen areas declined in the nineteenth century, Witney had a few manufacturers, who were often related,
such as the Earlys and Marriotts, so they combined to help each
other through difficult periods. By the twentieth century wool
was being shipped to Witney from all over the world—
Australia, New Zealand, South Africa and India, and the products were equally widely exported, the strong figured patterns
of Jacquard woven fabrics being popular in South America and
South Africa.

8th June 1906 was a red-letter day for the Earlys. Long before
the *Guinness Book of Records*, they had decided to challenge the
record of Sir John Throckmorton of Buckland, who, taking wool
from his Southdown sheep, had the cloth woven and a coat made
in thirteen hours twenty minutes, thus winning a 1,000 guinea
wager. So, at 3.46 a.m., as the sun rose, the men began to shear
the sheep (which had been kept inside overnight to prevent the
fleeces from being drenched with dew). By shearing only the
wool actually required for making the blankets—probably that
from the back and shoulders, they left strange-looking, partially shorn and rather confused animals. The wool was then
willeyed (blended), dyed, carded, spun and woven before being
rushed to the tuckers who completed the finishing processes of
washing, shrinking, dying and raising the nap. The entire process was completed in a mere ten hours twenty-seven minutes.

The Early family still makes its superb traditional blankets
but has now diversified into fibre-weaving, in which wool is
matted together instead of being spun, making a strong, hard-
wearing fabric. The big Early factory can be seen on the Burford
road, but the factories in Newland are now desolate and empty.

Banbury had its own wool-market by the fifteenth century. It
reached its heyday during the eighteenth century, when, with
the increase in horse transport, manufacturers began to specialize in webbing and girth cloths. Messrs Cobb opened a girth-
factory in 1701, supplying products to Birmingham, Walsall

and Bristol, and the last girth-factory in Banbury, that of Mr
Mead, closed only in 1932. From the mid eighteenth century
plush, a fabric with a pile similar to velvet, was predominant in
Banbury, providing employment not only in the town but in the
surrounding villages of Adderbury, Deddington, Broughton,
Wroxton and Shutford and on a smaller scale in Bourton,
Horley, Sibford, Tadmarton and Swalcliffe, where wool was
dyed, spun and handwoven in mills and cottages. In 1790 when
Banbury parish church was demolished, its timbers were much
in demand for making looms. By 1841 two-thirds of all plush-
workers operated in the Banbury area, but soon after that the
decline of the industry began.

In 1837 the firm of Cubitt's astutely purchased Henry
Bessemer's famous embossing-machine, on which he had embossed plush for furniture in Windsor Castle. At first it was
exclusive and expensive, but when the price of plush declined to
a shilling a yard, Bessemer decided to sell his machine. From
that time onwards embossed plush seems to have been made
exclusively in Banbury and was used for bus and railway seats
as well as stately homes such as Broughton Castle and Castle
Howard, according to quality. Special embossed designs were
created for the Houses of Parliament and the Reform Club. In
1851 plush from Banbury was exhibited in the Great Exhibition. In 1909 Cubitt's, the last remaining firm in Banbury,
sold its goodwill and its embossing-machines to Wrench's of
Shutford, a firm which had been in existence since the mid-
eighteenth century. Wrench's won two gold medals and one
silver for plush at the Brussels Exhibition of 1910. A disastrous
fire at the Shutford factory in 1913, in which the order books
were lost, the depredations of the wars, in which workmen were
lost, and the decline of the world's Courts, which lessened the
demand for livery plush, all contributed towards the closure of
the factory in 1948, when the ill health of Henry Wrench determined him to sell the business.

The fascination of plush is found in the great variety of types
and their uses—it can be made from wool, mohair, silk, cotton,
artificial silk and a mixture of these fibres, Livery mohair-and-
worsted plush was one of the principal products—Windsor
Green was worn by Queen Victoria's Royal Foresters in
Windsor Park, while cream plush went to the Netherlands and
Italian blue to Savoÿ; scarlet was worn at the coronation of Czar

Nicholas II of Russia—clients for livery plush were found all over the world, and this particular type was always handwoven and of superior quality.

The Japanese kept warm in the winter in blue and white silk-plush kimonos printed with designs of chrysanthemums, boats and birds; the natives of Africa purchased lengths of gaudily dyed plush, further decorated with sequins, which were folded in half, with seams sown down the sides, leaving arm-holes and a hole cut for the head. These proved very popular once a waterproof version had been developed to cope with tropical rainstorms. Plush was much in demand by Victorian ladies for their curtains, tablecloths, upholstery, picture- and mirror-frames; uncut plush—two layers of fabric with the nap in the middle—made strong trousers for workmen; one type of tussore-silk plush was woven with a particularly long, soft pile to imitate the fur underneath a rabbit's chin, required for colour printing. Other varieties were used in such diverse activities as tobacco-picking, panning for gold (black plush), covering machine rollers (green), powdering ladies' noses, scrubbing the bodies of athletes and those enjoying Turkish baths, and the manufacture of Irish linen.

Chipping Norton was a thriving woollen centre in the fif-teenth century and gradually developed a specialization in tweeds, when in 1821 the firm of Bliss & Sons (established in 1746), makers of kersey webs and horsecloths, began to manu-facture serges and tweeds. By 1852 they employed 150 hands and in 1867 won a gold medal at the Amsterdam Exhibition. The magnificent mill, rebuilt in 1872 after a fire, was designed by Lancashire architect George Woodhouse to look like a country house, and it forms a notable landmark with its tall tower. Unfortunately the firm closed in 1980.

There were a number of minor textile crafts and industries in Oxfordshire. Harris & Tomkins of Abingdon had one of the few factories where smocks for agricultural labourers were manu-factured. They had two smocks designed by the foreman, Thomas Watson, and embroidered by Esther and Hannah Stimp-son for the Great Exhibition of 1851, with intricate designs to illustrate the popular themes of universal peace and prosperity, with roses, agricultural implements, goddesses, "Success to Agriculture", "God Speed the Plough" and other exotic motifs embroidered in minute feather stitches—far more elaborate than any that graced the shoulders of the average farm labourer. This factory employed many outworkers in neighbouring villages such as Radley. Apart from those made for the factory, most smocks seem to have been made by village women on their own account or for *entrepreneurs*.

Henley had a thriving silk industry in the mid-nineteenth century. Pillow-lace making was very important to the labourers' wives in the west of the country, particularly around the Bicester, Thame and Henley areas, playing a vital role in supplementing sparse family incomes. Girls were despatched to lace schools at the age of four or five to learn lace making, and it was common to see women seated at their cottage doors in summer with heads bent over their pillows, clicking their wooden or bone bobbins with bead 'spangles' on their ends. These bobbins had quaint inscriptions, varying from "Kiss me quick for Mother is Coming", "Take this small gift I freely give and the Lord protect you while you live", and "Joseph Castle Hung 1860" (commemorating a wife-murderer), to personal names such as "Sarah Hunt Bicester 1843". Faced by increasing competition from the cheaper machine-made lace of Nottingham, the industry declined in the mid nineteenth century.

Sacking-manufacture was a speciality of the Vale of White Horse—in the eighteenth century a Thomas Westbrook of Abingdon was producing three hundred pieces of sacking each week. Later Abingdon firms made sailcloth for the navy, and products for local industries—sacks for millers, hop-pockets for brewers and biscuit-bags. Wantage produced hammocks for the army and the navy, and much of the hemp and flax required was grown locally in the Vale and fulled in the waters of Letcombe Brook.

The other major raw material was leather, used for deerskin and sheepskin gloves. The royal lodge of Woodstock, much frequented by royalty (from Henry II to James I) and their aristocratic entourage created a demand for high-quality gloves and hunting gloves such as ones made with fine chain between the layers of leather for hawking. A Glovers' Gild was formed in Oxford in 1461, and some Oxford products were of extremely high quality—in 1512 a scholar purchased Oxford gloves valued at 6s.8d. During the sixteenth century gloves became increasingly elaborate, fine ones being scented and embroidered, and they were frequently given as expensive gifts. The Ashmolean

Museum possesses an exquisite embroidered pair, said to have been presented to Queen Elizabeth I on her visit to Oxford and undoubtedly made in either Oxford or Woodstock. Tradition has it that Elizabeth discarded her gift because, despite their beauty, the gloves are rather large, and the Queen was inordinately proud of her small hands. During the sixteenth century Oxford ceded its gloving supremacy to Woodstock, and the making of gloves was confined largely to the villages and towns within Wychwood Forest, notably Leafield, Wootton, Hanborough, Bladon, Eynsham and Stonesfield, because of the proximity of deerskins and sheepskins and the necessity for crafts in the forest where there was little agricultural work. Towns involved in the manufacture included Bampton, Chipping Norton and Charlbury. Until machines were introduced, in the latter part of the nineteenth century, it was a cottage industry. Outworkers each had their own particular jobs—only men were cutters, as it required strong hands to stretch the leather, and a five-year apprenticeship. Women did the sewing, and children with their small nimble fingers tied the threads at the finger ends. Both hand-sewn and machine-made gloves and other leather goods are made in Woodstock today in the factory in Chaucer's Lane. The Marlborough family continues its patronage of Woodstock glovemakers—at the coronation of Elizabeth II in 1952 the Duchess of Marlborough wore locally made, hand-sewn, elbow-length, doeskin gloves.

Leather was tanned throughout the county, and fellmongers in the Burford and Bampton area specialized in making leather breeches and leather linings. Burford was so renowned for its saddles during the seventeenth and eighteenth centuries that they were presented to Charles II and William II. Today Pavlova Leather of Abingdon processes leather and makes leather clothing. Minor leather crafts such as shoemaking were practised in every town and the larger villages.

Oxfordshire has rich clay belts which provide the raw material for brick, tile and pottery industries. Pottery has been made here since Roman times. Nettlebed, Stoke Row, Leafield, Banbury and Barford St Michael all made earthenware pottery—pans, pancheons, jugs, flowerpots, money boxes—all sorts of practical objects, in addition to bricks, tiles and drainpipes. Leafield, being in the heart of Wychwood Forest, had few industries, so the presence of good clay to dig locally was a great boon. The Franklin family were noted potters in the nineteenth century, making honeypots, tobacco-jars and stands for flat-irons. The process was typical of local potteries: the clay was dug and the narrow band of yellow clay at the top reserved for pottery, while the blue and brown clay made drainpipes. It was cut up and treated in a horse-driven pug-mill, then sliced with a brass wire to remove pebbles. After pots had been turned, they were coated with red glaze and fired.

Nettlebed was unique in the county in making stoneware and had several potteries, employing a large number of men and boys. None is now in operation, though many people still have their rich red-brown wares with speckled orange-brown glazes. In many cases all traces of such industries have disappeared from the landscape as buildings have been demolished and clay-pits filled in and the resultant reclaimed land planted with trees.

North Oxfordshire is rich in ironstone, which was quarried to obtain iron from the mid nineteenth century at Fawler, Adderbury, the Wroxton area and Hook Norton. Hook Norton became the base for the Brymbo Iron Works established in 1896. There ore was calcined to remove water content and reduce it to red oxide for use in purifying coal-gas before sending it to be further processed. Remains of calcining-kilns and the cutting along which ran the narrow-gauge railway, used for removing the ore, are still visible, although calcining here ceased in 1926. The Oxfordshire Ironstone Company operated in the Wroxham area until 1967.

A number of iron-foundries were established: W. Lucy & Company of Oxford formerly made much street furniture such as lamp standards for Oxford streets, and iron and steel bookcases for the Bodleian Library and other famous libraries. Much of their work was unfortunately demolished for scrap during the Second World War. Their Eagle Ironworks has adapted to new technology, making distribution, switch and fuse gear. Lampitt's of Banbury, Wilder's of Wallingford, Nalder's of East Challow and the White Horse Foundry of Wantage made many types of agricultural machines, for example portable engines, steam-engines, rice-hullers, and malting- and brewing-machinery from the mid nineteenth century. John Allen's Oxfordshire Steam Ploughing Company was founded in Cowley in 1868, expanding to make steam-rollers and fairground models and to enter the engineering field.

The largest agricultural engineering industry in the county was that of Bernhard Samuelson in Banbury, and it is partially to his enterprise that Banbury owes its status as an industrial town. Until the mid nineteenth century it was a thriving market-town, with the woollen industry as its mainstay. There had been small foundries before Bernhard Samuelson acquired both Joseph Gardner's works in 1848 and the patent of his very successful turnip-cutter which became one of his major products, continuing in production into the twentieth century. Samuelson founded his Britannia Works in Fish Street (now known as George Street), and his factories and the houses of his workers spread throughout Grimsbury as his business brought many new people to the town. His firm produced such items as the American McCormick reaper, winnow-machines, chaff-cutters, root-pulpers, lawn-mowers, harrows, hoes, digging- and forking-machines and helped to build the Hook Norton viaduct.

The opening of the railway in Banbury in 1850 simplified export of this machinery. In 1872 the Britannia Works produced eight thousand reaping-machines, and Samuelson was reputed to be one of the largest manufacturers in the world; the business continued into the 1930s. Samuelson was a Member of Parliament for Banbury for many years, and a great philanthropist, financing a technical school, the Mechanics' Institute for Adult Education, and taking a keen interest in the welfare of the town.

The manufacture of Woodstock steel flourished from the sixteenth until the early nineteenth century. It is an elaborate craft, creating jewellery and small items from exquisitely hand-cut multi-faceted steel studs, alleged to have been made from old horse-shoe nails, riveted or screwed to a steel back. These studs glittered like diamonds when new—indeed cut steel must have been nearly as expensive as diamonds, since a chain made in Woodstock, weighing a mere 2 ounces, was sold in France in 1810 for £170. A box of polished steel was purchased for £37.16s.2d in 1802 and presented, together with the Freedom of the Borough, to Lord Clifton. The Duke of Marlborough owned a cut-steel Garter star costing 50 guineas. A wide variety of goods was made, including scissors, buckles, watch-chains, sword-hilts, chatelaines and jewellery, but when larger centres such as Birmingham began producing similar wares—albeit generally considered to be inferior, the trade of Woodstock declined, and it had disappeared without trace by the mid nineteenth century.

Most areas of the county have their own breweries, aided by the current demand for real ale, and their beer is well received by the populace. Beer once formed a much more important part of the diet, and home brewing was not uncommon. Many large households had their own brew-houses, and churchwardens used to brew their own beer regularly and sell it to raise money to repair the structure of the church. Oxford colleges, notably New College and Brasenose, had their own brew-houses— Queen's College was still brewing until the onset of the Second World War, and one of its brews, known as 'Chancellor' had an original gravity of 1,140, indicating a full-bodied strong brew.

Banbury Ale was so renowned in the thirteenth century that Eleanor, Countess of Leicester, employed a Banbury alewife to brew her beer at Odiham in Hampshire, and Richard Braithwait in *A strappedo for the Divell* (1615) quipped: "Stile it I might Banberrie of the North, famous for twanging ale, zeale, cakes and cheese." During the nineteenth century Banbury had fourteen maltsters, and brewers Richard Austen, Wyatt's, Barrett's, and Dunnells & Hunt & Co (later becoming Hunt Edmund's, which closed in the 1960s). Henley is also noted for brewing, and in the sixteenth century Evans Arderne "was authorized and allowed to be a beerebrewer and to brew good holesome drink for mans bodye".[4] Brakspear's Henley Brewery was established in 1779 by Robert Brakspear and Joseph Benwell, and members of the family are still attached to the firm. The brewery has 129 pubs in the countryside around, all within 15 miles of the brewery. As with so many breweries, the water for the beer is extracted from a well beneath the brewery, and the beers dry-hopped to make mild, bitter, a special bitter and Old Ale.

Brewing in Hook Norton began in 1849 when John Harris began brewing in his farm-house, but he soon found that the demand for his beer was so great that he built his own brew-house. His son went into partnership with A. A. Clarke. The brew-house is quite a village landmark—a striking brick building partially resembling a Chinese pagoda. Inside is a small museum containing the brewery's archives and illustrating its history. In 1976 a special brew, Old Hookey, was introduced, which is brewed only during the winter months.

Morland's Brewery, Abingdon, was established in 1711, making it one of the oldest breweries still in existence, operating in a 1911 tower-style building. It has taken over a number of other breweries in Shillingford, Wantage and Berkshire. Some of the hops for its cask beer are grown at Kingston Bagpuize. Morrell's brew at the Lion Brewery, Oxford, which was built in 1892, although the firm was established around 1782; its brews include 'Varsity Bitter', 'College Ale' and a 'Celebration Ale' first brewed to celebrate the wedding of Princess Anne and Mark Phillips. South Leigh has an unusual publican in the person of Tom Litt at the 'Mason's Arms' who has one of the few home brew-houses and has been brewing the beer for his pub since 1975. Brewing has now ceased in Wantage, Witney, Burford and Thame, but real-ale addicts still have their pick of several fine beers.

No description of Oxfordshire products would be complete without a mention of Banbury cakes. These delicious cakes consist of a sugar-and-lemon-dusted pastry case containing currants, peel, sugar, brandy, rum and other ingredients (the 'authentic' recipe used by Brown's of Charlbury, late of Banbury, descendants of the original makers, is a strictly guarded secret, passed only from father to son and never divulged to outsiders). The first reference we have to the cakes is in 1586, when Thomas Bright, in his *Treatise of Melancholie*, commented:

> Sodden wheat is a grosse and melancholicke nourishment and bread especially of the fine flower unleavened. Of this sort are bag puddings made with flower, fritters, pancakes, such as we call Banberrie cakes, and the great ones confected with butter, eggs, etc. used at weddings, and however it be prepared rye and bread made thereof carried with it plenty of melancholie.

Banbury was notoriously Puritan in the late sixteenth and early seventeenth century, and that such cakes should be used at pagan celebrations, such as weddings, was a source of great disapproval. Ben Jonson in *Bartholomew Fair* (1610) satirized 'Zeal of the Land Busy', a Banbury baker, who gave up his trade because "... out of a scruple, he took, that, in spiced conscience, those Cakes he made were served to bridales, maypoles, morisses, and such profane feasts and meetings".[6]

The cakes survived this Puritan onslaught, and in the eighteenth century, thanks to Betty White and her husband

Jarvis, they became a household name. Betty was a careful woman and jealously guarded her reputation—she used to claim, "My name is quiet Betty, I never meddles nor makes with anybody, no mealman never calls on me twice." Inflation was rife in the eighteenth century too, and when people claimed that her prices were rising, she justified herself: "Only think, there's currants, they be twice the price th' used to be, and then there's butter and sugar, they be double the price th' was formerly."[7]

Her husband Jarvis apparently spent most of his time leaning over the shop door, making outrageous claims about his wife's cakes, maintaining that they were so light that a sparrow could fly off with one in its beak, or the wind could blow one away. The Whites owned The Original Cake Shop in Parsons Street, which was sadly demolished in 1968. The Betts and Beesley families were both making Banbury cakes in the nineteenth century, selling them to India, America and Australia. Queen Victoria was of course presented with a box of them on the occasion of her visit to the town.

Oxford reigned supreme in the field of marmalade. Frank Cooper, an Oxford grocer, married a lady named Sarah Jane, who so endeared herself to her customers that, according to family legend, she was given a superb marmalade recipe by an Oxford don's family. She cooked this on a large scale in the kitchen of the Angel Hotel, marketing it in earthenware jars from Frank Cooper's shop at 83 The High. Demand soon exceeded supply, so the manufacture was transferred to a factory in Park End Street, where it was lovingly made together with concoctions such as horseradish relish and mint sauce as well as jams. Oxford Marmalade has travelled to the slopes of Everest with Sir Edmund Hilary and to the South Pole with Captain Scott. Coopers' products have long enjoyed royal and aristocratic patronage, and they proudly noted in their advertising that their marmalade formed part of the diet of the Oxford University Boat Race crew. A booklet published for the company extolled the quality of the products:

I can emphatically speak of the unique properties of the 'Oxford' Homemade Marmalade, which has a specially inviting and attractive delicacy and flavour, and is an article possessing a world-wide connection, and universally liked. It possesses valuable tonic and digestive qualities and is a welcome and wholesome addition to any meal. It is made from carefully selected oranges of the best type, and the finest sugar, and is appetising and satisfying in an eminent degree.[8]

The marmalade is now partially manufactured in Seville, to use the oranges at their freshest.

The presence of Oxford University, with many academics and scholars, has stimulated a consistent demand for parchment, paper, printing and publishing. During the Middle Ages parchment made from sheepskin was used for books and documents rather than paper. Paper was made in Oxford from Tudor times, and Wolvercote Mill soon became one of the main centres of production—in 1722 Hearne wrote that John Beckford, who then lived at Wolvercote Mill, made some of the best paper in England. Various other mills were operating during the nineteenth century at Eynsham, Sandford-on-Thames, Shiplake, Rotherfield Peppard, Oxford and Henley, all on the banks of the Thames. Canvas sails and cotton rags formed the raw materials, the snag with the former being the tarred thread used to sew them up, and the pitch from the decks splashed on them, while the cotton rags contained "a perceptible quantity of animal matter, the nature of which may be imagined, when it is stated that they are the cast-off garments of the lower class of society . . . The animal matter is very perceptible in the smell."[9] Wolvercote printed very fine India paper for Oxford Bibles, which was so strong that a fifteen-hundred-page volume could be suspended from a single leaf. In contrast, Adderbury Mill was producing special watermarked banknote paper in the latter part of the nineteenth century.

Oxford University Press had an uncertain beginning. The first book, issued in 1478, was most misleading—it has the date 1468 inside, now generally believed to be wrong, and it was an exposition of the Apostles' Creed, which, although credited to St Jerome, was really written by Tyrannius Rufinus. During this first period, until 1487, there were probably two printers in Oxford. Then the Press suddenly and inexplicably ceased production, not re-starting until 1517 and then in existence for only two years. It re-opened in 1585 to publish *The true difference between christian subjection and unchristian rebellion* by Thomas Bilston. The Earl of Leicester, then Chancellor of the University, encouraged the Press, and no one seemed aware that it had existed before. The new printer was Joseph Barnes, who, like John Cheney at Banbury a century later, combined printing with wine-selling. Archbishop Laud greatly encouraged the "learned" Press in the early seventeenth century, and the Civil War, far from disrupting it, increased its workload while Charles I was based in Oxford issuing proclamations. Dr Fell was the Press's benefactor during the Restoration, donating many type-matrices, and 1675 saw the beginning of the world-famous Bible Press which has been a mainstay to the Oxford University Press ever since. The Clarendon Building, such a feature of Broad Street, was the Press house from 1713, when it was built by Lord Clarendon to the design of Nicholas Hawksmoor, until 1830, when it became too small and new premises were erected in Walton Street.

The Press concentrated on its Bibles, Prayer Books and academic tracts but had now extended its range to include more general topics. The University has often been ambivalent about it, almost accusing it after the Second World War of deliberately not publishing the books required for academic courses, when the real cause of the problem was the running-down of stocks during the war and the drastic paper-shortage which continued until 1949. It has a large number of branches throughout the world and is one of the major employers in the city, consistently maintaining its high academic reputation.

Publishing is not confined to the University—Blackwell's must rank a close second, and there are many other small publishers. In Banbury printing is carried on by John Cheney, whose family has run the business since 1767, when the first John Cheney took up printing as a sideline while running the Unicorn Inn, selling French brandy and ales and at the same time printing ballads. In 1788 he abandoned the pub to concentrate on printing. The firm has superb archives of the items it has printed through the years, indicating a range of work from *Rasselas* to sermons, chapbooks, ballads and posters. The present John Cheney specializes in high-quality work and colour printing.

Every county has its quota of village crafts. Chair bodging was an important one in the Chiltern area. The beechwoods provided the raw materials, and the bodgers built primitive huts in the woods where they set up their pole lathes, felling trees between November and March, when the wood lacked sap.

The wood was chopped along the grain, shaved on the draw-shave horse, then turned on the lathe. Completed chair legs were sent to High Wycombe to be made into chairs. As the industry declined, their work was sometimes reduced to making tent-pegs. Often the bodger combined bodging with other jobs, as did Silas Saunders who ran the 'Crooked Billet' pub at Stoke Row, grew cherries in the orchard behind it and bodged in a hut adjacent to the pub. Silas is dead, and his bodging equipment is in the County Museum, but the pub is relatively unchanged, and visitors are entertained in the homely sitting-room, while beer is dispensed from the kitchen rather than a bar. The country crafts have almost disappeared, together with the rural life they served—blacksmiths have mostly set up garages, but one can still find the odd saddler and thatcher to meet modern needs.

The changes which have taken place in our way of life over the last century are well illustrated by the new industries. William Morris showed an astute appreciation of the new trends in the establishment of his Motor Company, which has become one of the major elements in Oxfordshire's industrial life. Even he can scarcely have realized the magnitude of what he would achieve. He was born in Worcester in 1877 and moved to Oxford at the age of three. His father, Frederick, had emigrated to Canada as a mail-coach driver but in 1876 returned to marry Emily Pether of Headington and became bailiff on her father's farm until his asthma forced him to take clerical jobs to support his family of seven.

William left the church school at Cowley at sixteen to become apprenticed to a bicycle-repairer but was astute enough to realize that he would do better working for himself, and nine months later, with a capital of £4, he started a bicycle-repair shop in the back of his parents' home in James Street and soon set up a showroom and shop in one of the front rooms. Not content with repairing bicycles, he soon had his first commission to make one, for Mr Pilcher, rector of St Clement's, a large man who required a 27-inch frame. His business rapidly outgrew his parents' house, so he took on premises at 48 High Street in 1901, making motorcycles. He cherished his employees—Alfred Keen, who became his apprentice in 1902, retired in 1953 as director of the British Motor Corporation. Employees wore white jerseys with 'Ride Motor Cycles' emblazoned in red on back and front. He realized that the age of the motor-car was beginning and started to garage cars in new premises in Longwall Street—alas demolished in 1979. Although the partnership he formed with an undergraduate and an Oxford businessman to create 'The Oxford Automobile and Cycle Agency' was a failure and was wound up after a year, it had the merit of starting him in the car busines.

Meanwhile he considered the possibility of creating a cheap, economical car of high quality and in 1910 began the initial work in his Longwall garage. His two-seater Morris Oxford appeared in March 1913, with a 10-horsepower engine, designed by White & Poppe of Coventry. The 'bullnose', costing £175 complete, became a familiar site. New premises were purchased on the site of a military training college in Cowley. He formed WRM Motors with himself as managing director and the Earl of Macclesfield as President. Their agents increased in number from ninety-nine in 1913 to 909 a year later, operating in Holland, Belgium, Denmark, Italy, Scandinavia and Uganda as well as Britain.

The Morris Cowley, which could be either a two- or a four-seater, was launched in 1915, despite the loss of many of its American-built engines which were sunk by German U-boats on their journey across the Atlantic. The firm, in spite of being adapted for munitions during the war, increased in strength, and Morris received an OBE. In 1919 Morris Motors Ltd took over from WRM Motors Ltd, and the first 'assembly line' was set up, although it was not mechanized until the 1930s. Morris survived the economic slump of the twenties and gradually bought up his suppliers. The MG began as an experiment to 'hot up' the Morris Minor, and in 1930 a new factory (which closed in 1980) was set up at Abingdon to produce the Midget.

In 1929 Morris was created a baronet, in 1934 a baron and in 1938 Viscount Nuffield of Nuffield, named after his home, Nuffield Place, still owned by Nuffield College, next to Huntercombe Golf Course, which he also owned and where he enjoyed playing golf. In 1952 the firm became part of the British Motor Corporation, merging with the Austin Motor Company. Morris was chairman for six months, retiring at the age of seventy-five. Now his firm is part of the unwieldy British Leyland, and in face of the oil-shortage and fierce competition its future is uncertain. The atmosphere of the family firm has disappeared within the amorphous body of a nationalized industry.

Morris was a generous philanthropist, giving much of his large fortune to further medical research—to hospitals and to form the Nuffield Institute of Medical Research. He founded Nuffield College, Oxford, for social studies, gave benefactions to St Peter's Hall and Worcester, Pembroke and Lincoln Colleges. He died a lonely man in 1963.

Pressed Steel Fisher Company's history has been closely linked with that of William Morris, who established the company in 1926, with finance provided by the merchant banker Henry J. Shroeder and with the American Edward J. Budd providing the technical knowledge, while Morris supplied the site and the work. The firm made, painted and trimmed car bodies. It soon became obvious that it could supply far more bodies than Morris could use, but other firms were reluctant to place orders because of Morris's interest, so he withdrew. Orders flowed in from Rover's, Hillman and Austin. In 1935 the American interests were withdrawn, leaving it independent. The previous year the company had introduced Prestcold Refrigeration. In 1939 2,500 motor bodies were produced each week by six thousand employees. The workforce increased to ten thousand during the war, and armoured cars, aircraft, submarine and mine parts were made. The company purchased several new factories after the war, starting new companies such as the British Executive and General Aviation Company which produced a range of light aircraft in 1960. This was taken over by the Government in 1967.

In 1965 Pressed Steel Fisher merged with the British Motor Corporation and after successive re-organization became part of British Leyland Components. The Cowley plant makes car bodies and manufactures tools and jigs for other manufacturing companies such as Vauxhall's, Ford's of Cologne, Simca, Volvo, Standard Triumph and Alfa-Romeo. The company was responsible for the introduction of the use of polystyrene in pattern-making, a notable development in this field.

The impact of the motor industry has extended to Banbury, where Automotive Products manufacture car parts, bringing immigrant workers to the area, as have the two major new industries in Banbury, which between them dominate the labour market in the town. These are Alcan Industries (UK) Ltd and General Foods, both part of multi-national companies which came to Banbury because it provided suitable land and facilities. They were at first regarded as alien, as they brought many outsiders to take advantage of the employment they offer, but now both have merged into the local community to form an integral part of the character of the town.

It was considered a *coup* to attract the Northern Aluminium Company in 1930, which, although it had sold aluminium products in England since 1909, had begun manufacturing here at a Birmingham factory only in 1926. Banbury was depressed and the prospect of new employment most welcome. The new steel-mill began production in its 39-acre site on the Southam Road in 1931, making hollow-ware such as panelling for motor bodies and aircraft, remelting pig aluminium from Canada and producing aluminium alloys. The firm then employed two hundred staff, giving a great boost to the town. In 1934 an extrusion department was added and a year later a tube-drawing department, and Alpaste, a pigment for paint and printing-ink, was developed. During the war the demand for strong aluminium alloys for aircraft bodies dominated the firm's production, and work for aircraft such as Comet and Britannia continued to utilize this capacity. Parts of the liner *United States*, holds for trawlers and hulls for launches, lifeboats and yachts were manufactured in Banbury. Alcan diversified to produce electrical equipment and bridges. The Alcan group is the largest supplier of aluminium ingot and the largest manufacturer of semi-fabricated aluminium articles in the United Kingdom, with products ranging from windows, doors, shopfronts, safety glass, vehicle bodies and refrigerated containers to aluminium gas-cylinders for diving and soft drinks. In 1979 the UK head offices of this great multi-national company were brought to Banbury, indicating the importance of its operations in the town.

The great green-glazed offices and factory of General Foods are an unmistakable landmark on the Southam Road. The green glass, designed to merge with the rural setting, is typical of the firm's attitude to its new home. Even before the firm of Alfred Bird & Sons, as it was then, actually moved its factory to Banbury in 1965, it took care to pave the way for its arrival with sensitive public relations, accustoming the town to the idea of its arrival and giving its Birmingham employees a chance to get to know their new home. Bird's has now become part of the massive General Foods Ltd, which has branches as far apart as Japan, Australia, Sweden, the USA and Venezuela. Banbury products include Maxwell House Coffee (which has occasionally caused problems when 'coffee fall-out' has covered washing and cars near the factory, but such problems have been rapidly solved) and a wide range of desserts. Banbury has been chosen as the head United Kingdom office.

Oxfordshire boasts two important international research centres. The Atomic Energy Research Establishment at Harwell started in 1945 to research all aspects of the use of atomic energy, with Nobel Prize winner Dr John Cockcroft as its first director. In 1954, when it became part of the Atomic Energy Authority, it had four research reactors, four accelerators for high-energy physics, a radio-chemical laboratory and over two thousand industrial staff. Since 1965 Harwell has widened its scope to tackle non-nuclear problems for industry—investigating industrial competitiveness and environmental problems, financed by Government and industry. Fourteen separate divisions cover physics, computer science, chemistry, environmental and medical sciences, metallurgy and engineering. The Environmental and Medical Science Division's work includes the sampling of radio-active fall-out, dating the sediment in lakes, investigating the effects of aerosol propellants and refrigerants on the stratospheric ozone layer, monitoring ozone by stratospheric sampling from Concorde, finger-printing and industrial land reclamation. The Analytical Department investigates the composition of drug tablets; the Material Physics Department is concerned with laser optics; the Chemical Department hopes to diminish pollution of the environment by developing a car-exhaust catalyst. Other projects cover geological exploration of the sea bed, study of marine structures, and mining developments. The research at Harwell affects the future development of the world in many different and vitally important ways, combating the pollution our society is creating, and augmenting attempts to conserve energy resources and develop alternatives.

Another research project which could revolutionize future energy-sources is the Joint European Torus project recently set up at Culham Laboratory. The Atomic Energy Authority initiated the project in 1961, aiming to create a new type of nuclear reactor to harness energy released when the nuclei of light elements such as hydrogen fuse together. The project has become one of the first major scientific research projects to be sponsored by the European Economic Community, and Culham was chosen despite strong competition from Italy and Germany. It will be many years before scientists know whether or not the project has worked or will be economic, as there are enormous difficulties to combat. The raw materials are cheap and readily available from the oceans which surround us—the main requirements being deuterium, or heavy hydrogen, and lithium, which is readily available in quantities estimated to be enough to last for at least five thousand years. A full-scale fusion power-station would require only a few pounds of fuel a day—the snag being that the 'hardware' is very expensive. To fuse atoms, rather than split them as is done at present, the temperature has to be raised to at least 100 million degrees Centigrade to make the atoms move so fast that they stop bouncing off one another and fuse instead. The maximum reached at present is 20 million degrees, and as current materials used for reactors cannot withstand such great heats, the reaction is isolated from its container inside an impenetrable magnetic field which deflects the particles—it looks rather like a hollow cylindrical tube with the ends joined to form a circle. According to present plans, there should be fusion reactions by 1988. It is fascinating to think of such research taking place in the heart of the Oxfordshire countryside. The impact the project has made is more than merely scientific, as a new European scientific community has been established here to work on the project forming a microcosm of Europe in Oxfordshire, complete with its own school.

4

The Thames, Canals, Roads and Railways

All in the golden afternoon
Full leisurely we glide;
For both our oars, with little skill,
By little arms are plied,
While little hands make vain pretence
Our wanderings to guide.

Ah, cruel Three! In such an hour,
Beneath such dreamy weather,
To beg a tale of breath too weak
To stir the tiniest feather?
Yet what can one poor voice avail
Against three tongues together?

Thus grew the tale of Wonderland;
Thus slowly, one by one,
Its quaint events were hammered out—
And now the tale is done,
And home we steer, a merry crew,
Beneath the setting sun.[1]

Lewis Carroll responded to the magic of the Thames, weaving his tale of Alice while enjoying boating expeditions on the river —his 'pool of tears' episode was probably inspired by a soaking he and the children had on an expedition to Nuneham. He epitomized the Victorian view of the Thames as a source of pleasure and amusement, which it still is to a lesser extent today. Punting expeditions are as popular as ever, and pleasure-steamers take eager tourists on river trips. But the Thames used to play a more important role. It even formed a defensive boundary between Saxon kingdoms—although the local inhabitants must have regretted their proximity to the river when the Viking longships sailed up it to make lightning raids.

Until the nineteenth century the river's main importance was a major transport route linking Oxford and the Thames Valley with London and the sea. The river had many shallows, where boats needed additional water to float them through—if this water was not available, cargoes had to be unloaded onto wagons. Mills created weirs, which could be used to help barges through the shallows, but they caused conflicts of interest which dogged the history of Thames improvement, as millers charged boatmen for the use of water, restricting the number of times they 'flashed' the water, perhaps only opening weirs once or twice a week. This led to delays for the bargemen, but the millers dared not antagonize them too far, because their grain and flour were transported by boat, and the cargoes carried by the bargemen belonged to wealthy, powerful merchants.

Repeated attempts were made to improve navigation— Edward the Confessor in 1066 denounced the hindrances caused by fish-weirs and mills, ordering that such hazards should be destroyed. The abbot of Abingdon rechannelled the river by the abbey in the eleventh century. In the fifteenth century navigation from London terminated at Henley, gradually improving so that by the sixteenth century boats could reach Buscot. The poor communications devastated trade between London and Oxford.

In 1605 Commissioners were appointed to clear the navigation between Oxford and Buscot, but they had insufficient powers, and it was not until 1624, when the town and university joined forces, that they were empowered to build wharves, locks and pound locks. The first pound lock was built at Iffley, Sandford and at Abingdon, where the lock was built on Switch Ditch, the old river channel earlier scorned by the Abingdon monks.

The river was open to Oxford in 1635, but the problems were not entirely solved, and during the dry summer months boats were frequently grounded. Further Acts were made to improve navigation, but the situation remained imperfect, hindered by the conflicts of interest between those who owned the fishing rights, and the bargemen. The end of the eighteenth century saw the building of several canals linked to the Thames, making good navigation even more vital. In 1789 the Thames and Severn Canal opened, linking those two rivers, providing a water route from the West Midlands and South Wales to Oxford and London. A year later the Oxford Canal reached Oxford, giving easy access to Coventry and the Midlands coalfields. In 1796 Isis and Louse lock linked the Oxford Canal directly to the river, and the Basingstoke Canal was completed. The Wiltshire and Berkshire Canal, begun in 1796, was completed in 1810, with links to the Kennet and Avon at Semington, and the Thames at Abingdon. The Thames became part of a network of waterways which increased its economic importance, but shortly canal and river traffic paled into insignificance in comparison with the railways. The powers of the Thames Commissioners were curtailed in 1857 as the Thames Conservancy took control of the river below Staines, although they retained control over the upper reaches until 1866, when the Conservancy took control of the entire river. The Commissioners attempted to compete with the railways by lowering tolls and even reducing lock-keepers' wages but were unable to stem the decline in barge traffic. The new Conservancy had few funds, but despite this they built new locks in the 1890s at Northmoor, Radcot, Grafton and Shifford and after the Second World War undertook the enormous project of mechanizing all the locks from Teddington to Godstow, changing electrical-mechanical systems such as that installed at Mapledurham in 1956 to hydraulic locks such as that at Shiplake. The Thames Conservancy was replaced in 1973 by the Thames Water Authority, which controls water-supplies, sewage and navigation in the Thames Valley area.

Most barges used on the Thames by the eighteenth century were flat-bottomed, to cope with the shoals, propelled by sail or towed. It could take six horses or sixty men to haul a laden barge over shoals, so it is hardly surprising that by the nineteenth century horses had replaced men. Living conditions aboard these barges were somewhat primitive, with a canvas awning at the stern, instead of a cabin. Because of the difficulties of navigation on the upper reaches, progressively smaller barges were used—70-ton barges could reach Lechlade, 100-ton barges travelled up to Oxford, and 140-ton barges went as far as Wallingford.

Bargemen tended to be a law unto themselves:

These boatmen pursue the same life from generation to generation . . . but they are remarkably exclusive, in daily life mixing as little as possible with the villagers with whom they come into contact. They are a class apart, and have an undisguised contempt for the ordinary rustic . . . They say, with some truth, that unless a man is born and bred to boating, he is never lissom enough . . . Their spirit of independence, amounting to a general readiness to fight, is a marked contrast to the opposite manners of the peasantry, especially noted by Oxford undergraduates, between whom and the 'bargees' there is an old-standing hostility.[2]

The pleasure-boaters of the nineteenth century resented the barges:

That they are useful may be taken for granted; that they are possibly ornamental, may be a matter of opinion; that they are a decided nuisance when a string of them under the convoy of a vicious steam-tug, monopolizes a lock for an hour or so, admits of no doubt. And the steam-tugs themselves are an abomination. They are driven along with a sublime disregard of the interests of persons in punts and small boats—in this respect resembling their more distinguished relatives, the steam-launches—and raise a wash which, one would suppose, can be as little beneficial to the banks of the river as it is to the peace of mind of the anglers and oarsmen. Nor are the manners and customs of their crews, or of their associates, the bargees, such as to conduce to the comfort of riparian proprietors or of pleasure-seekers.[3]

Evidently the average Victorian considered the pleasure aspect of the Thames of more value than the commercial one!

Bargemen and fishermen formed very distinct communities —perhaps epitomized by the close-knit community in Fisher Row, Oxford, in the parish of St Thomas. The first references to fishermen there occur in the thirteenth century, and they became established during the sixteenth and seventeenth centuries. Great continuity may be observed in the families of that area working on the river, adapting themselves as circumstances changed, some becoming bargemen when the demand for fish declined in the late seventeenth century as the practice of eating fish on fast-days was no longer rigorously observed. Later some bargemen changed to working narrow boats on the canals. The Beesleys and Bossoms, two of the major families in St Thomas's, feuded almost constantly. Thomas Bossom owned four barges on the Thames, and relatives were lock-keepers at Osney, Folly Bridge and Medley Weir in the early nineteenth century. Another Bossom, George, to the horror of his enemies

the Beesleys, was appointed water bailiff in the 1820s as part of
the Council's campaign to limit the fishermen's rights. Fishing
was becoming a popular amateur sport, and it was feared that
the fishermen of Fisher Row, who as freemen were entitled to
use the waters in Oxford, were over-fishing and thus destroying
their sport. This caused great controversy—nets were seized,
court cases held, all hastening the decline in the river fishing
trade, which received its death knell from cheap fish brought by
railway to the inland markets of Oxfordshire—Faringdon acquired its first fishmonger shortly after the railway opened
there. Abel Beesley was the last man in Oxford to call himself a
fisherman, but he eventually became more of a waterman and
was involved with pleasure-boating.[4] Fishermen diversified as
they needed additional income during the close season, becoming watermen carrying goods and passengers, or wild-fowling,
cutting osiers and rushes or even indulging in poaching.

The fishermen set traps, often at weirs, to catch eels:

> They are made of an elongated narrow basket, closed on every side
> except at the mouth and extreme end, about 56 inches in length, a
> yard in circumference at the largest part, 16 inches at the base of the
> entrance arch, about a foot high at the apex; the open end is round, 6
> inches in diameter, and closed up when in use by a movable stopper
> made of heavy unbarked pine wood. It must be effectually sunken, by
> wiring on half of a hard brick to each side of the narrow shoulder, and
> by another brick similarly fixed under the end; all the weights to rest
> level on the ground, and be sufficiently heavy to keep the flat base of
> the entrance perfectly level also, and to prevent the basket floating
> away or shifting. In the Thames, where gudgeons, etc., are plentiful,
> seven placed alive in each basket are the best of all baits. The use of a
> punt is necessary to store them in the well, also the eels when
> captured, and to carry the baskets and set them in likely places.[5]

The anglers have now superseded the professional fishermen
—there are now around five thousand of them based on Oxford,
and many more must use the other rivers. Crayfish are still
netted on the Windrush and the Evenlode. The Thames is an
angler's paradise, and salmon are being experimentally re-
introduced now that pollution has been drastically reduced.
Trout-fishing was a favourite pastime for Victorian anglers.
Trout-fishermen can join the Farmoor Fly Fishing Club and fish
Farmoor reservoir, which is stocked with brown and rainbow

trout. The lazy 'angler' can obtain his trout from one of the local trout-farms such as the one near Eynsham.

The river banks provided additional sources of income for the professional fishermen. Osiers, a type of willow, are grown in beds called holts or hams, often found on Thames eyots or islands and usually cut in March. After cutting they are sorted into different sizes and types ready for basket-making, such as Luke, Threepenny, Middleborough and Great; those spoiled by lateral shoots were called 'Ragged' or 'Rough'. Those to be used for brown baskets were stacked while those for peeled baskets required stripping in tools known as 'brakes', a convivial occupation:

> The first thing that strikes a visitor, on approaching the scene of the rod-stripping, is a hum of merry voices mingled with the ever-recurring musical 'ping' of the break; the shape of the instrument is not unlike that of a very narrow jews harp, and fully accounts for its resonance. The strong aromatic smell of the fresh peelings is probably what will next be noticed, as the air is quite laden with what is an agreeable, if slightly pungent, odour.[6]

During the nineteenth century Jacob Beesley, of Fisher Row, had an osier bed by Rewley Abbey, on a site which had previously been waste land, where the fishermen had beached their boats and laid out their nets to dry.

In August the fishermen cut rushes, which they sold for making rush chair-seats, rush lights (a cheaper form of lighting than candles, made by dipping rushes into mutton fat), mats and baskets, and for stuffing pack saddles and in barrel-making and thatching. These were harvested with a reaping-hook attached to a long pole, then tied in bundles and carried back home in the fisherman's punt. As rushes contract in drying, they were laid out in a field to dry for two to three weeks before being tied in bundles 40 inches in circumference called 'bolts'. Wild rushes were cut, but some fishermen propagated rush plantations, which took five or six years to mature from seed. The fishermen would have found it hard to survive without such additional sources of income.

Anglers are wary of the magnificent swans gliding along the river. Most belong to the Crown, and a Royal Swan Keeper has been appointed at least since the thirteenth century. The privilege of owning swans is shared by the Vintners' and Dyers' Companies. The Queen's swans are unmarked; those of the Vintners have a notch on both sides of the upper beak, those of the Dyers a notch on one side. Each July at Swan Upping, the cygnets are marked. The Dyers are allowed sixty-five birds and the Vintners forty-five, to the Queen's five hundred odd—their jurisdiction covers the area between Blackfriars and Henley, and the Queen's Swan Keeper organizes the event with the swan keepers of both Livery Companies, assisted by watermen, who do the hard work of rowing and actually handling the birds. Nowadays they use double-sculling skiffs, but at one time the old city Livery Companies' barges, or horse-drawn houseboats, were used, and the party stopped overnight at Staines, Taplow and Henley.

Pleasure-boating had begun as early as the seventeenth century. In the 1790s a young Trinity undergraduate by the name of Skinner sailed, rowed and towed the *Hobby Horse* from Folly Bridge to Iffley and Sandford, commenting on the dress worn by the boaters:

> Where a Dame
> Hooper yclept, at station waits
> For gownsmen, whom she aptly freights
> In various vessels moored in view,
> Skiff, gig, and cutter, or canoe.
> Election made, each in a trice
> Becomes transformed with trousers nice,
> Jacket and catskin cap supplied,
> Black gowns and trenchers laid aside.[7]

The year 1829 was memorable in the history of rowing, being the occasion of the first Oxford *versus* Cambridge Boat Race, held at Henley, following a challenge from Cambridge. Oxford won easily. Although the race was subsequently transferred to its London venue, the crews continue to train in Cambridge and Oxford. In 1858 the crew's special diet consisted of beef and mutton, occasionally varied with poultry or fish, and followed by a nourishing and substantial pudding of rice, sago or tapioca. The president was convinced that this gave his oarsmen great strength. The crew always comes from the Oxford University Boat Club, and the boat race is the culmination of months of hard work and training. The crew often trains at Henley and

Wallingford, and two weeks before the race they go to Putney. Training was demanding, as this description of its practice in 1861 shows:

> Feb 16th, rowed to Wallingford, dined there, came back by train. March 2, again rowed to Wallingford ... In the morning the old system of a mile run before chapel was dropped and a walk of half a mile substituted, which was found a great improvement. Breakfast of chops and steaks, bread and butter, and tea. Lunch, a half-pint of beer and bread and butter, or a sandwich and a glass of sherry and biscuits, which suited some men much better. At half-past two started for our row, after which we always had a run of a mile or half a mile. A clean jersey for rowing in every day was insisted upon. For dinner we had four days a week beef or mutton, and on the others fowls, fish for Sunday, and once or twice a light pudding. We were always careful to have the same (one pint) of beer every day. After dinner two glasses of port; never allowed large glasses, but occasionally, after hard work, an extra glass. For supper a basin of gruel or a cup of chocolate, and to bed at 10.30 sharp.[8]

Perhaps more immediate in their significance to the undergraduates are the Torpids races held in the Lent term, and the Eights in the summer term—eight-oared races extending over a week, during which each boat tries to catch the one in front and touch it and, if successful, takes its place in the next day's race, the ultimate winner being head of the river. Bernard Shaw disapproved of the importance given to rowing: "It is characteristic of the authorities in Oxford that they should consider a month too little for the preparation of a boat-race and grudge three weeks to the rehearsals of one of Shakespeare's plays."[9]

Max Beerbohm, on the other hand, captured the atmosphere in his fantasy *Zuleika Dobson*:

> The Judas Eight had just embarked for their voyage to the starting-point. Standing on the edge of the raft that makes a floating platform for the barge, William, the hoary bargee, was pushing them off with his boat-hook, wishing them luck with deferential familiarity. The raft was thronged with Old Judasians—mostly clergymen—who were shouting hearty hortations, and evidently trying not to appear so startlingly old as their contemporaries looked to them ...
>
> The enormous eight young men in the thread-like skiff—the skiff that would scarce have seemed an adequate vehicle for the tiny 'cox' who sat facing them—were staring up at Zuleika with that uniformity of impulse which, in another direction, had enabled them to bump

a boat or two of the previous 'nights'. If tonight they bumped the next boat, Univ., then would Judas be three places 'up' on the river; and tomorrow Judas would have a Bump Supper. Furthermore, if Univ. were bumped tonight, Magdalen might be bumped tomorrow. Then would Judas, for the first time in history, be head of the river. Oh tremulous hope![10]

Now the college barges such as the one used by 'Judas' supporters have been replaced by boat-houses. The earliest barges were purchased from the City Livery Companies in the mid-nineteenth century. In 1853 the university barge was commissioned—its hull being built in Pangbourne for £299 and the upper part in Oxford, at a total cost of £1,500. They were magnificent, richly ornamental affairs, with panelled saloons, changing-facilities for club members and dining-rooms, and they formed an ideal grandstand for spectators on race days. As recently as 1932 they stood in a long line by Folly Bridge. Alas, the wooden hulls rotted, and the barges became unsafe. The heroic efforts of the Oxfordshire Barges Trust to restore a few has been dogged by misfortune—they have completed the Jesus College barge, with the aid of the Sheriff of Maidenhead, and it is moored at Maidenhead, but the Hertford College barge was under repair when it was destroyed by fire. However, part of the Keble College barge is on display in the Museum of Oxford.

The international fame of Henley is based on its colourful regatta, which attracts rowers from all over the world, justly, as it is one of the oldest, having started in 1839. Various boat-races had taken place on Henley Reach, so it was decided to set these on a formal basis. In 1851 Prince Albert, the Prince Consort, extended his patronage, enabling it to become the Henley Royal Regatta, and it is still one of the 'events' of the social season, with the accompanying high standards of fashion—particularly in hats—maintained. A silver cup, the Henley Regatta Challenge Cup or Grand Challenge Cup valued at 100 guineas, was the main prize at the 1839 Regatta, rowed for by eight-oared boats, and the Town Challenge Cup was for four-oared boats, limited to clubs whose members lived within 5 miles of Henley.

The satirical magazine *Punch* realized that the social side could be of paramount importance to some spectators:

A Regatta Rhyme

On board the *Athena*, Henley-on-Thames.

I like, it is true, in a basswood canoe
To lounge, with a weed incandescent.
To paddle about, there is not a doubt,
I find it uncommonly pleasant!
I love the fresh air, the lunch here and there,
To see pretty toilettes and faces;
But one thing I hate—allow me to state—
The fuss they make over the Races.
I DON'T CARE A RAP FOR THE RACES!—
MID ALL THE REGATTA EMBRACES—
I'M THAT SORT OF CHAP, I DON'T CARE A RAP,
A RAP OR A SNAP FOR THE RACES!

I don't care, you know, a bit how they row,
Nor mind about smartness of feather;
If steering is bad, I'm not at all sad,
Nor care if they all swing together!
Or why do they shout and make such a rout,
When one boat another chases?
'Tis really too hot to bawl, is it not?
Or bore oneself over the Races!
  I DON'T CARE A RAP, etc . . .

Then the Umpire's boat a nuisance we vote,
It interrupts calm contemplation:
Its discordant tone, and horrid steam moan,
Is death to serene meditation!
The roar of the crowd should not be allowed:
The gun with its fierce fulmination;
Abolish it, pray—'tis fatal they say
To pleasant and quiet flirtation!
I DON'T CARE A RAP etc . . . [11]

Punting was popular from the 1840s, for both pleasure and racing. Racing was practised largely by watermen and fishermen using fishermen's punts and was a rough-and-tumble affair. The Beesley family of Oxford were superb punt-racers— S. Beesley won the 1842 punt-race, receiving a purse of 15 shillings. Abel Beesley rose to greater heights—he is credited with the introduction of an extension to the normal stroke, known as an 'after shove,' and was the first person to punt from one position rather than walking or running the punt. In 1877 he won the English championship, remaining champion until 1886 when the Professional Punting Championship was instituted—he won that six times and retired in 1890.

The demand for pleasure- and sporting-boats encouraged local boat-builders. Salter's is one of the oldest surviving boat-building firms in Oxford, established in 1858. They make, according to their advertising: "Boats of every Description, Canoes, Punts, etc., built to order on the shortest notice." They built and ran steam launches for hire, publishing their own *Guide to the Thames* with suggested tours. In 1905 they built the steamboat SS *Endeavour*, for the Baptist Missionary Society —it was dismantled and transported to Africa where it cruised the Congo River for some years. Salter's now make many boats from glass fibre, although they have not abandoned wooden racing-shells.

George Harris & Sons have their boatyard near Donnington Bridge. The business began with punt- and skiff-making in the 1880s and extended to include the hiring of boats and steam launches, specializing now in racing boats. Cedar hulls have been replaced by plywood, but old techniques of moulding and steaming continue. Hobbs & Sons, founded in 1870, operate from Henley, and one of their annual tasks is putting down the pilings which mark the Regatta course. They built three of the launches used by Regatta umpires, the *Amaryllis*, *Magician* and *Enchantress*.

A notable feature of the Henley Regatta, typical of the Victorian Thames, was the houseboat. They descended from barges and were at first used for carrying passengers, but by the 1880s they were frequently privately owned. They vied for position at the Regatta and were gorgeously decorated:

> Going down the line, the first boat to attract exceptional attention and admiration is unquestionably the *Ione*, which is a perfect flower garden on the upper deck, the predominant colours being yellow and white with large palms in green tubs, surrounded by marguerites, the whole rendered brilliant by the colouring of a huge Japanese umbrella, this combination of colouring, together with the red blinds which shade the many windows, render this floating house one of the most notable on the course. Next door, but one, is however, another palatial residence, appropriately enough named *Dolce far niente*, radiant with yellow and white flowers, blooming in the shade of a

green awning from which is suspended a number of hanging baskets full of blossom.[12]

Steam launches were popular among tourists but not with other river-users:

> Steam launches are too often the curse of the river. Driving along at an excessive rate of speed, with an utter disregard to the comfort or necessities of anglers, oarsmen and boating parties, the average steam launch engineer is an unmitigated nuisance . . . Perhaps the worst offenders are the people who pay their £5.5s a day for the hire of a launch, and whose idea of a holiday is the truly British notion of getting over as much ground as possible in a given time. Parties of this kind, especially after the copious lunch which is one of the features of the day's outing, stimulate the engineer to fresh exertions, and appear to enjoy themselves considerably as they contemplate the anxiety and discomfort of the occupants of the punts and rowing-boats which are left floundering helplessly in their wash.[13]

Many individuals enjoy holidays on the Thames—Jerome K. Jerome's epic *Three Men in a Boat*, first published in 1889, encouraged many people to follow his example, and indeed his route. He described the hard work of rowing and the amusements of such a trip, enjoying his stay at Clifton Hampden:

> Round Clifton Hampden, itself a wonderfully pretty village, old-fashioned, peaceful and dainty with flowers, the river scenery is rich and beautiful. If you stay the night on land at Clifton, you cannot do better than put up at the 'Barley Mow'. It is, without exception, I should say, the quaintest, most old-world inn up the river. It stands on the right of the bridge, quite away from the village. Its low-pitched gables and thatched roof and latticed windows give it quite a story-book appearance, while inside it is even still more once-upon-a-timeyfied . . . [14]

Until recently boats paid tolls at each lock as they went through —in 1875 the tolls were as follows, for boats travelling through and back in the same day:

> Class I for every pair-oared row-boat, skiff, outrigger, random, dinghy, punt, canoe or company boat, 3d.
> Class II for every four-oared row-boat (other than the boats enumerated in Class I) 6d.
> Class III for every row-boat, shallop and company boat over four oars, 9d.
> For every houseboat 2s.6d.[15]

Boats could alternatively be registered annually and pay 20, 30 and 40 shillings per class respectively and 100 shillings for a houseboat. The old system of paying at each lock has now been abandoned in favour of the annual registration system.

There are still many pleasure-boats, and many holiday-makers in small boats combine a trip on the Thames with one along the Oxford Canal, which, too, has lost its commercial aspect but is a very popular canal for cruising.

The Oxford Canal was designed to form a vital link between the coalfields of the industrial Midlands and, via the Thames, with London. It was considered an excellent investment by landowners, who subscribed to shares to finance its construction. The canal reached Banbury in 1778 and Oxford in 1790, eventually forming a major link in the national waterway network, linking with the Coventry Canal (1790) at Hawkesbury, the Grand Junction (1805–20)—later known as the Grand Union—at Braunston, the Warwick and Napton (1798) and the Thames at Oxford, which put Oxfordshire on routes between London and Liverpool, Birmingham and London, Hull and London, and London and the Severn.

The name of James Brindley is commonly connected with the canal, but his death in 1772 meant that he only decided the layout, and his assistants, Robert Whitworth and Samuel Simock, devised the final details. The navvies building the canal were considered something of a handful, as two pairs of pistols were purchased for the paymaster and the canal company's agents! As the canal took twenty-odd years to build, engineering techniques changed, and this is reflected, for example, in the simple lower gates found on some locks south of Banbury, used instead of mitred pair gates. This development, rather unwieldy and not altogether successful, is attributed to Robert Whitworth. A typical feature of this section of the canal is the carefully counterbalanced wooden drawbridges, easily lifted by the weight of a man. There are unique diamond-shaped weir locks at Aynho and Shipton on Cherwell, where the canal and river are joined.

Cropedy still has its own lock-keeper, with his cottage by the canal bank—the lock-keepers now help the lengthmen to keep the canal and towpaths in good condition. Thrupp is the British Waterways Board's administrative headquarters for the canal. After the beauties of the countryside the length of the canal,

Oxford proves a sore disappointment—Hayfield Wharf and the old canal basin were sold to Lord Nuffield in the 1930s, and now Nuffield College stands on the site, and the canal comes to an abrupt and untidy end.

Reductions in the price of coal following the opening of the canal were of great importance to local industry as well as to the general public. Industry had a new method of transport, particularly invaluable for heavy goods.

The rural side of the canal traffic was important, not least market-boats such as those of John Weaving, who carried goods and passengers to and from market between Banbury and Oxford, calling at the intervening villages, giving villagers a link with their market-towns and neighbouring areas. Such boats were very popular until the mid-1850s, when they were largely superseded by the railways. Passengers could travel on 'fly' boats (drawn by two or three galloping horses, their crews in smart uniforms) which were given priority at locks. Unfortunately the boats' washes damaged the canal banks, so they were discontinued.

A scarcely recognizable relic of the canal community is the boatmen's chapel in Hythe Bridge Street—now a shop selling beds!—which replaced the floating chapel, built in the late 1830s. This emphasizes the separation of boatmen from the rest of the community—they were travelling most of the time, often with their families aboard to provide extra crew members and avoid the necessity of paying for a home ashore. They tended to have their own pubs, such as the 'Nag's Head' and the 'Running Horses' in Oxford and the 'Strugglers' in Banbury.

Goods were transported regularly on the canal until the 1950s, when the operating expenses of the canal exceeded the receipts. The shortage of water in the top 'pound' section north of Banbury often meant that the canal had to be closed for weeks, and during the winter ice-breakers were insufficient to keep the canal clear.

Banbury has the only boat-building yard left on the Oxford Canal, and its future is precarious, as it is run by Herbert Tooley on his own, and he, alas, has no apprentice following in his footsteps. The boat-building yard has been there at least since 1790 and was taken over by the Tooleys in about 1900. The yard contains a dry-dock, large enough to accommodate a 70-foot narrow boat, and a smithy with a forge and workshops. Narrow boats have not been built here since around 1910, but people travel many miles to have their boats repaired. L.T.C. Rolt described how Tooley refitted his narrow boat *Cressy*. Herbert added painting to his skills, and Rolt vividly depicted the way he painted the elaborate roses and castles traditional to narrow boat art:

> Handling his fine camel-hair brushes with a wonderful sureness and delicacy, he first of all painted little shaded discs of sepia, ochre and pink on the green ground of the can and surrounded them with a garland of pale-green leaves. These were the centres of the roses. When they were dry, the petals, red on sepia, yellow on ochre and white on pink, were superimposed so simply and swiftly that only in the way a mere blob of paint seemed suddenly to blossom forth was the skill revealed. The bright work was completed when the veining of the leaves had been painted in with a very fine brush and a coat of varnish applied to preserve it.[16]

The Oxford Canal is still a flourishing waterway, busy with pleasure-craft and nurtured by the local branch of the Inland Waterways Association, but the Wiltshire and Berkshire Canal met a less happy fate. From the start it was a far less important canal, beginning at Abingdon, winding the 55 miles through the Vale of White Horse to Challow and Wantage, then on towards Bath, joining the Kennet and Avon at Trowbridge—very much a country canal, although it made coal from the Somerset coal-fields available to the Vale and Oxford. The canal opened in 1810 although opposed by the citizens of Oxford who feared that the Thames navigation to Abingdon would be injured by the new canal. Despite the traffic in coal, and the odd passenger fly-boat between Abingdon and Melksham, with connections to Bristol, the canal never became very profitable. It was badly hit by railway competition, rapidly losing its commercial viability —in 1863 only 564 boats passed the eastern summit. However, the Wantage wharf had a varied trade in coal, stone, manure, corn, groceries and salt—though the opening of the Wantage tramway connecting the town with the Great Western Railway boded ill. Various attempts were made to save the canal, largely by groups of merchants, who resorted to experiments with sectional boats—precursors of today's container-lorries—which proved too clumsy. In 1914 the canal owners closed it, and it is now one of the 'lost' waterways of England.

Prehistoric man had routeways along which he traversed the country, and roads have retained their importance throughout the centuries, road traffic being predominant in the twentieth century. Many roads have changed their status, and some are no longer recognizable.

Salt was an extremely important commodity, much of which had to be brought by road from Droitwich, and the county had several 'salt ways'—one, still known as Salt Lane, passed through north Oxfordshire, skirting Banbury; another crossed the centre through Chipping Norton and Kirtlington, heading off into Buckinghamshire, with routes forking off to Bampton and Shipton—all part of national routeways. Drove roads were used for the long-distance movement of animals from medieval times, to supply the London metropolis and other urban areas, but droving reached its peak from the seventeenth to nineteenth centuries. Welsh Black cattle and sheep were moved in large numbers by their drovers, being led 14–16 miles a day along wide, turf-covered routes providing grazing. Obviously it was better to keep herds (which could number a couple of hundred beasts) away from roads carrying other traffic. The increasing number of herds deteriorated the conditions of the roads, and it was partly to ease these problems that turnpike roads were developed, although many drovers preferred to use the old unmetalled drove roads, avoiding the hindrance of tolls.

Many animals come via Banbury:

A great number of cattle from Wales and Herefordshire used to be on trek through Banbury to Northampton and the grazing-lands of the eastern counties. I have known as many as two thousand pass through Banbury in a day; they would not travel more than 2 miles an hour. I have known them three hours marching through the town. Large herds of fat cattle would leave Banbury on a Friday and reach Smithfield Cattle Market on a Monday morning.[17]

Such visitations must have caused delays and aggravation to other traffic, and much mess. The Ridgeway became a drove road, despite the shortage of water, which was partially remedied by creating dewponds. Icknield Way and Portway, which followed the spring line of the Downs, were used in summer. Another route led from Wales through Faringdon, branching off to Abingdon, High Wycombe and Wantage. Some of the smaller local routes, such as the one near Woodstock, between the rivers Glyme and Dorn, leading to Over Norton, can still be traced, as greenways.

The Thames had few bridges over it until the twelfth century, when they were built at Oxford and Wallingford, with additional bridges at Caversham from the thirteenth century and Radcot in the fourteenth. Apart from these, people used fords or ferries, such as those at Bablockhythe, Swinford and Sandford. The organization of building and maintenance of roads was chaotic, being left locally to the lord of the manor or to monastic houses. Occasionally a tax was raised for road maintenance, and at Tetsworth in the fifteenth century a hermit collected alms for road repairs. Roads were a national as well as a local problem, as good communications were vital for the maintenance of trade, the collection of taxes and the control of rural areas by central government, so in 1550 an Act was passed making each parish responsible for all roads within its boundaries. However, roads continued to decay—even around Oxford they were so appalling that villagers were unable to transport their goods to market.

Little was done to improve this situation until the eighteenth century, when turnpike trusts were set up. By 1720 the road between London and Oxford had been completely turnpiked apart from 9 miles between Beaconsfield and Uxbridge. Other main routes rapidly .ollowed suit—by 1760 the routes between Oxford, Cheltenham and Gloucester, and Oxford, Banbury and Stratford had been turnpiked. Gradually the network extended to cover the whole country. Some new roads were built by the turnpike trusts, such as the new London road, avoiding the steep hill at Shotover; other roads were merely improved. The individual trusts were financed by private subscribers, so tolls were charged to cover the cost of the road building and if possible to pay a dividend. Tollhouses were set up to collect the tolls. Only the tollbridge at Swinford near Eynsham is still in use, now costing 2p per car to cross, but the tolls in 1769 were:

Carriage with four wheels	4d
Carriage with less than four wheels	2d
Horse, gelding, mare or ass, laden or not laden, drawing or not drawing	1d
Every ox, bull, cow, steer, or heifer	½d
Every calf, swine, sheep or lamb	¼d

Later tolls became more complex, to discriminate against heavy loads and vehicles with narrow wheels which did more damage to the road.

Tollhouses varied in design but were usually built in brick or stone, one or two storeys high, often with a bay or octagonal front, with a ticket hatch. Each one had its toll board prominently displayed. At Hinton Waldrist one can see the little thatched tollhouse with its rounded front, built for the Great Faringdon and Buckland Trust in 1735; a little brick tollhouse stands near Dorchester Abbey (Henley-Dorchester Trust, 1736), a smart whitewashed one at Attington (Thame United Trust c.1770); one stands on the Banbury road in North Oxford, another by Oxford railway station.

Many of the milestones still visible date from the era of turnpike trusts, but the earliest is one set up at Wroxton in 1686 by Francis White, a decorative stone with an urn-and-ball finial. The turnpike milestones vary in design: some are rounded pillars, others faceted, set up to comply with the Turnpike Act which demanded that stones should indicate the distance from each stone to major population centres. Many stones were defaced during the Second World War and are now illegible.

Coaching was the major form of transport for passengers and goods before the canals and railways were built. Travelling conditions before turnpike roads must have been execrable. Travel by goods wagon was slow, uncomfortable and cramped:

> The London waggon from Banbury was drawn by eight strong horses. It had very broad wheels. A large punt, or square-shaped boat was suspended by chains to the bottom of the waggon between the wheels. In this punt lambs, sheep, pigs and poultry of various sorts were carried, being fed at intervals on the journey. In the bed of the waggon goods of a heavy character were packed three or four in height, on the top of these were five or six tiers consisting of butter in flats, and carcases of sheep and pigs. The size of the waggon was 18 feet in length, 7½ feet in breadth at the bottom of the waggon and 12 feet to the top of the tilt . . . Good heavy mohair curtains securely closed up the back. Bags containing a large quantity of food for the horses hung in waterproof sheets in front. A light ladder to reach the top of the load was securely placed at the side of the waggon. Two huge horn lanterns were carried one in front and one behind the team. Two waggoners, with massive whips, always travelled with the team.[18]

Carriage and coach traffic was life-blood to market towns such as Banbury, Henley and Faringdon. Coaches stopped at particular inns, as did the battery of carrier carts which served the neighbouring villages. The coaches trundling through Oxford had fascinating-sounding names:

> Along that road, or into Oxford by the St Giles's entrance, lumbered at midnight Pickford's vast waggons with their six musically belled horses; sped stage-coaches all day long—*Tantivy, Defiance, Rival, Regulator, Mazeppa, Dart, Magnet, Blenheim* and some thirty more; heaped high with ponderous luggage and with cloaked passengers, thickly hung at Christmas time with turkeys, with pheasants in October; their guards, picked buglers, sending before them as they passed Magdalen Bridge the now forgotten strains of 'Brignall Banks', 'The Troubadour', 'I'd be a Butterfly', 'The Maid of Llangollen', or 'Begone, Dull Care', on the box their queer old purple-faced, many-caped drivers—Cheeseman, Steevens, Fowles, Charles Home, Jack Adams, and Black Will.[19]

The railway age led to the decline of such picturesque transport. The steam train had an important influence on the county, both town and country, and was not always as peaceful as Edward Thomas remembered it:

> Yes, I remember Adlestrop—
> The name, because one afternoon
> Of heat the express-train drew up there
> Unwontedly. It was late June.
>
> The steam hissed. Someone cleared his throat.
> No one left and no one came
> On the bare platform. What I saw
> Was Adlestrop—only the name.
>
> And willows, willow-herb and grass,
> And meadowsweet, and haycocks dry,
> No whit less still and lonely fair
> Than the high cloudlets in the sky,
>
> And for that minute a blackbird sang
> Close by, and round him, mistier,
> Further and further all the birds
> Of Oxfordshire and Gloucestershire.[20]

The railways brought hustle and bustle. Oxford fought against the invasion of the railway, but to smaller towns such as

Faringdon and Chipping Norton it was a life-line. Faringdon was stagnating until the Faringdon-Uffington branch opened in 1864, as it had been bypassed by the London-Bristol railway, Faringdon Road Station being 7½ miles from the town. This railway catered for agricultural produce, including milk, but apparently the job was not always adequately performed. An Uffington farmer, Mr. J. Whitfield, complained to the Company that some of the milk he sent by rail to London was being stolen en route.

Milk was an important product on the Woodstock Branch line too, where specially designed carts with low steps to facilitate loading and unloading were used. The Woodstock Branch was a small line (financed largely by the Duke of Marlborough) which opened in 1900. When the Duke wished to travel to Oxford, a special first-class coach was added to the train for him and his secretary, while businessmen travelled second class, the work-men and farmers third class, and goods wagons at the back hauled coal and Woodstock gloves. The other main freight carried on the Woodstock line was cattle and agricultural goods. The Blenheim and Woodstock station was famous for its garden, which several times won the 'Best Kept Garden' competition of the London Division. The line was never a great financial success and closed in the early 1950s—where the station once stood, on the Oxford Road, opposite the palace entrance, is now a garage, and traces of the platform can be seen in the garage yard. It is ironic that a garage, symbol of the petrol engine and its current, though far from stable, predominance, should have replaced the station.

The Wantage Tramway opened in 1875, linking the town with the Great Western London-to-Bristol Railway, 2½ miles away. The first trams were horsedrawn, but a year later the Wantage Tramway Company applied for permission to use mechanical traction and acquired steam-engines. Trams met all the trains stopping at Wantage Road station and, as well as passengers, carried ironmongery, building materials, groceries, corn and coal. The easy access to important goods caused a decline in some of the smaller town industries such as sack-making. After the First World War, the Great Western Railway introduced a bus service to Wantage and the surrounding villages, sounding the death knell for the Tramway, which struggled on with the help of its major customer, Clark's Flour Mill, until 1946.

There would probably never have been a station at Chipping Norton if it had not been for the Bliss family, who appealed for a branch railway to transport goods from their tweed-mill. This illustrates the vital role played by the railways in transporting manufactured goods and, by encouraging industry, helping to stem the failing prosperity of small towns such as Chipping Norton and Witney. The Witney and East Gloucestershire Railway to Fairford opened in 1861; easy access to coal enabled the Witney woollen-mills to introduce steam-power, and this was so successful that new mills were built. Mineral industries, such as ironstone-mining at Fawler, received great impetus from the railway but despite the railway project foundered in the 1880s.

Railways were built piecemeal, and the history of their planning and construction is riddled with petty squabbles between the various companies objecting to each others plans. The railways in Oxfordshire were the Great Western Paddington-Bristol Line, through the Vale; the Faringdon Railway; Didcot, Newbury and Southampton Railway; Wallingford and Watlington Railway; Great Western Railway, Henley Branch; Buckinghamshire Railway from Oxford to Bletchley, and from Banbury to Buckingham and Bletchley; the Great Central Railway (Banbury to Woodford Halse); Great Western Railway, Didcot-Oxford line; the Princes Risborough-Thame Railway; Great Western Railway, Abingdon Branch; the Oxford, Worcester and Wolverhampton Railway; the Oxford and Birmingham Railway; Woodstock Railway; Wycombe Railway; Great Western Railway, Chipping Norton branch; Great Western Railway, Banbury, Bicester and Wycombe line; the Witney Railway and the East Gloucestershire Railway.

The impact on the landscape was enormous, with the building of bridges, embankments and so on. The terrain was not always easy, as the engineers' report for the Princes Risborough, Thame and Oxford Railway indicates:

> Possession of land has been obtained as and where required, and the contractor has been enabled to make a satisfactory commencement at all the heavier portions of the work. Two temporary shafts have been sunk at the Horsepath Tunnel, and one length of invert and side walls at the end next to Oxford have been built. The material through which the tunnel is to be constructed will probably turn out to be blue clay, not involving any extraordinary difficulty, but requiring lining throughout.

The total quantity of excavation executed has been 81,000 cubic yards, leaving still to be completed 560,000. The following works have been completed: two occupation bridges, one public road under the railway, three overbridges to abutments and wings, and eight culverts, making a total of 1,600 cubic yards of brickwork, and 9,500 remaining to be executed. The contractor has been conducting the works in a satisfactory manner. He has lately purchased brick earth, has rented some quarries of good stone near Wheatley, has brought a locomotive engine to the ground, and has laid himself out for a vigorous prosecution of the works during the ensuing season.[27]

The disruption to local inhabitants was considerable—the Reverend Mr Elton of Wheatley commented that there were about a hundred navvies working and that they fetched buckets of spirits, carried on yokes, from the 'King and Queen'. The village of Cassington was swamped by 150 railway workers and their families, and the rapid opening of five pubs in the village did nothing to maintain moral standards. Osney, on the outskirts of Oxford, was another railway community. However, the populace in the towns and villages served by the railways achieved a new mobility—they could go on day trips to the seaside and tourist resorts. Trips from Witney went to Bala, Brighton, Weymouth, Liverpool, Torquay, Hastings, Southampton, Blackpool and Weston-super-Mare.

The railways upset other methods of transport—the Thames and canals lost their commercial importance, and the turnpikes declined. It is ironic that the success of the railways was in turn overtaken by the petrol engine, so that, with the advent of heavy lorries, many of the railways declined and some lines closed. Railways still play an important role in local transport, and the Transport 2000 group, taking into consideration the growing shortage of petrol and consequent high prices, recommends that some of the old lines, such as Didcot to Southampton, Banbury to Loughborough, Banbury to Buckingham, Oxford to Cambridge and Yarnton to Witney, should be re-opened, to ease pressure on roads and petrol. Other transport groups fulminate against the projects for new roads, such as the extension of the M40 motorway to Warwick, maintaining that the petrol engine has had its day. But only time will tell how transport problems will be solved in the future.

In the meantime one can explore old railway tracks—some, such as that at Hook Norton, have become nature reserves;

others still have traces of their origins to delight industrial archaeologists. Some original buildings survive, such as Culham Station, which illustrates early broad-gauge Great Western architecture. It was opened in 1844 and is an original Brunel station of 'Tudor Gothic Design', of red brick with stone quoins. Train enthusiasts of the Great Western Society have turned the engine-shed at Didcot, a town created by the railways, into a museum housing Great Western steam-engines and rolling-stock which they lovingly restore and regularly take on trips. The public can see the restoration work in progress and ride behind a steam-locomotive.

There is a 15-inch gauge railway in Blenheim Park taking visitors from the Palace to the Garden Centre, hauled by either *Sir Winston Churchill* built in 1846 or *Tracey Joe*. Blenheim is the headquarters of the Witney and West Oxfordshire Model Engineering Society which has a 3½-inch and 5-inch-gauge model-railway layout. A model railway has been constructed at Long Wittenham, and the landscape around it consists of exquisitely made, accurate scale models based on local buildings and villages, complete with furniture inside the cottages. The museum has ambitious plans to reconstruct a vista of part of the Vale of White Horse, and the trains speeding along the routes, again accurate scale models, are a source of endless fascination. Railways are by no means dead in Oxfordshire.

5

Wychwood Forest and Otmoor

Hailey, Crawley, Curbridge and Coggs,
Witney spinners and Ducklington dogs,
Finstock on the hill, Fawler down derry,
Beggarly Ramsden and lousy Charlbury.
Woodstock for bacon, Bladon for beef,
Hanborough for a scurvy knave,
And Coombe for a thief.

Wychwood and Otmoor were both remote areas until the mid nineteenth century, when the forest of Wychwood was disafforested and the marshes of Otmoor were drained. The history and traditions of both are many and varied.

Wychwood was one of the medieval kings' favourite hunting forests, and forest law, if not the forest itself, extended from Woodstock to Witney and Burford in the west and to Chipping Norton and Enstone in the north, when the forest was at its largest under Henry II. Yet that area has not always been wooded: prehistoric and Roman settlements indicate that the land was then extensively farmed by the occupants of villas such as Ditchley, Stonesfield and North Leigh. Akeman Street runs through the forest area, crossing the Rivers Evenlode and Cherwell.

After the decay of the Roman settlements, the forest again encroached—the area is bleak and inclined to be short of water in summer. Its poor grass did not suit sheep, so it was more profitable to have forest with common grazing. Saxon place-names such as Hailey and Spoonley indicate forest clearings which gradually became permanent settlements. Saxon kings enclosed the woodland round their royal manor of Wootton, building a residence at Woodstock.

The name 'Wychwood' derives from the 'Hwicca', a Saxon tribe centred on Cirencester, and the name 'Hwicca-Wudu', occurs in a charter of 841.

The Norman kings' harsh forest law dominated Wychwood as it did the royal forests of Shotover, Stowood and Bernwood. Only the king and those to whom he graciously granted permission were allowed to hunt within the forest area, the latter not forty days before or after the king's hunt, and the penalty for poaching was to have one's eyes put out.

The king and his licensed hunters were jealous of their prerogatives and appointed keepers to control the hunting and care for the deer. All dogs kept within the forest had their foreclaws removed with a chisel and mallet, to reduce the likelihood that they would be used as hunting-dogs. Under Richard II it was decreed that,

> If any man, not having 40 shillings per annum, or if any priest or clerk not having £40 per annum shall have or keep hound, greyhound, or other dog for to hunt or any ferrets, hags, harepipes, cords, nets, or other engines to take or destroy deer, hare, conies or other gentleman's game, and shall be convicted at the sessions of the peace, every such offender shall be imprisoned for one whole year.[1]

Such laws were relaxed in the fourteenth century, and great anger was aroused when Charles I, in his frantic pursuit of money, attempted to revive the forest laws during the seventeenth century. His attempts to re-impose the law failed, but he extracted a fine of £2,000 in 1636 from William Willoughby, who had illegally felled oaks worth 20 shillings, and £100 from Roger Gardiner, who had killed two does and a buck.

The Ranger, the chief forest official, was usually a royal favourite. This post was held by several generations of the Langley family in the late medieval period, and in the late sixteenth century a notable Ranger was Sir Henry Lee of Ditchley, the Queen's Champion. An eighteenth-century description of the forest (probably reflecting the medieval structure), says that under the Ranger were the launder, who controlled all the grazing rights, four keepers, two verderers (usually chosen from among the local gentry) and a woodward. The forest was regularly inspected by a group of twelve knights, or 'regarders', who ensured that it was kept in good condition and reported any offences.

The thirteenth-century Master Forester claimed 'horn tenure', and his privileges included two strikes of oats during

Lent from each forest tenant, to feed his horse; as much bracken as he required, except during the hunting season, when bracken provided cover for the game; grazing for his pigs and cattle; the windfalls and lops of felled trees; a halfpenny each for all cattle and goats taken at non-agistment times, and for all straying beasts caught between Michaelmas and Martinmas. He laid claim to all sparrow-hawks, merlins or hobbies, all swarms of bees, the right shoulder of every deer taken in the forest, the horns and skins of all those found dead, all waifs found in the forest, also the right to hunt foxes, hares, cats, weasels and vermin with his hounds or greyhounds. In addition he had the right to the best animal belonging to any man who committed felony or trespass in the forest. The forest court at which such offences were tried was called 'the Swanimote'.

The woodland was basically oak—pollarded trees were referred to as 'roers' and were frequently given away as firewood, and 'quercus' were well-grown, younger-timber trees. Oaks were used for the roofs of various Oxford colleges. It is alleged that Philip of Spain ordered the commander of the Spanish Armada to bring back Wychwood oaks with him as part of the spoils of the victory he envisaged. Nelson's famous flagship, the *Victory*, is said to have been built of Charlbury oak. Other trees included maple, ash, elm, hornbeam, crab, hawthorn, ivy, holly, hazel, blackthorn, elder, beeches and willows, suggesting some areas of scrubland with an undergrowth of brambles and bracken. The hazelnut crop was important, and the underwood provided poles and fuel. Woody areas were interspersed with large tracts of gorsy heathland, with some marshland by the river.

The cultivated land belonging to the villages gradually encroached on the forest areas during the medieval expansion of population. The village of Leafield is carved out of the heart of the forest. Although the first written reference to it dates only as far back as 1213, in the forest area the people of Leafield are even today considered a race apart—some people maintaining that they are of Celtic stock. They retained their reputation for aggression and an uncouth dialect until recently. Leafield has always been more remote than other Wychwood villages, not having its own church until after the mid nineteenth-century disafforestation. Other Wychwood villages appeared in the early Middle Ages—Finstock by 1135, Ramsden by 1146,

Fawler by 1205, Crawley by 1214 and Hailey by 1240. None became large settlements, and even today their appearance indicates how they were carved out of the woodland with irregular field systems and winding lanes and trackways. A major role was played by the monastic landowners, such as Eynsham Abbey, in carving settlements from the forest from the eleventh to fourteenth centuries. Although some of their assarting had royal permission, on several occasions the foresters reclaimed land for the king which the abbey had surreptitiously assarted round Spelsbury.

The king kept both red and fallow deer in the forest, with a predominance of fallow. Most of the deer were culled and salted in the autumn, because of the problems involved in feeding them over the winter. Salted venison formed an important portion of the provisions required by the king and his Court on their travels.

Wychwood received much attention from its royal masters. Woodstock was emparked by Edward the Confessor, then Henry I built a 7-mile stone wall around it, creating the first walled park in England. Woodstock became the royal headquarters in Wychwood, with a stone-built palace. Henry I also had a menagerie in Woodstock Park, described by William of Malmesbury: "He was extremely fond of the wonders of different countries, begging with great delight from foreign kings, lions, leopards, lynxes, or camels. He had a park called Woodstock wherein he used to foster favourites of his kind; he had placed there also a creature called a porcupine, sent to him by William of Montpelier."[2]

The village of Old Woodstock grew up on the outskirts of the park to cater for the needs of the courtiers. Henry II enlarged the forest to its greater extent, including within its bounds already established villages such as Shipton- and Ascott-under-Wychwood, Stonesfield, Fawler, Charlbury and Spelsbury, and more recent settlements like Asthall Leigh, Finstock, Ramsden and South Leigh.

Leland has embroidered the story of Henry II's romance, with Rosamund Clifford, his mistress, who, according to legend, was hidden from his jealous queen, Eleanor, in a bower or maze in the grounds of Woodstock Palace. Some silk from Rosamund's embroidery became attached to Henry's spur when he visited her, revealing the intricate path through the maze. Eleanor

followed the path to Rosamund's hiding-place, where she
angrily presented the cowering girl with the choice between
drinking poison or being incarcerated in Godstow Abbey. It
seems that Rosamund ended her days in Godstow Abbey—though
maybe Henry merely tired of her. She was buried there in great
style, and her tomb was treated almost as a shrine until the visit
of Hugh, Bishop of Lincoln in 1191, who was so appalled that an
immoral woman should be so worshipped that he banished her
tomb to the churchyard.

The forest was still popular among Tudor royal hunters, and
Elizabeth was several times entertained by Sir Henry Lee at
Ditchley. Sir Henry Lee was made Seneschal, Lieutenant of the
Manor of Woodstock and Master of the Leash around 1673, his
duties including that of Ranger. Lee had several properties in
the area but resided chiefly at Ditchley or at High Lodge, near
Woodstock. He resigned the post of Royal Champion in 1690,
aged fifty-three, because of gout, but he continued to maintain
the two to three thousand deer in the forest, to account for
Crown rents, to graze his cattle and horses on the demesnes, to
claim his rights to firewood, brushwood and hay and even to
hunt with his royal masters. He kept the trophies of deer shot by
royal hands in his hall at Ditchley, with inscriptions beneath
them such as:

1608 August 24th, Saturday
From Foxhole Coppice rous'd, Great Britain's king
I fled. But what? In Kiddington pond he overtook me dead.

1608 August 26th Monday
King James made me run for his life, from deadman's riding
I ran to Gorrell Gate, where death for me was biding.

1610, August 2nd, Wednesday
In Henley Knap to hunt me King James, Prince Henry found me.
Cornbury Park river, to end their hunting, drowned me.

Sir Henry was immortalized romantically but far from accu-
rately in Walter Scott's *Woodstock*, where he plays an important
role in a Civil War plot—long after the real Sir Henry Lee's
death.

The privilege (greatly prized by the villagers of Witney, Brize
Norton, Leafield, Bampton, Charlbury, Crawley and Finstock
until the nineteenth century) of hunting deer in the forest each

Whit Monday may go back to Saxon times. The Whit Hunt was a great festive occasion—the young men made crude horns from willow-bark, coiled into conical shape and held in place with thorns, with a reed as mouthpiece. At midnight on Whit Sunday these horns were blown to rouse men for the hunt, and at daybreak they all met at Hailey, where the keepers organized the hunt. They were permitted to kill three deer, one each for the villages of Witney, Charlbury and Hailey. The man first in at the death laid claim to the horns, and everyone tried to secure a piece of the skin to ensure good luck and fertility.

The Whit Hunt began a week of holiday and celebrations. A 'bowery', or hut covered with green boughs, was set up as a drinking-hall, where much beer was consumed, games were played, and the Wychwood teams of morris men came from Ascott- and Shipton-under-Wychwood, Asthal Leigh, Brize Norton, Ducklington, Field Assarts, Leafield, Finstock and Spelsbury to dance, then spent the next week dancing from village to village.

The people of Burford once had a similar right to hunt deer, but this right was commuted in 1593, because of plague. Instead on Whit Sunday afternoon the churchwardens led a procession to Capps Lodge Plain, near the town, where the boy and girl chosen to be 'lord' and 'lady' demanded from the keepers "a brace of the best bucks, and a fawn, without fee or regard, with their horns and hoofs", on behalf of the town of Burford. They received the deer during the first week in August, when the church-wardens provided a venison feast in the church hall for several hundred people. This right was so firmly established that the Award of the Commissioners for Disafforestating Wychwood Forest (1857) awarded the people of Burford £150 as compensation.

The Wychwood Forest Fair, held in the autumn, was said to have originated when a group of Methodists, disapproving of the drunken antics of Witney Feast, instead organized a picnic near Charlbury for their friends from nearby villages. However it started, the fair became a great attraction, quite as notorious as Witney Feast for drunkards, pickpockets and similar un-savoury characters—so much so that one year Lord Churchill, the local magistrate, had so many cases to deal with that he limited the fair to one day. It struggled on until 1855 and was finally discontinued after Lord Churchill banned it and dug

A view of Woodstock across the lake at Blenheim Park.

Manor Farm, Cogges, now a museum of farming and the countryside,
run by the Oxfordshire County Museum.

Bloxham village.

The maze at Troy Farm, Somerton.

Wroxton village.

Cottisford church.

The 'Red Lion', Steeple Aston—a pleasant village pub with a superb restaurant.

The almshouses at Ewelme.

The 'Falkland Arms', Great Tew.

Arabella's Cottage, Letcombe Bassett, so named after the character in Thomas Hardy's novel *Jude the Obscure*.

Blewbury village.

East Hendred village.

Ardington.

Broughton Castle.

Childrey village pond.

trenches to prevent wheeled vehicles being driven across the plain. Clothiers came to sell such fabrics as flannels, homespun linen and other types difficult to obtain locally; children could purchase farthing and halfpenny chapbooks while adults paid only one penny for *Lives of Notorious Criminals* and were entertained by a Wild West Show, Wombwell's Menagerie, a travelling theatre and a shooting-booth where the target around 1854 was the Russian Empress; they watched Monsieur Columbier and his French company display their fireworks, danced at the Vauxhall dancing salon, listened to fiddlers, clarinet players and the Charlbury Yeomanry Band and gorged themselves on food.

With so many deer roaming the forest, and poverty among the villagers, poaching was a foregone conclusion. The Magna Carta of 1215 ended hanging for poaching, but it remained a serious crime. Many tales relate the exploits of the poachers, who were obviously local heroes. Although deer were the main victims, other mammals, such as hares and rabbits, and birds, such as pheasants, must have been trapped or shot. Hiding the carcases from the sharp eyes of the keepers involved much ingenuity—some were hidden in the tiny chamber above the church porch, inside churchyard altar tombs or in hollow hayricks on the downs. One woman had a venison pie in the kitchen when a keeper called unexpectedly, and with great presence of mind she placed it in the crook of her arm, with the baby on top, its long clothes carefully arranged to hide the offending piedish—if her husband had been caught, he would have been sent to prison. The keepers seem to have been easily outwitted—on one occasion they found a skinned deer carcase before the poachers had time to carry it away. They put it on their wagon, proceeded to the 'Crown' for a drink and enjoyed a convivial evening, little realizing that while they were being entertained the poachers had steathily reclaimed their booty.

Actually catching the deer was not always easy: a Shipton man had his eye on one grazing the forest edge and took a pot shot at it—to his horror a terrific braying sounded, and he discovered that he had shot a gypsy donkey—the poaching gang had to recompense the distraught gypsy woman handsomely. On occasion the keepers actually solicited the aid of the poachers, as in the 1840s: they heard that a large group of men was coming down from the Black Country to poach and appealed to the men of Milton Quarry, notorious poachers, to help. Their leader, Jack Smith, carried a flail as weapon. In the ensuing fight he accidentally killed his opponent by hitting him on the head with the flail, but in court he produced his billycock hat, which had had the crown ripped off by his opponent's stick, and was discharged, with a verdict of justifiable homicide.

The most notorious highwaymen in Wychwood were the Dunsden brothers—Tom, Dick and Harry—who were born in the mid eighteenth century, of respectable yeoman stock at Fulbrook. They are said to have become highwaymen because of a grave injustice done to one, starting their career in a small way by robbing farmers on their way to market of stock and money. Their first big haul was £500 secured by robbing the Oxford coach. They became too sure of themselves after this, boasting of their intentions, so that when they went to rob Tangley Manor, the occupants were forewarned. Dick slid back the small shutter in the door and put his hand through to push back the lock—his arm was grabbed and securely fastened inside so there was no escape. In panic the other brothers severed his arm, and all three made their escape, but Dick is heard of no more, and it is assumed that he died of his injuries. Tom and Harry did not learn their lesson, and on Whit Sunday 1784 they unwisely drank their fill at Capps Lodge, became quarrelsome and were overpowered and arrested by the local constable. They were sentenced and hanged at Gloucester, but their bodies were brought back to Capps Lodge and gibbeted, to deter others from following in their footsteps. The gibbet was a local sensation—a favourite Sunday afternoon activity for sometime afterwards was a journey to the ghoulish scene to ascertain how much was left of the bodies, and the letters 'H.D. T.D. 1784' can still be seen cut on the tree near where the gibbet stood.

In 1792 the Commissioners reporting on the state of the Crown woods wrote unfavourably about Wychwood, commenting that deer were damaging the trees and underwood. At that time the herd numbered about a thousand, and sixty-one bucks and forty-two does were culled annually, only six of each going to the king. The state of timber had deteriorated—from 1700 to 1786 the oaks had not been of high enough quality to supply the navy. The Duke of Marlborough, who was, as Ranger, responsible for coppicing the trees at eighteen years old, was equally disparaging, seeing no sign of it becoming more productive in the future.

Despite these unfavourable reports, nothing further was done until 1837, when the antiquary and lawyer Stacey Grimaldi was appointed to enquire into the Crown's rights in the forest, and the decision was taken in 1853: 3,780 acres, 2 roods and 31 perches were disafforested; the office of Ranger ceased, and compensation was given to all who had the right of pasture. Wychwood became a parish, and a church was built in Leafield. New roads were built, trees were grubbed up and new farms created. The task of destroying the woodland was an enormous one:

> Hundreds and hundreds of men and boys were engaged, some cutting the light wood and laying it in drift, some tying the firewood into faggots, some preparing the larger pieces for posts and fencing, and others busy felling the timber trees, or stripping off the bark. Gradually and steady was the advance like that of an invading army, however, as might have been looked on with pleasure, even by a member of the Peace Society. It was heralded by the rustling sound of the brushwood, and the crashing noise which echoed through the glades when some spreading oak, a forest sire, fell prostrate, and intimated that the sylvan glories of old Wichwood were drawing to a close.[3]

Lord Churchill purchased some of the land and retained Cornbury Estate as it was when held by the last Rangers. Now the principal remaining portions of Wychwood forest are found in Cornbury and Blenheim Parks, Cornbury being run as a sporting estate.

What of Wychwood Forest today? It has little of its former glory, but there are still oak standards, a few large beech trees scattered around, some sycamore and increasing numbers of ash. The hedgerow maples are some of the tallest in Britain, and other trees include sweet and horse chestnut and hornbeam, with lime avenues. Dutch elm disease has decimated the elm population. The scrubby areas and hedgerows have shrubs of buckthorn, blackthorn, hawthorn, hazel, spindle, elder, sallows and holly. Wild flowers such as the pyramidal orchid, eyebright and gromwell are found in limestone areas, and in the damper land autumn-flowering meadow saffron, now localized in the Cotswolds. Hidden in the woodland are the greater butterfly orchid, columbine, dog's mercury, bugle and patches of stinking hellebore. Many of these are found in the area now a nature reserve. As Wychwood has not been managed for forestry for over a century, there is considerable natural regeneration of wood. Titmice, nuthatch and finches thrive in the woodland, and rarer visitors are bittern, buzzard, roughleg and the odd falcon. The red deer all disappeared with disafforestation, being killed or taken to other deer-parks, but now Muntjac deer and Sika deer dwell in the forest. Frogs, toads, grass snakes and slow worms abound; twenty-five species of butterfly enjoy the sanctuary of the woodland, which also houses a vast and varied fly population. Much research is needed to assess all the species, and the Biological Records Centre at the Oxfordshire County Museum is constantly processing new information.

> For some minutes Alice stood without speaking looking out in all directions over the country—and a most curious country it was. There were a number of little brooks running from side to side, and the ground was divided up into squares by a number of hedges, that reached from brook to brook.
>
> "I declare it's marked out just like a large chess-board!" Alice said at last. "There ought to be some men moving about somewhere—and so there are."[4]

Thus Lewis Carroll described the view from the Beckley over the northern portion of Otmoor in *Alice through the Looking-Glass* after its taming in the nineteenth century by enclosure and drainage.

Otmoor used to be a remote, wet, marshland area where fishing and fowling were more profitable than farming, Otmoor itself being considered merely the common land attached to the estate of the manor of Beckley. Even after enclosure and drainage it was liable to flooding, as the Reverend C. E. Prior wrote:

> ... the meandering Ray was insufficient to drain the moor. Consequently there were 'flits', or marshy hollows, and 'pills', or accumulations of quaking bog. There is at the Beckley end of the Roman Road ... a boggy piece of land still known as 'Fowls' Pill'. Any little pond is called a 'lake', and Fencott, Murcott, Marslake, as well as a piece of land at Fencott known as 'Splash', tell of the former condition of that district.[5]

The 2,000-odd acres of Otmoor form a bowl of land lying below 200 feet, with alluvial peat and humus overlying a band of Oxford Clay, intersected by the River Ray. Charlton-on-Otmoor and Oddington are densely packed villages perching on 'islands' of cornbrash, while later settlements such as Fencott and Murcott, on the northern fringe of the moor, are on ill-drained Oxford Clay. The Corallian escarpment to the south rises to a height of over 450 feet, contrasting with the flatness of the moor. Part of the southern portion came within the bounds of the medieval royal forests of Shotover, Stowood and Beckley, and remnants of woodland still persist in Noke Wood and Prattle Wood. Other parts were rough heathland and common land.

The scatters of flint implements and fragments of knapped flints found in the fields indicate that the area has been regularly visited, and subsequently settled, since the Mesolithic period. Bronze Age cremation burials have been discovered at Oddington, and the Roman road linking Alchester and Dorchester-on-Thames is still visible today as a hedged green lane. A broken lump of stone known locally as 'Joseph's stone', is situated near the centre of the moor and has been claimed (probably wrongly) as a Roman milestone. Whatever the truth of this, by the nineteenth century it bore more resemblance to a mounting-block, and an 1871 drawing in the Bodleian Library quotes the inscription:

> Joseph Guilder brought this stone
> To help people up when they were down.

Local opinion thought the inscription read:

> Joseph's stone of high renown
> To help me up when I am down
> On my way to the seven towns.

The stone is said to be a 'half-round stone', turning round once every twenty-four hours.

There was considerable Roman settlement in the vicinity of Otmoor, with villas at Beckley, Islip and Woodperry, a Roman temple at Woodeaton and a smelting works at Druns Hill.

Villagers of the 'Seven Towns'—Beckley, Charlton-on-Otmoor, Oddington, Noke, Horton-cum-Studley, Fencott and Murcott—claimed common rights on the moor, with various traditions as to how they arose, such as the legend of the burning oatsheaf. Alexander Croke, who was anxious to enclose the lands during the nineteenth century, wrote scathingly of the legends:

A false notion has prevailed amongst the people, that Otmoor had been granted to them by Queen Elizabeth, or some other Queen, who gave them as much land as she could ride round while an oat sheaf was burning. Another story assigns the gift to King Charles the First. These are evidently, upon the face of them, some of those improbable and ridiculous old women's tales which are current in many places, and impose upon the credulity of the vulgar.[6]

By Domesday each of the 'Seven Towns' had common pasture lands. The fisheries formed an important part of the economy; Islip men not only enjoyed fishing available on the River Cherwell but probably used the River Ray. They were famed for their eel traps, or 'weels', made from local osiers. An Islip fisherman by the name of Beckley was granted exclusive fishing-rights at Islip in 1645 as a reward for ferrying Oliver Cromwell's troops across the river before the battle of Islip bridge. Islip eels were sent as far as London where they supplied the Ship Inn at Greenwich. James Price, who died in 1939, put stakes and wires across flooded areas of the moor to catch the fish as they drained back into the River Ray, catching golden carp, which he sold locally. The Beckley fishing has now been taken over by the Oxford Angling Society.

Wildfowling was another right owned by the Lord of the Royalty. Lord Abingdon, as Lord, employed his own fowler, who, instead of receiving a salary, had the right to any game caught not required by his master.

The Moor Courts which controlled common rights over Otmoor from the Middle Ages were based at Beckley, seat of the lord of the manor. Only commoners were allowed to take cattle onto the moor, and each village had a brand with the first letter of its name—such as 'B' for Beckley—to mark its cattle. Unbranded animals became the property of Lord Abingdon. Each village (except Fencott and Murcott, which had an allowance of fifteen hundred sheep between them) could have a thousand sheep grazing on the moor, except between Candlemas—2nd February—and All Hallowtide—in October—when certain portions of the moor had to be kept free. Ringed pigs could be kept on the moor except between Christmas and 1st April. The scope for the spread of disease with so many animals grazing together was wide, and despite the precaution that no diseased animals were to be brought on to the moor, 'moor evil' was notorious—it was a 'flux of the belly', which reduced cattle to skin and bone, often killing them, although water from the medicinal wells at Oddington was said to cure it.

The villagers had the right to dig peat, except on the roadways, provided that the holes were filled in afterwards. Some villagers kept large flocks of geese which formed a valuable cash crop, being sold to buy winter fuel. Such common rights gave the villagers a strong measure of independence and self-sufficiency. Few substantial landowners or clergy actually lived on Otmoor, and many villagers became Dissenters in the nineteenth century.

This independence was much treasured, and when schemes for draining and enclosing the moor were broached, there was much disquiet. The Earl of Abingdon's surveyor made the first suggestion in 1728; then Sir Alexander Croke of Studley Priory put an enclosure bill before Parliament in 1786, which would have confiscated common rights, but the Earl of Abingdon brought about its defeat in 1788.

The villages strongly opposed enclosure, which would curtail their common rights, and made very plain their feelings against the Reverend Philip Serle, Rector of Oddington, who supported it:

> It was narrowback, the parson,
> As I have heard 'em say,
> Who employed the Parish Clerk
> To stop the River Ray.
> He blocked up the water
> For four foot high or more,
> To injure other farmers
> And keep it out of Otmoor.[7]

On the death of the Earl of Abingdon in 1799, Croke renewed his call for enclosure, and after a prolonged struggle the Otmoor Enclosure Act was passed in 1815, despite counter-petitions by the moormen. A Commissioner was appointed to distribute the land according to rights, to start drainage operations, which involved altering the course of the River Ray, and to sell off land to defray expenses. Only seventy-three people received land from a population of seventeen hundred and of these forty-eight received allotments of 10 acres or much less. Most of the land went to the Earl of Abingdon, Alexander Croke, the Reverend Theophilius Leigh Cooke of Oddington, Balliol, Oriel and

Magdalen Colleges and various clergymen and trusts.

All was peaceful until 1830—the lull before the storm. The disturbances were spearheaded by the small farmers of Charlton, Fencott and Murcott, whose lands were being flooded as a result of the drainage operations, which failed in their intention of drying out the moor—the new channel cut for the River Ray merely succeeded in flooding previously dry areas.

Nocturnal raiders broke down the new embankments. Warrants were issued for the arrest of twenty-nine farmers from Charlton, Merton, Fencott and Murcott, but they maintained that the embankments were a public nuisance and that one of the prosecutors had the year before destroyed some of his own embankments to relieve flooding. They were acquitted, which the people of Otmoor took as an admission that their rights to the moor were vindicated and that the whole Enclosure Act was wrong. They considered they had a right to reclaim the moor and made night forays, armed with billhooks and axes, to destroy the enclosure hedges, fortified by beer and food.

The Reverend Theophilius Cooke described the forays:

On the Tuesday night [August] (the 31st) the depredators increased in number greatly, and came in disguise with their faces blackened, and some with partly women's clothes; they began cutting down some trees of about ten years' growth on the Oddington side of the Moor, and a watching servant of Mr Serle's was struck at with an iron bar, as it is alleged by one of the rioters, Charles Busby. Whenever a tree fell, a shout of exultation was raised with a blowing of horns, heard at the distance of 2–3 miles. The assemblage had begun between eight & nine o'clock & continued their ravages of pulling up posts & rails, cutting the live quickset hedges & trees till about twelve, when they retired; the watch were completely paralysed by the opposed numbers.[8]

A man by the name of Price was captured and imprisoned for two months, but the attacks shortly began again. The Oxfordshire Militia and Lord Churchill's Troop of Yeomanry Cavalry were called in to help. The commoners were not in the least deterred and on Monday 6th September decided to conduct a daylight perambulation of Otmoor, as had been done before enclosure, and to break down all hedges in their way. Between five hundred and a thousand people, including women and children, took part, many armed with billhooks, hatchets, bludgeons and pitchforks. The Riot Act was read, and sixty-six people were arrested and taken to Islip, where twenty-five were released on bail and the other forty-one taken by wagon to Oxford. However, the journey to Oxford proved eventful:

> The civil authorities, not having anticipated any attempt at rescue, did not think it necessary to secure the prisoners in any manner, and therefore it required constant attention of the escort to prevent their escape from the waggons. At some distance from this city, the detachment were met by the mob, which continually increased, and which attacked them with stones, bricks, sticks, etc., calling out to the prisoners to make their escape. The fair at St Giles . . . had assembled vast numbers of the worst description of people, and in passing through the streets the yeomanry were assailed with the utmost violence, and many of them seriously injured . . . The rioters had latterly increased to the number of several thousands, and it became utterly impossible for the small party of the military to prevent the prisoners, consisting of double their number, and who were unbound, from making their way out of the waggons, assisted as they were by the mob.[9]

The prisoners were rescued at the corner of Beaumont Street and St Giles. The rescue marked the beginning of a new phase of fierce resistance. The community stuck closely together, as evidenced by the local rhymes which date from this time, referring to attempts to find informers:

> I went to Noke,
> But nobody spoke.
> I went to Beckley,
> They spoke directly.
> Boarstall & Brill
> They are talking still

or:

> I went to Noke
> And nobody spoke.
> I went to Brill
> They were silent still.
> I went to Thame
> It was just the same.
> I went to Beckley
> They spoke directly.

Another rhyme indicates the bitterness of feelings:

> The fault is great in Man or Woman
> Who steals the Goose from off a Common:
> But who can plead that man's excuse
> Who steals the Common from the goose.

The disturbances continued intermittently throughout the next five years, despite repeated attempts to restore law and order. The farmers gradually veered towards the enclosers' viewpoint, and the movement lost momentum. The small people, who had most to lose, lost their battle, and the proprietors strengthened their hold.

The great enclosure movement did not live up to its expectations, with flooding continuing, as indicated by a report from the *Bicester Advertiser* for 12th September 1879:

> An account of the present state of the Fencott and Murcott hamlets in the parish of Charlton-on-Otmoor will be found in our columns today. The present continuous wet weather renders almost any locality not over pleasant, but those of our readers who have never visited the hamlets . . . should do so without delay, but let the journey be taken either on horseback, or with proper water-tight Wellingtons, so that none of the interesting nooks be overlooked. We feel sure the visitor will afterwards have an exalted opinion of the tenacity of human life which exists, apparently in so healthy a state, amid the stagnant mud pools on the borders of the celebrated Otmoor, whose thousands of acres now form an immense lake. The only beauty in this paradisiacal locality, is that, probably of the ducks, fine creatures of the pure Aylesbury breed, who are quite at home in their favourite element . . . To the naturalist this watery track is a happy spot, many of our most rare aquatic species having been found there.

Otmoor is still a fascinating area for the natural historian, but even at the end of the nineteenth century botanists lamented the deteriorating number of flower species, and the twentieth century has seen further drainage and agricultural improvement at the expense of flora and fauna. The army bombing-range, used from 1920–58, which is now a rifle-range, has preserved the natural habitat in that area, by keeping it remote. The Berkshire, Buckinghamshire and Oxfordshire Naturalist Trust has a nature reserve, the Spinney, a 15-acre strip of oak woodland, which protects the black hairstreak butterfly, flora such as the rare fox sedge, *Carex vulpina*, and many birds including nightingales.

The central unimproved area of Otmoor is dominated by *deschampsia*—a rough tufty pasture. Pepper saxifrage and meadow rue are found on damp pasture land, and in the dykes marsh bedstraw, marsh stitchwort, water violet, frog-bit and the rare *Viola stagnina*. All these are in gradual decline. The area is still changing and drying out. In 1964 the whole moor was under permanent pasture, but since then new dykes have been built in the south-west of the moor and hedges removed (5 miles of them since 1968), and the land is used for large-scale arable cultivation.

The villages have changed little and maintain an atmosphere of remoteness. Beckley, whose name means 'Becca's clearing', was in the eleventh century the largest Otmoor 'town'; its Norman church was rebuilt in the fourteenth and fifteenth centuries. Richard of Cornwall built a palace here in 1227, which was sacked and burned five years later. A park was laid out below the palace, first recorded in 1175—it was stocked with deer, walled, with deer-leaps. The ruined manor house was replaced by a hunting lodge. Its triple concentric moats remain, but the house there now was built in 1540 by Sir John William, whose descendants became earls of Abingdon. The house has plum-coloured bricks with a diaper pattern, and stone-mullioned windows, and the garden is set out to reconstruct its appearance in the sixteenth century.

Charlton-on-Otmoor has declined. Its thirteenth-century church dedicated to the Virgin Mary has a beautifully restored and repainted rood screen. It is said that there were once two magnificent statues representing the Virgin Mary and St John the Baptist on the rood screen, which were destroyed during the Reformation. The people of Charlton objected strongly to this desecration and instead created figures on a wicker frame covered with greenery. The Rector C.E. Prior described the ceremonial attached to it in the late nineteenth century:

The large cross made of wood, with a circular base, which stands on the rood-screen, is known locally as 'The Garland'. It is completely covered with spring flowers and evergreens and placed on the screen on the first of May. The old woman who has lately superintended the dressing of 'The Garland' speaks of it as "My Lady", talks about "giving her a waist" and calls the flowers down the front "buttons". The arms of the cross are "her arms" . . . In earlier days there used to be two crosses, a larger and a smaller one . . . The two crosses were carried about bedecked with flowers, the larger by the men, the smaller by the women, but this custom has fallen into disuse. At such times the Cross would be set down at the corner of the Churchyard, and the morris dancers would dance up and down before it. The Garland is now dressed and placed on the screen on May Day. Children sometimes carry about little crosses decked with flowers and sing a May Day song, but compulsory school attendance has nearly put an end to the custom. There are people living who can remember the great cross being carried over Otmoor to Studley Priory, where Lady Croke used to give the party 10s. It was accompanied by the morris dancers . . . [10]

Oddington had a Cistercian abbey in the twelfth century, but despite the Cistercians' love of remote areas, Leland remarked that "this site upon the moor was more fitted for an ark than a monastery". Its site is probably what is now Oddington Grange. The village has shrunk and has few old houses.

The Rogationtide blessing of the crops is still carried on each year by the rector, who assiduously touches a portion of each field, well, farm, barn and wall in the village. Oddington's most unlikely inhabitant was a Maori princess, Maggie Papakura, who married an Englishman and died in 1930. She set up a *pietà* in the churchyard to commemorate Maoris who died during the First World War.

Noke probably originated as a clearing in the oak forest. The church contains the tomb of Benedict Winchcombe, a notorious huntsman, who died in 1623. It is said that on a winter's night he and his hunt speed through the village—here the old legend of Odin's Wild Hunt, which brought death to all who saw it, has been given a historical personality. Another charming story attached to the village is that Lily, Duchess of Marlborough, who died in 1887, lost Noke at cards!

Horton-cum-Studley had a small Benedictine priory founded in about 1176, which was purchased after the Dissolution by John Croke, who began building the present mansion. Fragments of tracery from the priory have been built into an arch in the garden. Sir George Croke built brick almshouses in 1639. He ruled that each inhabitant was to be given 2 shillings each week and provided every two years with a London russet broad-cloth livery gown. They were threatened with expulsion if not of sober temperament.

Fencott and Murcott are two tiny agricultural villages once frequented by gipsies. The land has always been low-lying and marshy.

Otmoor has, despite its drainage and enclosure, remained remote. It has been threatened with being turned into a reservoir to provide Londoners with water, and its peace is now threatened by the forthcoming extension to the M40 motorway, to link Oxford with Birmingham.

6

Villages

The character of Oxfordshire is multi-faceted, the variety being clearly expressed in its villages. Building materials reflect the underlying geological structure, so we find grey oolitic limestone in the west, golden-brown Hornton stone in the Banbury area, flint and brick in the south, and half timber and chalk in the Vale, giving each its own distinct character.

A village's topography and buildings can reveal much about its development and history—the age of the buildings indicate when the village was prosperous; the character of the buildings shows whether it was industrial or agricultural. Uniformity of cottage design, as at Lockinge, raises the suspicion that it is an estate village, with most of the buildings erected by the lord of the manor. The village church, too, often situated at the heart of the village, encapsulates its history.

Village development has been influenced by many factors. Most were established before or during the Anglo-Saxon period, some, such as Bloxham, Benson, Shipton-under-Wychwood, Kirtlington, Wootton and Headington, having considerable importance as *villae regales*[1]—royal Saxon administrative centres for their area. Coombe, a sub-manor of Woodstock, changed its situation. The old village nestled in the valley by the River Evenlode. Between the eleventh and thirteenth centuries the area of arable increased from 500 to 800 acres, as trees, furze and underwood were brought under cultivation, and in about 1350 the village was moved to a new site on the hill, possibly because of depopulation by the Black Death and to improve its position in relation to the arable. For a while the old church remained in use; then in 1395 a Perpendicular-style one was built in the new village, somewhat unusual in that it was built largely at one time. Inside, the walls are decorated with a series of fifteenth-century wall-paintings, depicting the Last Judge-

ment, the Crucifixion, St Catherine, the Angel of the Annunciation and St Christopher (it was considered especially lucky to
see the image of St Christopher as one entered a church, so it is
surprising that it was overpainted in the seventeenth century to
illustrate Moses, Aaron and the Ten Commandments).

Coombe has acquired the nickname of 'Silly' Coombe. 'Silly'
originally meant blessed, but the folk-tales attached to Coombe
make the villagers sound stupid. It is said that they became
dissatisfied with the height of the church tower, considering it
rather squat, so they piled manure around its base and waited
for it to grow. During the night rain washed away the manure,
and next day the jubilant villagers were convinced that their
plot had worked! This legend is attached to several English
villages. Other stories in the same vein tell of balancing a pig
precariously on a wall so it could see the village band go by, and
that once the band was playing in the church when villagers
told them how good they sounded from outside—upon which
they put down their instruments and rushed outside to hear
themselves! Coombe has had a mill at least since 1086, originally used for grinding corn. The present water-powered saw-
mill was built around 1852, with additional power from a beam-
engine which could be used in time of drought or flood, and was
used by the Duke of Marlborough's Blenheim Estates for building and equipment maintenance. It contains a workshop with a
forge, where the horses which hauled the timber were shod;
another workshop has woodworking equipment. The Coombe
Mill Society, which is actively restoring the mill, opens it to the
public several weekends a year.

The medieval expansion of cultivation reached a peak before
the early fourteenth century, and after this a number of villages
were either deserted or diminished in size, becoming what we
term 'deserted or shrunken' medieval villages. Some had always been small settlements, struggling to make ends meet
using marginal land—the number of tenants at Langley near
Leafield had shrunk from eighteen in 1279 to only four in 1316.
Such settlements were more vulnerable to disasters such as the
Black Death, although this has been given more prominence as
the cause of village-desertion than it deserves. However, it does
seem that Tusmore was depopulated by the Black Death. Its
name means 'Thur's Pool' or, more romantically, a 'lake
haunted by a giant or demon', and in the fourteenth century it

was the poorest and smallest village in Ploughley Hundred. In 1358 the land was enclosed by Sir Roger de Cotesford as there were no inhabitants left. No visible traces of the hamlet remain, and the church disappeared after the Reformation.

Cogges, on the outskirts of Witney, was a Saxon village which after the Conquest became the principal estate of the Arsic family who owned considerable lands in Oxfordshire. They built a moated manor-house by the River Windrush, and Manasses Arsic in the late eleventh century endowed a small priory close by, which he presented to the abbey of Fécamp in Normandy. The Norman connection accounts for the unusual octagonal church tower with its pyramidal roof. The present vicarage was originally the priory (dissolved in 1414) and retains medieval features such as a thirteenth-century trussed-rafter roof, probably the oldest example surviving in an Oxfordshire domestic building. Although the priory housed only two or three monks, some, such as William Hamon, surgeon and diplomat to Edward II, held notable offices.

As Witney and the planned twelfth-century village of Newland flourished, Cogges declined. When the de Grey family took over the manor in 1242, they moved the manor-house from its damp location by the river to higher ground. In doing so they probably evicted villeins from their homes along Church Lane. Earthworks indicating sites of cottages can be seen to the west of the manor-house. The village now consists of Manor Farm, church and vicarage, thus qualifying for the title of 'shrunken village'. Manor Farm is being preserved as an agricultural museum, with the house set up as an Edwardian farm-house.

Some villages were affected by early enclosures. Eaton Hastings in the Vale was a prosperous village with thirty-nine households before the Black Death, but in the sixteenth century the lord of the manor, a member of the Fettiplace family, dispossessed peasants by enclosing over 200 acres of arable land to provide grazing for 3,500 sheep. The peasants complained to the king, to little avail, and Eaton Hastings still consists of pasture, with a solitary church, farm and field-names such as 'Little Old Town' and 'Old Town', indicating the former site of the village.

In some areas of the county between a quarter and a third of the villages either disappeared or shrank, the majority probably between 1350 and 1550. The sites of many such villages may still be discerned in the landscape in the form of mounds (house sites) in the fields, sometimes accompanied by the ridge and furrow from the medieval open fields.

The pattern of villages continued to change—emparking, particularly during the eighteenth and nineteenth centuries, moved the site of several, for example Heythrop, a model village of gabled stone cottages built in the 1870s by Albert Brassey, complete with school and school-house, and a church designed in 1880 by A. W. Blomfield, which replaced a Norman church, whose chancel has been preserved as a mortuary chapel.

In the village of Mixbury the old cottages were destroyed and new semi-detached stone ones built in 1874 by order of the Court of Chancery, in a narrow ribbon-development down the road from Mixbury House, opposite the site of the Norman Beaumont Castle.

Lord Faringdon commissioned Sir Ernest George to design new cottages, a village hall and a well for the centre of Buscot in the 1890s, built in local stone, the hall decorated with a cupola. As recently as the 1930s Cornwell near Chipping Norton was almost entirely rebuilt to the designs of Clough Williams Ellis in a distinctly 'model' fashion, with coursed rubble cottages leading downhill to the stream and water-splash, with a village green enclosed by elaborate stone walls and decorated ball finials. The village hall, once a school, is apsidal and neo-Georgian, with Art Deco combined belfry and air-raid siren.

Other villages have fairly recent origins—Freeland, near Witney, consisted of just a few houses in the mid seventeenth century, increasing to about twenty by 1738. The village was clustered around a green in 1800; then expansion was encouraged by nearby Eynsham Hall and by Freeland Park, both of which were surrounded by their own parks, becoming a ribbon-development of mixed types of houses.

William Carter purchased land near Brize Norton in 1901 from the Duke of Marlborough to create Carterton as a small-holders' colony, but the venture was not a success. However, it has attracted much new housing since the 1920s, following the establishment of RAF Brize Norton.

Some villages such as Didcot have grown in size. It was an ordinary Vale village until the arrival of the railway revolutionized the community. Initially the railway, being a third of a mile to the east, did not have a dramatic impact, but gradually in the 1860s the area around the station became the centre of commerce, with a corn exchange, a coal depot, shops and hotel. The new settlement was called 'Northbourne' or 'Didcot New Town'. A variety of houses—detached, semi-detached and terraces—was built, some on the initiative of Stephen Dixon, a local farmer who purchased 119 acres for development. Most houses were constructed from imported yellow and red brick, with decorative string-courses and quoins, utilizing dog's-tooth pattern and moulded brickwork. The new settlement was largely for railway workers and remained a community distinct from the original village, and a considerable rivalry developed between them. In 1904 the Great Western Railway built houses linking Northbourne with the station, of brick, with cleverly designed stepped slate roof-lines and contrasting brick bands to emphasize that they are on a hill. The population more than doubled between 1841 and 1871, to a total of 594 people.

Kidlington was a small village of grey stone cottages, not notable in the history of the county except in 1569, when there was an ill-fated armed uprising of labourers, who, protesting against Tudor enclosures, intended to murder the gentry, steal corn and break down the hedges delineating enclosures. It was not until the 1930s that the village grew rapidly and was designated a 'Garden City'. The 1930s ribbon-development consists of unimaginative semi-detached houses, and it is this that people see as they drive between Oxford and Banbury, perhaps not even realizing the charm of the old village. Kidlington Airport was used during the Second World War and is now a commercial airport, with an active training school for pilots, many students coming from abroad. The population nearly doubled between 1941 and 1965 from 4,800 to 8,514, and it serves as a dormitory town for Oxford. Thomas Beecham, founder of the pill firm, came to live in Kidlington in 1840, where his uncle was a shepherd. He is said to have developed the formula for his pills from a particular grass growing behind the shepherd's cottage, and he began his career by supplying the local doctor.

The area radiating out from Banbury, with its circumference reaching Tysoe, Hook Norton, Great Tew, and Clifton and extending into Northamptonshire and Warwickshire, has such distinctive vernacular architecture that it merits an entire book, *Traditional Domestic Architecture in the Banbury Region*, by R. B. Wood-Jones. As a prosperous farming area it is rich in yeoman houses, particularly dating from the sixteenth to eighteenth centuries. The building stone is Middle Lias marlstone, containing iron, varying from rich rusty brown to a greyish colour, generally known as 'Hornton stone', but many villages had their own quarries. The quality of the stone varies, so at Hook Norton the stone courses are narrow rubble; where the stone is of good quality, it can approximate to ashlar. Occasionally ironstone is mixed with grey limestone, again as at Hook Norton. Thatch was the most common roofing material, though in many cases it has been replaced by Stonesfield or Collyweston slates. The regional style is medieval in character, with distinctive features such as decorative main façades, mullion windows and, from 1650-75, elaborate gable windows.

The buildings of Bloxham epitomize the yeoman-farmhouse architectural tradition, and the layout of the village reveals much of its history and development. It was an important Saxon administrative centre for the Hundred, or *villa regalae*. Because it straddles both sides of the valley created by the Sor Brook, the village is divided into two and, during the Middle Ages, consisted of two manors, which were reunited in 1545 when Richard Fiennes, Lord Saye and Sele, purchased the second manor, having inherited the first. The Fiennes family still retains the lordship of the manor. The larger southern section of the village is dominated by the magnificent church, celebrated in rhyme:

Adderbury for length,
Bloxham for strength,
And Kings Sutton for beauty.

Local legend alleges that at both Bloxham and Adderbury churches there was one mason who worked consistently hard and well, producing superb workmanship, until one day he tripped with his barrow load of stone, which turned into Crouch Hill, the high eminence on the outskirts of Banbury—the man disappeared leaving a sulphurous smell behind him, and it was only then the workmen realized that their companion had been the Devil. Most of the present church dates from the fourteenth century, featuring fine carving, some evidently created by the fourteenth-century school of north Oxfordshire masons who also worked at Adderbury, Alkerton and Hanwell. The sculpture round the west doorway depicts the Last Judgement, with Christ surrounded by angels and with intricate carvings of birds, leaves and ballflower trailing around the blessed and the damned. The west window is unusual in having carved figures in the tracery, similar to those at Dorchester Abbey, and Christ, decorating the central hub of the rose, is the principal feature. The fifteenth-century Milcombe Chapel has windows decorated with gargoyles similar to those at Adderbury. Some of the stained glass dates from the fourteenth century, but the church is noted more for that designed by William Morris and Edward Burne Jones in 1868 and 1869, depicting the heavenly city, saints and angels, with a splendid Art Nouveau cloud formation designed by Philip Webb. Burne Jones designed the St Christopher in the chancel and the figure of St Martin in the north aisle window.

Several other medieval buildings survive, hidden by later exteriors, such as the manor-house in Chapel Street, which, though largely seventeenth and eighteenth century in character, has a fourteenth-century arched doorway, a lancet window and part of its medieval timber roof. The village has a maze of ancient winding lanes with frontages of early buildings along them. The focus of the northern portion of the village is the crossroads by the 'Elephant and Castle' pub; this, the Old Bridge Road, High Street and Workhouse Lane parallel to it, appear to be a planned medieval development. The 'open' village character of the village is seen in the irregular way the houses are built, close together and sometimes encroaching over greens and streets. The prosperity of the farming community is shown by the number of houses belonging to the 'great rebuilding phase' of the sixteenth and seventeenth centuries. Sycamore Terrace started as a medieval three-bay hall-house, being enlarged in the seventeenth century and converted to weavers' cottages in the nineteenth century. Weaving was an important village industry, especially in the eighteenth and nineteenth centuries, with a woollen manufactory and extensive plush weaving. Weaving shops in Queen's Street were demolished in the 1950s and a wool warehouse on Stone Hill was burned down in 1850. The courthouse by the church was rebuilt in the 1680s and repaired in the 1880s but still has a fourteenth-century doorway. Some buildings were 'smartened up' and refronted during the eighteenth century, presenting a new ap-

pearance with ashlar ironstone façades and symmetrical fronts
with elaborate doorways and sash or casement windows replacing the mullions. New buildings, such as Stonehill House and
Cumberford House, were erected.

In the nineteenth century the Banbury and Chipping Norton
Turnpike Trustees constructed the present High Street through
the centre of the village—previously the main route wound
round Church Street, Unicorn Street, Old Bridge Road and
Humber Lane. Estates have been built recently as Bloxham
became a commuter village for Banbury. Another vital influence in the nineteenth century was the establishment of All
Saints' School, which dominates the northern portion. Its first
foundation by the Reverend J. W. Hewitt in 1853 was not altogether successful, but it was refounded in 1859 by the Reverend Philip Egerton as a 'middle-class' school for boys, especially
intended to give a sound general education in the distinctive
principles of the English Church! It is now part of the Woodard
Foundation and a flourishing public school.

In addition to its value as building stone, local stone was
quarried for its iron content during the nineteenth century, and
tunnels have been found in Queen's Street surviving from the
ironstone mines.

Adderbury, like Bloxham, is divided into two by the Sor
Brook—and its church was probably worked on by some of the
same masons. Considerable rivalry existed between the villages, leading to the saying, "Bloxham dogs, come to Adderbury
to buy your togs."

The magnificent church is a basic thirteenth-century cruci-
form shape, enlarged in the fourteenth and fifteenth centuries.
Carved around the cornice of the aisles is a frieze of charming
figures, birds and beasts, each depicted playing a musical in-
strument. Other carving includes pillar capitals depicting
knights, similar to one at Bloxham and another with ladies'
heads. The tithe barn stands near the church, probably dating
mainly from the fourteenth century. Some village architecture
is somewhat grander than that of Bloxham, for example the
sixteenth-century manor-house which has diamond-patterned
brick chimney-stacks, and the Grange, built by John Bloxham
of Banbury for Sir Thomas Cobb in 1682. 'Capability' Brown
made a plan for Adderbury House Park, and in 1796 the vicar
complained that ninety cottages had been demolished in the

landscaping process. Much of the house was demolished in 1808. Adderbury West Manor has a fourteenth-century core, and the old school on the Green was founded in 1589 by Christopher Rawlins, whose name is preserved in the current school. Adderbury, too, was a centre for plush weaving and ironstone mining —the latter particularly after the building of the railway. Rather surprisingly Adderbury provides employment for over five hundred in manufacturing, largely through a firm making concrete garages and garden furniture.

North Oxfordshire abounds in such 'double' settlements— originally separate—such as Barford St John and Barford St Michael, each of which has its own church. Other villages are close together, yet different in plan and character, such as the 'open' and 'closed' villages of Middle Barton and Sandford St Martin. Dr Edwin Guest, Master of Gonville and Caius College, Cambridge, who purchased Sandford Park in 1849, largely rebuilt the latter village with neat labourers' cottages along both sides of the single village street flanking the church. Its compact and planned appearance contrasts with the sprawl of neighbouring Middle Barton, inserted between Westcote and Steeple Barton, its confused boundaries making it seem an afterthought. Here there was no overall control by a lord of the manor, and Nonconformity flourished in the nineteenth century. The standard of living was lower and far more precarious in the 'open' village economy.

Hook Norton, an industrial village, has a complex plan. The rich colour of its building stone reveals the ironstone content, and although the Brymbo Ironworks no longer operate, the brewery thrives and some cottages have long rows of weavers' windows. It is one of the larger Cherwell villages, with the splendid church dedicated to St Peter matching its character with a fine Norman chancel, several wall-paintings and a Norman font revealing the medieval belief in astrology, with signs of the Zodiac mixed with Adam and Eve.

The Cherwell Valley, with the Oxford Canal running alongside, has many picturesque villages. Somerton may have formed the summer pastures of a Saxon unit linked with Souldern and Fritwell. The de Grey family had a castle here, already uninhabited when the manor became the home of the Fermor family in the sixteenth century. They moved to Tusmore in 1625, and their once magnificent Tudor home is a ruin, mostly demolished during the eighteenth century, leaving only part of the hall wall with a forlorn traceried window and extensive earthworks. Several family monuments may be seen in the church, including the brass of William Fermor and his wife, who died in 1552, the alabaster effigies of Thomas Fermor and his wife, who died in 1580, and an elaborate canopied effigy with obelisks carved for John Fermor (died 1625). Thomas Fermor endowed the free school in 1580, and a sixteenth century mullioned window from the original school building is incorporated in the present eighteenth and nineteenth century school.

The oval maze situated near the village at 'Troy Farm' in the farm-house garden, measuring 57 by 50 feet, is surrounded by trees and shrubs; unlike the hedge maze at Hampton Court, this consists of banks and ditches approximately a foot wide. It is impossible to get lost, but the brave soul who follows its meandering path will find himself walking 400 yards before he reaches the centre, and 400 yards back. The origins and purposes of mazes are shrouded with mystery, and even the date of this one is unknown, although it is probably medieval, being similar to the pattern on the tiles of Toussaints Abbey. Although it is the only maze preserved in the county, it is possible that there was one at Muswell Hill, near Piddington, which has an earthwork with a low bank around it, known as 'The Wilderness', a term once used to denote a horticultural or hedge maze; there is another site, possibly moated, south of Caldecott near Abingdon, also called 'The Wilderness'.

Lower Heyford's name indicates that it was important as a ford before the thirteenth-century bridge was built—'Hey' suggesting its use particularly at the time of the hay harvest. The square at the heart of the village served as a market-place in the nineteenth century, but the village is now a quiet backwater despite the addition of council houses, built between 1925 and 1954, and its club room and library, built in 1926, and must cede importance and bustle to its other half, Upper Heyford. This was known as Heyford Warren until the fifteenth century. Its changed importance stems from the building of an RAF station, which opened in 1927. The Oxford University Air Squadron trained here, and it was a base for Bomber Command during the Second World War and then became No. 1 Parachute Training School for the Strategic Air Command. The site has been leased to the United States Air Force since 1951 and is one of their most important tactical fighter bases in Europe. The peace of the village is frequently shattered by the noise of F111 fighters taking off and landing, and the sound of American accents contrasts with the Oxfordshire dialect. On the base, life is a microcosm of America—the employees are paid in dollars, buy American food in an American-type supermarket and educate their children at an American school. Many live on the base, but some prefer to live in the surrounding villages and integrate themselves into Oxfordshire life.

Kirtlington with its grey stone cottages is dominated by Kirtlington Park, built in 1742–6 for Sir James Dashwood. It was a Saxon royal manor, important enough for a 'Witenagemot' to be held there in 977, attended by Archbishop Dunstan, and in the eleventh century it belonged to Edward the Confessor. It was a wealthy parish during the Middle Ages, becoming a centre for fulling and dyeing cloth and quarrying. In 1801 it ranked third in size in Ploughley Hundred behind Bicester and Islip. It is noted for a curious custom known as 'lamb ale' which, together with the Kirtlington morris team, has recently been revived. The ceremony began each Trinity Sunday, when the young men of the village elected a Lord who chose his Lady. They processed round the village, carrying maces and ribbon streamers, accompanied by a Fool in motley, morris dancers and musicians, and two men carrying decorated wooden clubs known as 'Forest Feathers'. The jollifications continued for the next eight or nine days, the lamb itself being carried in procession on the Monday, Tuesday and Wednesday before being killed, cut up and made into pies, one of which contained the whole head, with some of the wool still on it—this was sold whole, while the others were cut up and distributed among the villagers. During this time a 'bowery' was set up where drink was available in abundance. The festival merged in the late nineteenth century with the village club day, with its attendant procession, church service and celebratory dinner. The revival, although it includes the procession, no longer involves the sacrifice of a lamb.

Further downstream are Hampton Gay and Hampton Poyle. Hampton Gay manor house is a romantic ruin, while nothing is left of the village but a farmhouse and a lonely church with extensive earthworks. The village is named after its former owners, Rainald and Robert de Gaie, who held it at Domesday. The water-powered paper-mill was in use until about 1888, but when that closed, several villagers moved elsewhere in their search for jobs. Their cottages fell into ruin and have now almost disappeared, and the manor-house itself was destroyed in a disastrous fire in 1887.

Cottisford has been immortalized as 'Fordlow' by Flora Thompson in *Lark Rise to Candleford*. The village she knew in the 1880s had been substantially altered about forty years before by William Turner, who removed the main road away from Cottisford House and improved his view by demolishing the houses by the church, rebuilding them further away and replacing them with trees. She describes it as

> a little, lost lonely place, much smaller than the hamlet [Juniper Hill], without a shop, an inn or a post office, and 6 miles from a railway station. The little squat church, without spire or tower, crouched back in a tiny churchyard that centuries of use had raised many feet above the road, and the whole was surrounded by tall, windy elms in which a colony of rooks kept up a perpetual cawing. Next came the Rectory, so buried in orchards and shrubberies that only the chimney-stacks were visible from the road; then the old Tudor farmhouse with its stone mullioned windows and reputed dungeon. These, with the school and about a dozen cottages occupied by the shepherd, carter, blacksmith and a few other superior farm-workers made up the village. Even these few buildings were strung out along the roadside, so far between and so sunken in greenery that there seemed no village at all. It was a standing joke in the hamlet that a stranger had once asked the way to Fordlow after he had walked right through it.[1]

One of the dead commemorated on the church war memorial is Flora's brother, Edmund Timms. The village is even smaller today than in Flora Thompson's day. Juniper Hill began as cottages built for the paupers of Cottisford and soon exceeded it in size. Fringford, just down the road is the 'Candleford Green' of *Lark Rise* (although in the book it is mixed with elements of Grayshott, Hampshire). The forge-cum-post office is still there, though no longer operating as a forge. The lovely church is little changed, and the village has a peaceful unspoilt air.

West Oxfordshire too is stone country. One of its most picturesque villages is Great Tew, with golden Hornton stone buildings topped by thatched or Stonesfield slate roofs. The two cottages on the green, combined to form the 'Falkland Arms', date from the sixteenth century, and much of the village was rebuilt in the seventeenth century. Sir Lawrence Tanfield, the dreadful overlord of Burford, purchased the manor in 1614. His memory is so strong that his coach and horses are said to haunt the manor house at the stroke of midnight. His grandson, Lucius Cary, Viscount Falkland, and his wife Lettice had a far more beneficent effect on the village, giving stone for reconstructing cottages. He brought his academic friends such as the Oxford scholars Dr Sheldon and Dr Morley and playwright Ben Jonson to the village, making it a cultural centre. This tranquillity was destroyed by the Civil War, which Cary strove to prevent. He was no coward, however, proving his courage in battle. A sad legend attaches to his death. Charles I was based in Oxford and decided to divine his fortune in the war by opening Virgil's *Aeneid* at random, the verse on which his finger alighted proving his fate. The chosen verse, from the fourth book, prophesied the loss not only of his kingdom but of his friends, and his own early death. Understandably he was somewhat downcast by such an evil omen, and Lord Falkland tried to cheer him by reading his own fate, but his disastrous one, foretelling his death in battle, must have entirely failed in its object. The ill omens of both men were fulfilled, Lord Falkland dying at the battle of Newbury in 1643.

The seventeenth- and eighteenth-century village was somewhat different in plan, having several nuclei, one around the present village green, another to the east across the stream known as 'The Square', surrounded by orchards and enclosures, while another group occupied the site of what is now Great Tew Park with a small linear settlement across the road from the walled gardens of the manor, with a number of outlying farms. The nineteenth century saw a period of great change in the village. In 1808, General Stratton of Tew Park, who was in financial difficulties, heard of J. C. Loudon's advocacy of the profitability of Scottish farming methods using arable and grass and invited him to try them at Great Tew. Stratton dispossessed the existing tenants, and the new tenants, faced with high rents, sublet to a dozen Scottish farmers. Loudon established an agricultural college at Tew Lodge, for the sons of the landed proprietors, laid out pleasure gardens at Ditchley and put his 'beauty with utility' theory into practice at Tew, aiming to create a model village and a practical *ferme ornée,* utilizing the natural landscape. He built the farm-house with a view across the valley and the farmyard at the bottom on a diagonal axis giving a view over the whole farm. The kitchen, flower, alpine and American gardens were laid out in rectangular and ovoid plots. The kitchen garden contained a specimen of almost every variety of fruit tree, shrub and vegetable known in Britain. The lake provided water for the water-powered threshing-machines. The lanes followed natural contours to lessen the burden for the farm horses and were constructed with a paved winter or wet-weather section 9 feet wide and a summer or dry-weather section of packed earth, 11 feet wide. The decorative temples overlooked fields instead of parkland; plantations graced less fertile slopes, and 201 fields were amalgamated to form one hundred. Loudon's new agricultural methods increased the land value but were not an enormous success. He left Tew in 1811, and only a few exotic trees, rhododendron plantations and Cedars of Lebanon remain as evidence of his improvements. Tew Lodge has been demolished, and the park vistas are obscured.

The Jacobean house was replaced by a Georgian dower house, extended in Tudor style in the mid nineteenth century. The Gothic-style school encroaching on the village green was built in the 1850s. Many of the cottages were given additional picturesque details, following the ideas of Loudon, by Matthew Boulton—dripstones were added above the windows and doors. Porch House acquired Gothic tracery, and a few new cottages with Stonesfield slate roofs were added. A mound indicates the site of an ice-house, and a strange edifice of Gothic arches known as 'the Dog Kennel' may be the site of an animal burial. The only industrial building remaining in the village is the ruined smithy, with its decaying forges open to the elements and in grave danger of imminent collapse. The tools from the smithy and other items are on display in a small private museum at the forge.

The village is unique in having sixty-nine Grade II listed buildings and has been declared an area of outstanding interest, thus qualifying for Government grants towards the upkeep of the buildings, which may help the houses, which are in a grave state of disrepair, owing largely to the lack of money available to the estate, which has maintained the village as a closed village, not allowing weekenders and commuters to buy houses, thus avoiding jarring modern development.

The slates used on some of the roofs not only at Great Tew but in many Oxfordshire villages come from Stonesfield. It is easy for the stranger to become hopelessly lost in Stonesfield, with its maze of streets laid out with no apparent logic. Paradoxically the name 'Stonesfield' has no connection with roofing-stone, deriving from the Saxon 'Stunta's Field'. The 'slates' are of brown or grey sandstone or blue and grey limestone which occurs in solid chunks of stone known as 'pendle', or from 'pot-lids', formations of sandstone occurring in oval masses, often containing fossils.

Dr Plot gives us the first reference to the industry in the seventeenth century. Most slate was then extracted from surface outcrops, but as these were used up, adits had to be mined. Most shafts are only 4—5 feet high, and the winding tunnels are uncomfortable and eerie. One has to work with bent knees and back, until the muscles in the backs of the legs feel as though they will never straighten out again, and it is possible for it to be completely silent in one part of a tunnel, when one knows that there is a party of people round the corner. Slates were mined in autumn—the pendle was brought to the surface and carefully dampened, then protected by straw topped by an earth clamp to prevent the sap in the stone from evaporating, as it played an essential part in the splitting process. If there were no sharp frosts over the winter, it had to be buried even more deeply during the summer and turfed over. As soon as a hard frost came, the men uncovered the pendle and spread it out over the fields to give the frost a better chance of splitting it to the required thickness, and the slater then trimmed slates to size and put a hole through the top end. Some sources give distinc-tive names to the various sizes, such as 'Jenny-why-gettest-thou', 'rogue-why-winkest-thou' and 'long and short hag-hatters', but the basis for such names is doubtful. More authentic names include Short, Middle and Long Cock (7–8 inches long), Muffity (9½ inches) Short and Long Bachelor (11-11½ inches), Short and Long Wippet (13½–14 inches) and so on. The sites of the mines and chipping banks are scattered throughout the village, but only Spratt's Barn, which remained in use later than the other mines, until 1914, is occasionally opened. The industry died at the turn of the century—perhaps easy accessibility of Welsh slates, the need to extend the area of mines, the poor wages and conditions of the labourers, and mild winters all combined against it. There are fewer Stonesfield slate roofs in Stonesfield and the surrounding area than one might expect, as the prices commanded by slates, particularly between the wars, caused many to sell their slate roofs and replace them with corrugated iron, Welsh slates or tiles. Some unusual buildings include the stone village lock-up with its stout iron grille, built in the yard of the 'Rose and Crown', and the restored cockpit in the grounds of the former rectory, said to have been used by a rector who coached students to augment his income, in an attempt to keep them out of mischief.

Stone quarries, particularly those at Taynton, have been in use much longer than Stonesfield slate. A block of stone carved into a Roman coffin may come from Taynton, and its stone may have been utilized for villa building. The Taynton quarries were important enough to be mentioned in Domesday Book. In the thirteenth century Taynton stone was used for the tower and spire of Oxford Cathedral, and in the fourteenth century for Merton College and Windsor Castle. When quarried, it is bright yellow in colour, weathering to a mellow brownish grey. Traces of old quarries abound, and the stone is still quarried today. Other quarries were found at Milton, Swinbrook and Minster Lovell.

The Windrush villages, such as Fulbrook, Swinbrook and Minster Lovell are delightful, with lovely stone cottages. Swinbrook has seventeenth- and eighteenth-century farmhouses mixed with some Tudor-influenced Victorian cottages. Its church has monuments to the Fettiplace family, who lived here for generations—including sculptured recumbent effigies of 1613 to Sir Edmund Fettiplace and 1686 to his namesake. More recently it has been the home of the Mitford family.

Fulbrook church has wall-paintings with a design of red stars over the chancel arch, and two merchants' wool-pack tombs in the churchyard, emphasizing the local importance of the woollen industry.

Filkins is more typical of a Gloucestershire Cotswold village than of Oxfordshire. Its neat houses have lovingly tended cottage gardens, some fenced with solid stone slabs similar to those used to hood doorways. St Peter's Church was designed by G. E. Street and built in the 1850s in French Gothic style. The village

houses the Swinford Museum, a fascinating folk-museum consisting of material collected by stonemason George Swinford,
who was born here in the late 1880s. He assiduously collected
local craft and agricultural material, tools and examples of
locally made pottery, encapsulating the flavour of the way of life
in a Cotswold village.

Another private museum with the same aim has been
founded by Chris Walker at Asthall Barrow, on the outskirts of
Burford, again reflecting the Cotswold tradition but with
material gathered from a wider area and collected within the
last few years.

Standlake is a long, straggling village near the River Thames
in an area liable to flooding. Its church has remains of Norman
work but was enlarged in the fourteenth century and has an
unusual octagonal west tower. Moated Gaunt House is largely
sixteenth century but retains some fifteenth-century features
and was fortified and besieged during the Civil War. The manor-
house is half-timbered, dating from roughly the same period as
Gaunt House, but most of the buildings are stone. Stone is the
most prominent but not the only building material used in west
Oxfordshire. Nearby, Yelford Manor is timber-framed on stone
footings. It is moated and retains the late-medieval hall house
layout with solar and service-wings plus a sixteenth-century
walled-in staircase although the hall has been given a ceiling to
make it two storeys, instead of being open to the roof. Above the
dais in the hall is a hexagonal bay window, and the parlour has
seventeenth-century panelling carved with caryatids and a
frieze of dragons.

Brick has been used for buildings of lesser quality and in some
larger houses, such as Aston House, near Bampton, built in the
eighteenth century, in an area where building stone was
readily available. There were several brickworks in west
Oxfordshire, including the Duke of Marlborough's nineteenth-
century estate brickworks at Bladon and later at Ascott-under-
Wychwood, Combe and Leafield.

South Oxfordshire has a shortage of building stone, and a
glance at Nettlebed indicates the importance of clay, as most
buildings are of local brick, the principal building material of
the area. Even Nettlebed church is built of grey brick, with
stone dressings, and a speckling of red bricks on the tower. It is
dedicated to St Bartholomew and was built in 1845-6. A notable

feature is a stained glass window designed in 1970 by John Piper. The past importance of brickmaking here is also echoed by the bottle-kiln, the only one of its type still standing in the county, now a forlorn appendage to a modern housing-estate. Clay industries have dominated the village at least since the fourteenth century, when 35,000 Nettlebed tiles were used in the building of Wallingford Castle, and Flemish brickmakers who had emigrated to Crocker End, Nettlebed, made bricks for Stonor manor-houses. Some bricks have a vitrified glaze, and these are used in conjunction with the normal bricks to create patterns. The clay was so plentiful that several brickworks existed concurrently.

Stoke Row, another centre for clay industries, was notoriously short of water, so the villagers must have been astounded and delighted when in 1863 the Maharajah of Benares presented them with their first well. This came about because E. A. Reade of Ipsden organized a water-supply scheme in Benares and once told the Maharajah about the problems faced by the villages such as Stoke Row. Perhaps the Maharajah had not realized the extent of his munificence—the well had to be dug 368 feet deep. It appears an outpost of India, despite being made by Wilder's of Wallingford—having an oriental canopied dome supported on eight cast-iron columns, and above the machinery stands a cast-iron elephant. Close by is a neat well-keeper's cottage. The well provided only drinking water, so the servants and children sometimes ventured far from the village in dry seasons searching for water for washing.

Ewelme is dominated by medieval brickwork. Its name derives from the Anglo-Saxon 'Iaew[i]elm', meaning 'spring whelming'—the stream, now known as 'King's Pool', which courses through the village, is thought to have curative properties and is ideal for growing watercress. The principal buildings date largely from the 1430s, when William de la Pole, Earl of Suffolk, and his wife Alice Chaucer (granddaughter of the poet Geoffrey Chaucer), who owned the manor of Ewelme, rebuilt the church, retaining only a portion of the early fourteenth-century tower from the previous building, and endowed alms-houses and a school. These buildings now form the core of the village, as the medieval palace was largely in ruins by the early seventeenth century, although in the sixteenth century Henry VIII and Catherine Howard honeymooned there,

and Elizabeth I stayed there. Fragments of the palace are incorporated in the present Georgian manor-house.

The church, dedicated to the Virgin Mary, has chequer flint-
work, with an embattled brick parapet, and is unusual in having no chancel arch or division between nave and chancel. This
design and the building techniques may have been influenced
by those of the church at Wingfield in Suffolk, another manor
owned by the de la Poles, which has a similar arrangement of
carved screens dividing the church. The fifteenth-century rood-
screen has an unusual design of hand-wrought iron mullions
and ogee tracery and fragments of the medieval paint colours.

St John the Baptist's chapel contains the tomb of the church's
patron, Alice, who died in 1475 at the venerable age of seventy-
one. She was a notable national figure in her time—she had
been married three times by the age of twenty-eight, each time
rising in the social scale: her first husband, Sir John Phelip, was
a mere knight, who caught dysentery at the battle of Barfleur in
1415, leaving her a widow at eleven; her second husband,
William, Earl of Shrewsbury, was a victim of the siege of
Orleans, defending the besieging army from the secondary
attack of Joan of Arc. Alice's marriage to William de la Pole,
who became Duke of Suffolk in 1448, ended in tragedy when he
was attacked by jealous nobles in 1450, impeached for treason
and banished. He was on his way to France, aboard the omin-
ously named ship *Nicholas of the Tower* (his astrologer had
foretold a shameful death and warned him to beware of the
Tower), when the crew seized him and hacked off his head with a
rusty sword.

Alice had the strength of character to surmount her difficulties: her son married Elizabeth of York, and she herself
acted as custodian to the captive Margaret of Anjou, widow of
Henry VI, at Wallingford Castle. Her brightly painted tomb
matches the magnificence of her life; golden-haired angels with
peacock-eyed wings flank her alabaster effigy, depicted in a
coronet and a stately robe decorated with the Order of the
Garter (she was one of few women to receive this honour, and it
is said that Queen Victoria, who wanted to know exactly how
she should wear her own Order of the Garter at her coronation,
sent to Ewelme for information). The open crypt below this
ornate tomb illustrates the medieval belief in the transitory
nature of life, with another effigy of a rather gruesome shrunken

figure in her shroud. The underside of the canopy above the crypt has paintings of John the Baptist, St Mary Magdalene and the Annunciation, but one has to lie on the chancel floor and crane one's neck to see them. A tomb in the churchyard is that of Jerome K. Jerome of *Three Men in a Boat* fame.

The alms-houses are perhaps the first to be planned as separate dwellings around a cloister, rather than following the earlier plan of a monastic infirmary. They were built in 1437 by royal licence to house two chaplains and thirteen inmates rather than to provide shelter for travellers as well as the aged and infirm. The inmates used the south aisle of the church instead of having their own chapel—it must have had rather a segregated air, as until recently men sat in the left aisle and women in the right. Inspiration for the novel layout may have come from Carthusian priory design, one at Hull having been founded in 1378 by the Duke's grandfather, Michael de la Pole, first Earl of Suffolk and Lord Chancellor of England, which has a layout of cells round a central quadrangle on the plan followed at Ewelme. Another notable feature of the Ewelme alms-houses is the early use of local pink-red brick, with plain bricks cunningly used to create herringbone, triangle and chevron patterns. The porch and the gateway to the schoolmaster's house have bricks of a wide variety of shapes, curved, concave, beaked and chamfered. The gables have beautifully carved bargeboards and are filled with brick nogging. Each inmate had two rooms with fireplaces, connected by a staircase. This layout remained unchanged until 1970, when the number of alms-houses was reduced to seven. The muniment room and the master's lodgings are still substantially unaltered, the former with its fine sixteenth-century panelling. The grammar school was founded at the same time, and one of the alms-house chaplains gave free teaching to the children. It was greatly altered in the Georgian period, but much of the fine fifteenth-century brickwork has been preserved, and it is one of the oldest school buildings in current use, now as a state primary school.

The eighteenth-century alms-houses at Goring are also of brick—two storeys high with casement windows, situated south-east of the eleventh-century church, dedicated to the Virgin Mary, which was built by Robert d'Oilly, drastically altered in the twelfth century when it was rededicated to St Thomas of Canterbury and given to the Augustinian nuns of

Goring, who in the process of erecting their own priory church demolished part of the Norman church, extending it to make a much grander edifice. Stone from the priory buildings was used to build local houses after the Dissolution.

The buildings of the village are constructed from a wide variety of materials—the Miller of Mansfield Inn, which amalgamates three different buildings, has a seventeenth-century wing of typical Chiltern materials—flint and brick, a main block of Georgian brickwork, topped by red tiles, and a nineteenth-century addition. Some sixteenth-century half-timbered buildings with brick nogging, such as the Catherine Wheel Inn, survive, and from the eighteenth century onwards flint and brick became the characteristic materials—flint was being used as late as 1913, when Flint House, designed by Ernest Newton, was built in Tudor style.

In the terrible winter of 1850–1 the River Thames froze, and the ice was so thick that people travelled on it by pennyfarthing bicycle all the way from Goring to Wallingford. Oscar Wilde stayed there, perhaps acquiring his inspiration for 'Lord Goring' and 'Lady Bracknell'. Edwardian Goring proved a popular resort—there was a boom in rented holiday accommodation, people flocked there for picnics and tea-parties, and members of the theatrical world such as George Grossmith and Sir Frank Benson threw parties. Regattas were held with processions of gaily lit boats, fireworks and a fun fair. The river was also used for industrial purposes, and seventeenth-century Cleeve Mill, a water-mill on the river bank, has recently been restored to working condition, with the water-mill providing much of the electricity for the house. More recently the village has become a commuter area for Reading, Harwell, Benson and London, with considerable residential development, so that the population has increased from just under two thousand in 1931 to about four thousand in 1980.

Goring and Goring Heath are typical of many Chiltern parishes in having a river-bank portion and a secondary hill settlement. Goring Heath is set in heathland among trees, about 4 miles from Goring. Its large brick alms-houses were donated by Henry Alnut, lawyer of the Middle Temple and Lord Mayor of London, who died in 1724. They consist of one-storey apartments clustered around three sides of a courtyard, with a central chapel of red and grey brick with decorative stone acorns and a wooden clock-turret. Other buildings in the village vary from timber-framed cottages and farm-houses, with brick nogging, to the delightful post office built in 1900 with weatherboarding and tile hanging.

Dorchester-on-Thames was no longer a town after the Roman era and declined in the late-Saxon period, after the establishment of Wallingford and Oxford. An Augustinian abbey was founded around 1170, and the present abbey church was built. The church is a glorious building, with a fine Tree of Jesse window dating from about 1320. It contains gems such as the memorial to Sir John Holcomb, who died during the second crusade, which shows him twisting as though in the act of pulling his sword from its scabbard, and the corbel showing sleeping monks, with the Devil blowing his horn. The church radiates peace and tranquillity, in contrast to some of the past history of the abbey, which in the mid fifteenth century had a riotous monk by the name of Ralph Carnelle in the community:

> The same brother Ralph is disobedient to the abbot as regards his lawful commands and makes conspiracies with the young canons against the abbot and against the institutes of the rule. The same Brother Ralph takes the young canons out of the monastery by night to eatings and drinkings in the town with women, and other secular folks; and that he may be able to go out freely, he breaks the doors, windows and the other wooden enclosures of the monastery.
>
> Also if the abbot says to the said Ralph or enjoins anything upon him for his offences, straightway he breaks forth into words of abuse, despising and reviling him; and he is very unbearable in the house . . . [2]

The abbey was dissolved in 1557, and little remains of the abbey buildings except the guest-house dating from the fourteenth and fifteenth centuries, which was later used for the grammar school founded by John Fettiplace in 1652. Now the building houses a small museum, illustrating the history of Dorchester, with a display rich in Roman items found in the town.

Many of the buildings are pre-eighteenth century, including the fine George Inn, with its galleried courtyard dating from about 1500. The earlier buildings are timber-framed with brick nogging, some of their thatched roofs decorated with straw birds, while some flint-and-brick and chequered-brick buildings date from the eighteenth century.

At the entrance to the town by the bridge stands an eighteenth century tollhouse. The massive lorries thundering along the narrow high street shake the houses, but this situation will shortly be remedied by the building of a bypass, although this may contribute to further diminution of the town. However, it is this stagnation, and lack of new building, which gives Dorchester its coherent and vaguely old-world charm.

The Chiltern villages have delightful churches, including that of Checkendon, dedicated to St Peter and St Paul and built of flint and stone, its Norman doorway carved with eagles and monsters and diaper patterns. The internal arches have Norman designs of interlacing and palmettes, and there are still some medieval tiles *in situ* in the sanctuary. The restored wall-paintings which fill the apse depict Christ seated on a throne, under a canopy with St Peter and St Paul, these three figures being larger than those of the other apostles, the whole painted in red ochre. An unusual monumental brass commemorates William Beauchamp (died 1430) with a design of the deceased soul, in a winding-sheet, being transported to Heaven by two angels. The village focuses round a trianglar green surrounded by typical Chiltern houses of timber framing, brick and flint with red-tiled roofs. Some of the bricks may have been made at Neal's kiln, buried deep in the woods.

North Stoke church, too, has some fascinating wall-paintings. The church belonged to the abbey of Bec, Normandy, and a new chancel was built in the thirteenth century, the nave and tower a century later. The oak door dating from 1300 has its original ironwork. The mass dial which is probably Norman has the head and hands of a priest holding the dial—which marks the hour of twelve and alternate hours with a cross. The little church is full of wall-paintings which, combined with the simplicity of the architecture, impart great charm. Subjects include the Last Judgement, either St Stephen or St Lawrence accompanied by a priest in vestments, a small Crucifixion scene with the Virgin Mary and St John, a portion of the Resurrection, a three-tier painting of the Last Supper, Christ's Betrayal, Trial and Flagellation, and some faded, damaged portions which may show Christ bearing the Cross, His Descent from the Cross and Resurrection and, over the south door, a possible Annunciation. The north wall illustrates the legend of three dead kings warn-

ing the living, "What you are, we were; what we are, you will
be." Between the windows are the martyrdoms of St Catherine
and St Stephen, and the figures of the cruel stone-throwers on
the latter have villainous hooked noses. The martyrdom of St
Thomas à Becket on the east wall is marred by the loss of St
Thomas himself. Another painting shows St John, identified by
the *agnus dei*, and a winged demon. The ochres and blacks are a
little sombre, but the overall effect of all the paintings is over-
whelming.

The Baldons, with their delightful *mélange* of half timber,
brick and stone, form a transition between areas, situated on
the edge of the Oxford Heights. The church at Baldon Row,
slightly remote from the village is the parish church of Toot
Baldon. Marsh Baldon is the larger village, a short walk from
Toot Baldon, with most of its houses clustered round the
spacious village green. Many of the thatched, half-timbered
cottages that once stood round the green have been destroyed
at one time or another by fire. Some are now tiled instead of
thatched, some whitewashed; others have brick nogging perhaps of local brick. Decorative Victorian brick is used not only
for the farm-house of Durham Leys Farm but also for its barns.
The village school has been in existence for over two hundred
years, thanks to the generosity of Mrs Elizabeth Lane, who died
in 1771. One of the village lanes has been known as 'Tinny
Lane', since Pressed Steel Fisher dumped waste trimmings
along there in the 1920s to make it less muddy!

St Peter's Church has a bell tower with an octagonal top, and
the crudely carved sundial above the porch door is probably
twelfth century. Its homely character is typified by the inscription to one of its much-loved residents, Anne Pollard, who died
in 1701 of smallpox, at the age of sixty-four:

> Illustrious women deserve the
> Praises of this Marble.
> Bright in her Extraction
> Allied to many of the Nobility,
> And to WILLIAM OF WICKHAM,
> The Glory of her Family,
> And the Ornament of her Age,
> Beautifull even to Envy,
> Hearts were her victims,
> Her mind wholly Divine,

Her face in its lively portraiture
Heaven her Ambition was,
The world her Scorn,
Encircled with a Crown of Virtues,
And prudence equal to her piety.

Wheatley is a straggling village of largely stone-built cottages, still with its hexagonal village lock-up, built in 1834. Once it stood on the main road from London to Oxford. Stones from its now disused quarries were used to build Merton College and Windsor Castle, but its popularity was outshone by Headington from the fifteenth century. Later the stone was used for lime, the ruins of a lime-kiln still remaining, although the brick-kilns have long disappeared. Its proximity to Oxford has made it a popular commuter village, as attested by the new housing estates which contrast with the fine seventeenth-century buildings of the village centre.

The Vale of White Horse was until very recently part of Berkshire and still retains a distinct character. The chalk supports a different flora from the rest of the county, as found in the BBONT nature reserve at Aston Upthorpe, including the burnt-tip and frog orchids, chalk milkwort and pasque flower, in the juniper habitat. Such a haven as the nature reserve becomes increasingly vital as much of the Downs are put under plough, destroying the habitats for the flowers. The chalk, together with half timber, and later brick, is the main building material of the Vale, since, except for its northern extremities, there is little building stone.

A neat line of villages lies along the spring line at the base of the Downs. Uffington is set a little apart from the famous White Horse Down—almost all its buildings are of chalk (including the seventeenth-century schoolhouse) topped by thatched roofs. Styles Cottage is typical of an agricultural labourer's cottage. It was built before 1699 by the Craven Estate and consists of a single room with a loft above; in the eighteenth century a second cottage with similar accommodation was built on to one end. Life in such a tiny cottage must have been cramped and squalid—in the mid nineteenth century each housed a farm labourer and his family, one with six children and the other with nine. Mercifully it was converted into one cottage in the early twentieth century, when a dairyman and his wife lived in it.

Uffington church was fondly referred to as 'the cathedral of the Vale', a dominating building in Early English style with a central octagonal tower. In 1743 the church spire was struck by lightning, leading to the rhyme:

> Poor Uffington, proud people:
> Has a church without a steeple,
> But what is more to its disgrace
> Has a clock without a face.[3]

The old faceless clock has now been replaced by one with hands.

Thomas Hughes, author of *Tom Brown's Schooldays* and *The Scouring of the White Horse*, was born in Uffington in 1822, the son of the vicar. His memorial may be seen in the church, although his career took him away from the village to become a Queen's Counsellor, County Court Judge and Member of Parliament for Lambeth and Frome.

Kingston Lisle also has chalk cottages and even thatched chalk barns. The small church dedicated to St John the Baptist, with much Norman and thirteenth-century work, has great thick chalk-walls and wall-paintings depicting scenes from the life of St John the Baptist, including his beheading, with large figures of St Peter and St Paul painted in brown and black.

Flints occur plentifully in the chalk, and these, together with fossils, have been used to decorative effect, in conjunction with the chalk in Manor Farm House. The fertile chalk, which makes the Vale such a prosperous market-gardening area, is used by Kingston Lisle Nurseries, centred on the kitchen garden of Kingston Lisle House, specializing in pot-plants and such flowers as carnations and gladioli, plus fruit and vegetables.

Although the twin villages of East and West Hendred, linked by the Ginge Brook, are also situated at the foot of the Downs, they make little use of chalk, most of the sixteenth- and seventeenth-century houses being of half timber. West Hendred is the smaller of the two with a largely fourteenth-century church, still with many slip-decorated medieval floor-tiles set into the nave and chancel. East Hendred is considered one of the most beautiful Vale villages. It has a complex plan and is a failed market-town, probably because of its proximity to Wantage. The Downs provided good grazing, and East Hendred shows the profits to be made from sheep and wool. The Ginge Brook provided the motive power for fulling-mills, and cloth may have been dried on terraces near the church. Some of the fine houses doubtless belonged to merchants, and memorials to several, such as the brass to Roger Eldysley, who died in 1439, may be found in the church. Some of the timber framing has been infilled with brick nogging, and the village is given further character by the thatch-topped cob walls lining some streets. A village museum is housed in Champs Chapel with its adjacent fourteenth- and fifteenth-century priests' house.

Blewbury was for many years the home of Kenneth Grahame, author of *The Wind in the Willows*. Its delightful grey-stone cottages are surrounded by colourful gardens, interspersed with black-and-white timber-framed buildings and eighteenth- and nineteenth-century brick-and-tile ones, winding down narrow lanes with the stream with its watercress beds gurgling through the centre of the village. The church contains much Norman work, and the chained books echo the days when books were immensely valuable and required protection. Here we find *Paraphrase of the New Testament*, written by Erasmus in 1548, *Defence of the Apology of the Church of England* (1567) by Bishop Jewell, and a Bible published in 1613, all chained to reading-desks.

The red-brick village school was founded by William Malthus, a wealthy merchant, as a chantry school in 1709, designed to educate fifty—later sixty—children, each of whom received £1 a year for clothing; £1 was paid to each child whose parents were unable to pay the parish rates. To encourage children to attend the school, this money was paid at a rate of one penny six days a week, forty weeks a year, and if the child was absent, he or she did not receive the penny. Children did not learn arithmetic until they were considered proficient at reading and writing—reading being mainly from the Bible and Prayer Book. They were also taught practical skills such as knitting and sewing, and on the site where the house called 'Swallows' now stands was a workshop (which also served as a workhouse) where they learnt spinning and weaving. In 1713 the pupils wove 120 yards of cloth which was dyed green to make their school clothing, so the school became known as 'Green School'. Now the school is housed in a 1960s building in Westbrook Street.

Ardington and Lockinge, at the foot of the Downs, are distinctive villages. They, together with West Ginge and East and West Betterton, were combined to form the Lockinge Estate by

Lord Overstone in the mid nineteenth century, so that when his daughter received it on her marriage to Colonel Loyd-Lindsay (later Lord Wantage), it was the largest estate in Berkshire, comprising over 20,000 acres. In 1860 cottages clustered round the church were demolished to give the manor greater privacy, being replaced by model cottages to the south. These are typical of the ethos of the estate, which was to create a harmonious environment, self-contained as far as possible, for the hard-working labourers. The accommodation in most of the new cottages consisted of a living-room, a kitchen, three bedrooms, a coal-shed, a built-in copper for heating water, an earth closet and a garden—extremely generous compared with the size of many labourers' cottages. They were largely half-timbered with the timbers left brown and the plaster painted yellow. A reporter for the *Daily News* described the venture in 1890:

These villages of Ardington and Lockinge are well worthy of a visit . . . The estate is beautifully timbered; the cottages with their ornamental eaves and pointed gables, their fanciful chimney-stacks and pretty porches overgrown with ivy and roses, their grass slopes and lawns and shrubs and flowerbeds, all present innumerable points of view with which the artist would be enraptured. Every villager has, or may have, his allotment. There is an admirable reading-room and a public house in charge of a salaried manager who has no interest whatever in pushing the sale of drink but who is especially required to provide soup in winter and tea and coffee and other non-intoxicants at all times. There is a first-rate co-operative store, with commodious premises, at which the people can get all the necessaries of life, clothes, grocery, bread, meat and provisions, on profit-sharing terms. The bakery is a beautiful little place, with patent ovens and the newest machinery. In addition to all this, over a hundred villagers are employed in municipal workshops, so to speak —shops fitted with all kinds of the latest machinery and the best appliances—saw-mills, carpenters' shops, blacksmith's shops, painters' shops, wheelwrights' shops—all for the building and repairing and general maintenance of the property on the estate. There are two churches and an excellent school. In short, it is a little self-contained world in which nobody is idle, nobody is in absolute want, in which there is no squalor or hunger. While in the midst of it all is the great house of Lockinge, the beautiful home of Lord and Lady Wantage, always ready to play the part of benevolent friends to all who need their help and who . . . seem sincerely desirous of promoting the happiness and well-being of the people.[4]

Everything was forward-looking, with up-to-date steam-driven machinery and innovative agriculture, including an excellent Shire-horse stud. In the 1920s the farming was re-organized, with less arable and more milk production and pedi-gree breedings of Jerseys and Shorthorns, with increasing num-bers of sheep and poultry. The agricultural depression of the 1930s halted progress and continued the trend of fewer village men employed on the Estate (at one time they had all been). Forestry declined, but a racing stud was started. Shooting was important, and agricultural production continued to alter to suit the commercial market.

Many inhabitants now commute to Harwell, Didcot or Wan-tage, but the estate is far from being in decline. It proves that rural areas can be successful sites for small industries—the old co-operative store houses a flavour-chemist; plastics are made in the old forge; Ardington pottery has taken over the dairy, producing varied stoneware and softly glazed semi-porcelain products, including kitchenware, tableware, vases and com-memorative wares. Rush-bottomed-chair makers occupy the grain-dressing shed, and furniture is made in the water-mill, enabling the Estate to remain vital, adapting to a new age.

Charney Bassett and Goosey are both in the low-lying Vale but are very different in character. Charney Bassett is by the banks of the River Ock, and the water-mill on the river bank is currently being restored by volunteers. It is a nucleated settle-ment with a small church, containing some Norman work in-cluding a carved tympanum illustrating a modified legend of Alexander being carried to Heaven, and a Jacobean bellcote. The cross on the green is now a war memorial. The manor-house has elements of its thirteenth-century predecessor, including the solar wing and early windows. Charney and Goosey both came under the control of Abingdon Abbey, but Goosey is en-tirely different in appearance, dominated by its enormous vil-lage green, with houses scattered loosely around it. It is on low-lying, rather marshy land, and, as an Otmoor, goose raising was a profitable activity. The small village of Baulking too is dwarfed by the size of its village green.

Village life today is changing rapidly. Villages are no longer self-sufficient; many are even losing their post offices and stores and becoming commuter villages. Rising petrol costs are isolat-ing them, and public transport is decreasing, so there is a growing contrast between the remote villages, which are diminishing, and those near towns, acquiring vast acres of housing estates, but as commuter villages in many ways lacking a heart and a centre of community. There is a crying need for more encouragement of rural industries such as those at Ardington to stem rural decline.

Country Houses

Ride a cock horse to Banbury Cross
To see a Fiennes lady on her white horse.

Oxfordshire is rich in fine houses, built by the premier families of the county, which reflect the changes in architectural and garden fashions. Many were built as show-pieces to indicate the wealth and power of their owners.

Broughton Castle, an important medieval house, has its origins in a thirteenth-century moated house, enlarged around 1300 by Sir John de Broughton. It is built in orange-brown ironstone, with a magnificent great hall flanked by the family's private apartments and the kitchen and other offices. The solar wing is little altered. The present dining-room with its sixteenth-century linenfold panelling was the undercroft of the medieval house, retaining a fourteenth-century vaulted ceiling. The family chapel, licensed in 1331, has many original decorated floor-tiles and contemporary armorial glass.

William of Wykeham, Bishop of Winchester and founder of New College, Oxford, purchased the manor, which on his death in 1404 passed to his nephew Sir Thomas Wykeham, who obtained a licence to crenellate the house and probably built the battlemented wall. It passed to the Fiennes family through his granddaughter Margaret who in 1451 married Sir William Fiennes, second Lord Saye and Sele; the same family lives at Broughton today. In the mid sixteenth century the castle was given a fashionably symmetrical north front with oriel window; a decorated ceiling was put in the great hall, and two rooms including a long gallery were built above it. The kitchen, buttery and pantry were moved, and a dining-room was built in the new west range of buildings which consisted of two major rooms lit by mullioned and transomed windows. The sixteenth century

interior decoration is very sophisticated, its style being linked
with that of Fontainebleau, and may have been executed by
the same Italian craftsmen who worked for Henry VIII at
Nonsuch Palace, the only place in England with similar decoration.

Broughton was the home of William Fiennes, nicknamed 'Old
Subtlety', a Puritan who strenuously opposed the Crown, con-
spiring against Charles I before the Civil War. A small room at
the top of the house, known as 'the Council Chamber', which
could only be reached by one staircase, was the scene of countless meetings between Hampden, Pym, Lord Warwick, St John,
Lord Brooke, Sir Henry Vane, William Fiennes himself and his
son Nathaniel. When the Civil War finally broke out, William
Fiennes raised a regiment for the Parliamentarians, but dis-
associated himself from the execution of Charles I, and at the
Restoration he was pardoned and appointed to the Privy
Council. Celia Fiennes, his granddaughter described Broughton about 1694: "Broughton . . . an old house moted round and a
parke and gardens, but are much left to decay and ruine."[1]
Evidently the state of the house had been improved when John
Byng visited it in 1785:

> Broughton Castle, 2 miles from Banbury, is a noble old place, with a
> bridge and gateway of approach, and a moat around it, clean and
> transparent; the two distant gateways with the old wall are gone, but
> much of the turreted wall remains. The bedrooms are clean and
> convenient, with good old chimney pieces, and nice oaken floors; the
> chimney piece in the kings bedchamber, where King Charles lay, in
> several of his marches, is of superb stile. But the ornament of the
> house are the dining and drawing rooms, which are noble apart-
> ments of compleat proportion with lofty chimney pieces. The en-
> trance to the dining room I much admired, and the ceiling of the
> drawing room is one of the most beautiful I ever saw, a model for such
> work.
>
> The whole house is well fire-grated, and looks comfortable; in short
> it is a place worthy of inspection; and we congratulated each other in
> having come to view it.[2]

During the 1760s much of the interior was redecorated in a
Gothic style, possibly by Sanderson Miller. The house was let for
much of the nineteenth century and fell into disrepair—in 1837
many of the contents were sold to pay debts. Towards the end of

the century it was let to Lord Algernon Gordon Lennox, and Edward VII was a frequent visitor. Now the Fiennes family again live in their castle, and they contribute much to the local community.

Broughton church is situated in the castle grounds and dates from about 1300. The fourteenth- and fifteenth-century wall-paintings, depict the Annunciation and life of the Virgin, St Christopher and St George. The family tombs and effigies include that of John de Broughton, builder of the castle, who died in 1315, and a pair of effigies obviously ill-matched during the Victorian restoration. The woman's effigy is that of Elizabeth, wife of Sir Thomas Wykeham; that of the man was originally thought to be her husband, but the armour is later, so he probably represents William Fiennes, second Lord Saye and Sele, who died fighting for Edward IV at the battle of Barnet, in 1471.

Stonor Park, remarkable for its early brickwork, is situated at the foot of the Chiltern Hills, and its deer-park, created in 1395, merges with the beech woods. The architectural history of the house is complex: an arcade of arches survives from the thirteenth-century aisled hall, built by Sir Richard Stonor; a detached chapel was added in the fourteenth century, built partly of local bricks including elaborately moulded ones with designs of hearts and flowers—many made at nearby Nettlebed. The chapel brickwork is varied with horizontal layers of tiles laid between the courses of brick, and plaster simulates quoins and dressings. The chapel was enlarged around 1349, and a timber-framed hall, a solar and service wing were added to the house. This complex structure was rationalized in the sixteenth century to make a more symmetrical E-shaped building, with a brick façade, ornamented with brick, flint and stucco. Leland, wrote in the 1530s: "There is a fayre parke, and a waren of conies, and fayre woods . . . the mansion place standithe clyminge on an hill and hathe two courtes byldyd with tymber, brike and flynte."[3] The Elizabethan gables are now gone, and the house and parklands appear largely eighteenth century in style. Some of the interior of the house has been remodelled in 'Gothick' style.

The Stonor family has lived there since the twelfth century and has a distinguished history—Sir John de Stonore (1280–1354) was Chief Justice of the Common Pleas for twenty-five years, Privy Councillor and Chief Baron of the Exchequer among other posts. Succeeding generations were knights of the shire, sheriffs for Oxfordshire and Berkshire and Members of Parliament. Family fortunes changed abruptly with the Reformation as the Stonors remained the premier Oxfordshire Catholic family, acting as a focus for recusants, suffering heavily for their continued allegiance to Rome—in 1577 Dame Cecily Stonor's annual fine for recusancy was set at the modern equivalent of £50,000, and she was imprisoned several times. Father Edmund Campion set up his printing-press at Stonor in the space behind the chimney in the room in the gable above the main door, where he printed *Decem Rationes*, and the furore caused by this led to his capture in 1581 and execution. As recusants the family were deprived of public office and were compelled to sell many estates to pay fines. They made Stonor a centre for Catholic learning, building up a magnificent library of recusant books, many secretly printed or illegally imported. The Catholic Emancipation Act of 1829 enabled them to resume their role in society, and Thomas Stonor was immediately elected Member of Parliament for Oxford.

Shirburn Castle is another example of early brickwork; in 1377 Warin de Lisle was granted a licence to build a castle. The moated castle has a quadrilateral plan, with four corner towers. An inventory of 1539 lists the rooms as: a wardrobe, great chamber, inner chambers, "Brusshynge howse", hall and chamber, parlour, cellar, buttery, chambers each for the butler, priest, horse-keeper, cook, chamberlains, plus a low parlour, kitchen, larder, boulting-house, fish-house, garner, brew-house and other outhouses.

In 1716 the castle was purchased by Thomas Parker, Earl of Macclesfield, who became Lord Chancellor. He spent about £7,000 altering the house, including remodelling the library. Formal gardens were laid out, and in 1741 a circular temple was built by Westby Gill. It is not accessible to the public.

Fyfield Manor, a stone house dating from around 1320, was built by John de Golafre, with a medieval hall, porch and service-wing, with decorative ballflower mouldings over the doorways, hidden by an Elizabethan front.

Mary Russell Mitford described Greys Court (now a National Trust property) in the mid nineteenth century:

> Framed like a picture by the rarest and stateliest trees . . . stands
> Greys Court . . . erected among the remains of a vast old castellated
> mansion . . . the rich yet wild country in which it is placed . . . the
> park so finely undulated and so profusely covered by magnificent
> timber . . . the huge old towers which seem to guard and sentinel the
> present house: . . . the far extended walls whose foundations may yet
> be traced in dry seasons among the turf of the lawn . . . [4].

The "castellated mansion" (of which the crenellated flint-and-brick Great Tower and three smaller towers survive) was built by the first Lord de Grey, a Knight of the Garter in the mid fourteenth century. The main portion dates from the late sixteenth century, probably built by the Knollys family who acquired the property in 1514. Francis Knollys, who married a granddaughter of Sir Thomas Boleyn, first cousin to Elizabeth I, was Treasurer of Elizabeth's Household from 1572 to 1596, and for a time guarded the captive Mary, Queen of Scots. Materials from the fortified manor were re-used to build the red brick and flint mansion with its mullioned and transomed windows and moulded brick arches. They also built the brick Bachelor's Hall, so called from the seventeenth-century inscription over the door: "*Malius nil coelibe vita*" ("Nothing is better than the celibate life"); the stables, used as a messroom by Cromwellian soldiers; and the early Tudor wheel-house built over the ancient well, 200 feet deep, from which water was raised by a donkey on a treadmill—the largest surviving example of a donkey-wheel.

Francis's son William may have been the inspiration for Shakespeare's 'Malvolio'. He was created Earl of Banbury in 1626 but made a disastrous second marriage to Elizabeth Howard, the nineteen-year-old daughter of the Earl of Suffolk, nearly forty years his junior, who behaved so scandalously that her sons were debarred from succeeding to the earldom. The house passed to the Stapleton family, who built the main wing in about 1750, decorating the drawing-room with a rococo plaster ceiling depicting bows and arrows and lovebirds, possibly commemorating Sir Thomas Stapleton's wedding in 1765.

Some of the trees in the garden are very old, including a tulip-tree and a weeping ash. Japanese cherries grow by the old tithe barn, and in the courtyard are many varieties of roses. The kitchen garden is laid out with an octagonal tank, approached along an avenue of morello cherries, or along a stone path delimited by éspalier apple trees and peonies. A lily-pond graces the Tower garden, and a Chinese Bridge and Moongate lead over the ha-ha. Robert Gittings vividly created a vision of the garden:

> Peace—a country peace
> Here in the garden at Greys . . .
> Walk free in the formal maze
> Box hedge, privet and yew,
> And camomile under the feet,
> All that the gardener grew
> Whose nature is known to be sweet,
> Alleys of blossom and scent,
> The old walls breathing it back
> Render an ancient content.[5]

Greys Court has a link with Minster Lovell, as Alice, grand-daughter of the fifth Baron de Grey married William, Lord Lovell, in 1422. A chest at Greys Court is claimed to be the Mistletoe Bough chest, in which, according to legend, a Lovell bride was suffocated while playing hide-and-seek on her wedding day. However the chest is of a later date than the legend.

Minster Lovell is a picturesque ruin by the River Windrush. The manor-house was built around 1430 by William, seventh Lord Lovell, incorporating a twelfth-century building. The large house was built round three sides of a courtyard. Portions of the chapel remain, with a traceried window and glowering gargoyles, and the entrance passage in the north wing has roses and oak leaves on the vault bosses. Nearby stand a late medieval dovecote, with conical roof, and a barn. After the Battle of Bosworth in 1485 the Crown confiscated the estates of Francis, Lord Lovell, who subsequently fought for Lambert Simnel at the Battle of Stoke 1487, after which he disappeared and was assumed dead. His disappearance was never explained, and legend said that he returned to Minster Lovell, where he was hidden by a faithful retainer. What happened after that is a mystery—perhaps the retainer died or betrayed his master—but Lord Lovell was never seen again. In 1728 some workmen building a chimney discovered a secret chamber containing the skeleton of a man sitting at a table with his dog at his feet—these crumbled to dust on exposure to the air. In 1602 Sir Edward Coke purchased the manor, and his descendant Thomas Coke, Earl of Leicester, dismantled the house in the eighteenth century; the ruins were used as farm buildings until rescued by the Ministry of Works in the 1930s.

The medieval manor-house at Stanton Harcourt was deserted in the late seventeenth century and demolished in about 1750 when the Harcourt family moved to Nuneham. The magnificent fourteenth-century detached kitchen still stands. Dr Plot wrote: "By way of Riddle one may truly call it either a Kitchin within a Chimney, or a Kitchin without one; for below it is nothing but a large square, and Octangular above ascending like a Tower, the Fires being made against the Walls, and the Smoak climbing up them, without any Tunnels or disturbance to the Cooks."[6]

The kitchen is 31 by 33 feet, 64 feet high at the centre, with a fifteenth-century octagonal pyramid roof and windows. There were two fires for spit roasting, and three ovens. Smoke escaped through shutters below the roof, which could be angled according to wind direction.

Alexander Pope, who lived in the adjacent fifteenth-century tower from 1718 to 1719 (named Pope's Tower in his honour) while translating the *Iliad*, compared it with Vulcan's forge or the cave of Polyphemus, and with Moloch's temple: "The horror of it has made such an impression upon the country people, that they believe the witches keep their Sabbath here, and that once a year the Devil treats them with infernal venison, viz. a toasted tiger stuffed with tenpenny nails."[7]

The formal gardens are opened to the public, and the lake, canals and ponds have been painstakingly restored. These gardens abound with stone and lead ornaments, and there are a terrace, rose garden, nut grove and woodland in the area of the medieval fishponds. The Rotunda was erected in 1965 as a tribute to Elizabeth, Viscountess Harcourt, who did much to recreate the garden from the late 1940s until her death.

Culham manor-house contains part of a fifteenth-century building, which belonged to the abbots of Abingdon. It has a timber-framed upper floor above stone, with a kingpost roof, and became a manor-house after the Reformation, with sixteenth century linenfold panelling.

Hanwell Castle was built in 1498 when the manor was granted to William Cope, Henry VII's cofferer. The castle is of brick, the earliest example in north Oxfordshire with stone dressings—a surprising choice in view of the ready availability of stone. It was built around three sides of a court and in 1665

had one more hearth—twenty-seven—than Broughton Castle.
It was never a true castle, having battlements and turrets for
their decorative effect. Much of the house was demolished in the
eighteenth century, but one corner tower with two octagonal
turrets remains, and the north front of the south wing has a
diaper pattern of blue bricks. Anthony Cope lived in great state
at Hanwell, and although he never fulfilled his ambition of
entertaining Queen Elizabeth, James I and Charles I both
visited. In the late seventeenth century the elaborate gardens
contained a 'House of Diversion' on an island in the middle of a
fishpond, which had waterworks with a ball tossed by a column
of water, an artificial shower and a water-clock. The ponds have
now been replaced by a lake.

The dissolution of the monasteries released monastic buildings and estates. One beneficiary was Lord Williams of Thame,
who acquired houses at Thame Park, Rycote and Beckley.
Thame Park incorporates portions of thirteenth- and
fourteenth-century Cistercian abbey buildings and the
sixteenth-century abbot's lodgings. His houses at Beckley and
Rycote were built of purplish-coloured brick with a black diaper
pattern. Rycote Park was a magnificent Tudor house, burnt
down in 1745. It was built in about 1520 for John Heron, Henry
VIII's treasurer, and taken over by Lord Williams in 1542.
Rycote chapel still stands, complete with very fine seventeenth-
century fittings. The house and chapel are said to be haunted by
the ghosts of Sir Thomas More and his youngest daughter,
Robert Dudley, Earl of Leicester, and a monk. Formal gardens
were created in the eighteenth century by 'Capability' Brown
for the Earl of Abingdon.

Cornbury Park was a royal hunting-lodge in Wychwood
Forest, normally granted to the Ranger of the Forest, and tenants included Harcourts, the de la Poles and Robert Dudley, who
died there, allegedly after a death-warning from the ghost of his
wife Amy Robsart. The sixteenth-century house was improved
in 1631 by Nicholas Stone who created a seven-bay wing of
classical design, altered in the later seventeenth century by
Edward Hyde, Earl of Clarendon and Lord Chancellor. Cornbury was a centre of Jacobite intrigue, and it is said that Prince
Charles Edward visited the house secretly in 1750.

Mapledurham is a large mellow red-brick mansion with
towering chimneys, built in about 1588 by Sir Michael Blount,

to replace a fifteenth-century timber-framed house, a fragment
of which still remains. Sir Michal Blount was Lieutenant of the
Tower of London, as his father, Richard, had been, and served as
Sheriff of Buckinghamshire and Oxfordshire. Building Mapledurham House was part of his plan for self-aggrandizement,
necessitating raising a loan of £1,500. The H-plan house has an
attractive red and blue diaper brick pattern. Some of the interior decoration, including elaborate plaster ceilings, is early
seventeenth century, and alterations were made a century
later. Michael's son Charles, a Royalist, was so extravagant
that he had to sell off household goods to pay his debts. The
house was sacked by the Roundheads and the estate sequestered
by Parliament after Charles's unfortunate death during the
Siege of Oxford, when he was killed by one of his own sentries.
Alexander Pope was a frequent visitor in the eighteenth century and a great admirer of Martha and Theresa Blount—he
made no secret of his admiration, writing poems based on the
girls and Mapledurham. The Blounts were Catholics, and in
1789 they built a chapel, with a Strawberry Hill Gothic
interior—apparently making the proviso that the exterior must
appear an extension to the servants' quarters. The house
belongs to the Eyston family, descendants of the Blounts. The
gardens were laid out in about 1740 in the style advocated by
Alexander Pope and William Kent, with a ha-ha dividing the
former deer-park and the gardens, once known as 'The Pleasure
Ground', where stands a late-Georgian Gothick farm-house
built in banded flint and brick, with pointed windows; an arch
leading into the kitchen garden was part of an eighteenth-
century summerhouse.

The main interest of Kelmscott, an unpretentious grey stone
manor-house dating from about 1570, with later additions, is
that William Morris made it his holiday home, and it has now
become a shrine to him and his work. Morris found it quite by
chance in a house agent's list in 1871 and immediately leased
it—his wife Jane and Rossetti went down there for the summer.
His poem about the house was embroidered on bed-hangings for
his four-poster:

> The wind's on the wold
> And the night is a-cold,
> And Thames runs chill

Twixt mead and hill,
But kind and dear
Is the old house here,
And my heart is warm
Midst winter's harm.
Rest then, and rest,
And think of the best
Twixt summer and spring
When all birds sing
In the town of the tree,
As ye lie in me
And scarce dare move
Lest earth and its love
Should fade away
Ere the full of the day . . . [8]

His daughter May Morris purchased the house, and it devolved, via Oxford University, to the Society of Antiquaries, who preserve it much as it was when William Morris lived there, with many of his embroideries, tapestries, carpets and wallpapers, some products of the Kelmscott Press and paintings of the family, including Rossetti's portrait of Jane Morris in her blue silk dress.

Chastleton House was built between 1603 and 1604 by Walter Jones, a wealthy Witney wool merchant and Member of Parliament, who used his wealth to establish himself as a country gentleman, purchasing the estate from Robert Catesby, a Gunpowder Plot conspirator. The house is typical Jacobean design, virtually unchanged, with a front of five tall, narrow gables flanked by staircase towers. An inventory made in 1632 gives a vivid impression of the house: the hall was furnished with a long table, four long forms, six stools and a court cupboard; the little and great parlours had cushions in the deep window-seats; the great chamber had twenty-four pictures, probably those of the Sybils and Prophets there today; the chamber above the little parlour contained three large pieces of Arras tapestry. Leading out of the 'Chamber over the Parlour' is a secret room called 'the closet' where Walter's grandson Arthur hid after the Royalist defeat at the battle of Worcester. The Roundheads thought that the exhausted horse in the stables was that of Charles II and determined to stay overnight in the house to prevent his escape, settling in the room adjacent to the secret chamber. With great presence of mind, his wife offered them wine, copiously laced with opium or laudanum so that they fell into a deep slumber and her husband was able to escape. The top storey consisted of the Gallery, Tower Chamber and three others, and outside were the wool-house (reflecting Walter Jones's occupation as a wool-merchant), meal-house, milk-house, stable and barn. The Great Chamber was richly decorated in Flemish style with panelled walls divided by fluted pilasters, a frieze of caryatids and a carved and painted stone overmantel bearing the arms of Walter Jones and his wife, Eleanor Pope. The tunnel-vaulted 72-foot-long gallery runs the whole length of the top storey, with plasterwork patterned with daisies, roses and *fleurs-de-lis*. Such rooms were invaluable for providing exercise in poor weather. The topiary garden, one of the finest in the county, was set out in about 1700.

Wroxton Abbey, on the site of an Augustinian priory, was built by Sir Thomas Pope, treasurer of Henry VIII's Court of Augmentations and the founder of Trinity College, Oxford. William Pope, later Earl of Downe, did major work on the site in the early seventeenth century. Fragments of the ruins are incorporated into the basement, including a thirteenth-century blocked arch and a fourteenth-century moulded doorway. Celia Fiennes described the house at the end of the seventeenth century:

> There is about 2 mile off the Lord Guilffords house Roxton which is a good house within a parke, you enter a large hall, on the left hand leads to a little parlour down to the kitchins; the halfe pace att the upper end of the hall leads into dineing roome, drawing roome, and a large staire-case with good pictures, there you enter another large dineing roome with great compass windows, fine Pictures of the family; within is a drawing roome and chambers and closets well proportioned, little or no furniture was up, only in the worst roomes, in one closet att each doore was Queen Mary and Queen Elizabeths pictures to the foot in bibb and apron very pretty, in one room was the Lord North and Ladyes picture, which was Lord Chiefe Justice, and their sonnes picture in the middle, all at length; many good pictures in most roomes, there was a part new built all the new fashion way, which was design'd for the present Lord Gilford and Lady, the gardens are very good the out houses and stables handsome.[9]

By then Wroxton had passed to the North family, through the marriage of Francis North to Frances Pope, who used it as their country house. The alterations Celia Fiennes refers to were building a withdrawing-room and changing some windows, which had previously "made the rooms like bird-cages".

Horace Walpole was much impressed by his reception at Wroxton in the mid eighteenth century but less so by the house itself:

> But now I am going to tell you how delightful a day I passed at Wroxton. Lord Guildford [sic] has made George Montagu so absolutely viceroy over it that we saw it more agreeably than you can conceive; roamed over the whole house, found every door open, saw not a creature, had an extreme good dinner, wine, fruit, coffee and tea in the library, were served by fairies, tumbled over the books, said one or two talismanic words, and the cascade played, and went home loaded with pine-apples and flowers ... The house was built by a Lord Downe in the reign of James the First; and though there is a fine hall and a vast dining room above, it is neither good nor agreeable; one end of the front was never finished, and might have a good apartment. The library is added by this Lord, and is a pleasant chamber. Except loads of old portraits, there is no tolerable furniture. A whole-length of the first Earl of Downe is in the Bath robes, and has a coif under the hat and feather. There is a charming picture of Prince Henry about twelve years old, drawing his sword to kill a stag ... There is too a curious portrait of Sir Thomas Pope, the founder of Trinity College, Oxford, said to be by Holbein. The chapel is new, but in a pretty Gothic taste, with a very long window of painted glass, very tolerable. The frieze is pendent, just in the manner I propose for the eating-room at Strawberry Hill. Except one scene, which is indeed noble, I cannot much commend the without-doors. The scene consists of a beautiful lake entirely shut in with wood: the head falls into a fine cascade, and that into a serpentine river, over which is a little Gothic seat like a round temple, lifted up by a shaggy mount. On an eminence in the park is an obelisk erected to the honour and at the expense of "optimus" and "munificentissimus" the late Prince of Wales, "in loci amoenitatem et memoriam adventûs ejus". There are several paltry Chinese buildings and bridges, which have the merit or demerit of being the progenitors of a very numerous race all over the kingdom; at least they were of the very first. In the church is a beautiful tomb of an Earl and Countess of Downe, and the tower is in a good plain Gothic style, and was once, they tell you, still more beautiful, but Mr [Sanderson] Miller, who designed it, unluckily once in his life happened to think rather of beauty than of water-tables, and so it fell down the first winter.[10]

The Prince of Wales's obelisk was erected in appreciation of his hospitality at Wroxton when he attended Banbury races in 1739, as guest of Francis North. North did extensive work at Wroxton, employing Sanderson Miller who designed the grounds to draw one's eye from the house, via water, a fanciful circular temple and polygonal crenellated Gothic dovecote into the countryside beyond. So much money was spent on the house and garden, on remodelling the chapel, inserting a false plaster ceiling with pendant in the great hall and so on, that it put the family in financial difficulties, and his son Frederick, Prime Minister between 1770 and 1782, was given over £16,000 by George III. The house remained the home of the North family until 1932 and in 1963 was bought by Farleigh Dickinson University.

Ashdown House has a romantic fairy-tale origin. It was built in about 1660–65, possibly designed by William Winde, of cream-coloured blocks of 'clunch' or chalk, with grey Bath stone dressings. It looks like a dolls' house because it is tall and square, topped by a cupola surmounted by a golden ball. Its remote situation, originally standing alone in the centre of a large dense wood, approached by four symmetrical avenues, of which only one remains, augments the fairy-tale atmosphere. Its builder, William, Earl of Craven, was the son of a Lord Mayor of London, a self-made Yorkshireman who became wealthy in Elizabethan England. William never married, perhaps because of his hopeless romantic attachment to Elizabeth, 'the Winter Queen', daughter of James I. He spent much of his fortune attempting to keep her husband, the Elector Palatine, on the throne of Bohemia and later supported Charles I during the Civil War. Legend has it that Ashdown was built as a sanctuary for Elizabeth, but she died of the plague in London before it was finished, bequeathing her papers and pictures to her benefactor. When Ashdown was given to the National Trust by Cornelia, Countess of Craven, in 1856, it was empty, but several of the original portraits were repurchased and again grace the walls of Ashdown, including portraits of 'the Winter Queen' herself and William, Lord Craven.

Several generations enjoyed the hunting and riding at Ashdown, making few alterations to the house. Elizabeth, wife of the sixth Baron, deserted her husband and six children in 1780 to live with the Margrave of Brandenburg, Anspach and Bayreuth, whom she later married, and both lived at Ashdown, where she wrote plays such as *Le Philosophe Moderne* and *The Robbers* and the opera *The Princess of Georgia*.

Milton Manor near Abingdon was built in about 1663, possibly designed by Inigo Jones. It is red brick, identical front and back, its five bays divided by enormous Ionic pilasters with festooned stone capitals and *fleur-de-lis* decoration opposite the first-floor windows. The simple classical lines have been lost with the addition of two eighteenth-century semi-octagonal wings. It was built by Paul Calton, great-grandson of the London goldsmith who had purchased the manor after the Reformation, before which it had belonged to Abingdon Abbey. On his marriage to a wealthy heiress, he used his new wealth to build a mansion worthy of his position. William of Orange stayed there, quartering his troops at Abingdon, while on the march to London to usurp the throne of James II. Admiral Benbow, father-in-law of Paul Calton III, lived in the Dower House, and Peter the Great of Russia stayed with him after receiving an honorary degree at Oxford. Milton Manor was purchased from the Caltons in 1764 by Bryant Barrett, a wealthy 'lace-man', who numbered the Prince of Wales among his clients. Barrett was a strong supporter of Bonnie Prince Charlie and was converted to Catholicism by Richard Challoner, Bishop of London, whose robes are housed in Milton chapel. Barrett added the Georgian wings, which used 700,000 bricks and included a large kitchen and domestic offices. He purchased fourteenth-century stained-glass windows from Steventon church for the chapel, which, like the library, is decorated in Strawberry Hill Gothick style. The house is the family home of the Mockler family, Mrs Marjorie Mockler being a descendant of Bryant Barrett.

Fine seventeenth-century houses include Shipton Court, Shipton-under-Wychwood, built in about 1603 by the Lacey family, one of the largest Jacobean houses in the county, but with the interior gutted by twentieth-century alterations; the remains of the Gilbertine priory at Clattercote were incorporated into a large house, again largely destroyed or altered; Cote House was rebuilt in the early seventeenth century by Thomas Horde, later surrounded by eighteenth-century stone walls and cobbled paths; Baldon House has an irregular early-seventeenth century façade, with an eighteenth-century back and wing with bell turret. The stone tower incorporates details from Nuneham church, demolished in the eighteenth century, and the folly in the grounds has a thirteenth-century window from the church incorporated during eighteenth-century landscaping. Nether Worton House is stone-built with an embattled parapet and stepped gables, dated 1653, and remodelled in about 1920. North Aston Hall is an enormous seventeenth-century ten-bay building with mullioned windows, refronted in about 1850. Radcot House and Finstock Manor are probably both c.1660 with unusual oval attic windows. Castle House, Deddington, is largely seventeenth century, incorporating medieval work. Prescote Manor, Cropredy, built in about 1691, is now largely Victorian in appearance, and the outbuildings house a craft centre, Prescote Gallery.

Shotover Park was mainly rebuilt in the early-eighteenth century, a tall, narrow house of Haseley stone with rusticated pilasters and a slate roof. The surviving formal gardens date partially from 1718, with additional work by William Kent. The original formal layout had long avenues and cross walks, with a canal and temple, one of the earliest Gothic garden buildings. William Kent designed a domed octagonal temple and an obelisk, linked by serpentine walks. The pond, like that of Rousham, is octagonal. This garden, like Blenheim's, illustrates the change from a formal geometric style to the desire for perambulations.

Rousham House was built in about 1635 by Sir Robert Dormer on an H-plan, with mullion windows. He lived there during the Civil War, and the door has holes through which muskets could be trained at marauding Parliamentarians. The house was remodelled in Gothic style in 1738–40 by William Kent, with a battlemented parapet, an ogee cupola, lead statues of classical figures and octagonal windowpanes. Kent designed the interior decoration and added the library, which was remodelled in rococo style in 1764. He excelled in the Painted Parlour, which is grand but in scale. Kent himself painted the ceiling and designed furniture and carved wall-brackets which display the collection of Italian bronzes. The gardens gave him immortality and are the best-preserved of his creations. He visualized a romantic naturalistic effect, in the Italian manner, with a series of idyllic scenes, intended to be seen in a particular sequence, linking woodland with the natural barrier of the

River Cherwell and the house on a terrace above it. The formal garden north of the house was replaced by a bowling-green and lawn with gravel walks; the slope to the river was smoothed—a mammoth task involving seventy or so labourers. From the house one proceeds via the bowling-green to the Vale of Venus, with pools linked by cascades and fringed with trees augmented by statues. The woodland path leads to a serpentine rill which runs into the octagonal Cold Bath. The Doric temple nearby is called 'Townsend's Building' after its architect. The path that leads to a statue of Apollo with its view of the medieval Heyford Bridge, the 'Temple of the Mill' (a ruin created from a mill) and the 'Eyecatcher', a 'ruined' arch positioned on the skyline to encourage the visitor to look beyond the estate to the landscape outside. The lime walk leads back towards the Praeneste, with its terrace and arcade, with Kent's specially designed garden seats. Nearby, overlooking the river, is a 'natural theatre', which once housed a 40-foot fountain. Below the north lawn stands the Pyramid building and the old walled garden. Even the barn was designed in Gothic style. Horace Walpole was delighted by the effect:

> But the greatest pleasure we had was in seeing Sir Charles Cotteril's at Rousham; it has reinstated Kent with me: he has nowhere shown as much taste. The house is old and was bad. He has improved it, stuck as close as *he* could to Gothic, has made a delightful library, and the whole is comfortable—the garden is Daphne in little; the sweetest little groves, streams, glades, porticos, cascades and river imaginable; all the scenes are perfectly classic.[11]

Blenheim was designed by Vanbrugh as a symbolic tribute to a great man, John Churchill, Duke of Marlborough, given by the nation and Queen Anne after his magnificent victory at the Battle of Blenheim in 1704, during the War of the Spanish Succession. Vanbrugh was assisted in his monumental task by Nicholas Hawksmoor, a more experienced architect. The project was fraught with difficulties; although a model had been made of the proposed palace, and estimates prepared, they proved woefully inadequate—by 1712, £220,000 had been spent, greatly exceeding the original estimate of £100,000, and a further sum of £45,000 was still owing to the masons, and moneys after this had to be supplied reluctantly, by the Marlboroughs themselves. Sarah, Duchess of Marlborough, had never wanted Vanbrugh as an architect and railed perpetually against his extravagance, eventually dismissing him, so vengefully that, when he brought friends to see his work, she refused him entry. Building such a palace was an achievement—over fifteen hundred workmen were on site at one stage; the building is 850 feet long, and it and its courts cover 7 acres.

Vanbrugh's design was influenced by Palladio and by the Palace of Versailles. The view from the Grand Bridge is dramatic—the Corinthian pillared entrance, with flanking wings, the four square towers, which look oddly unfinished, the myriad sculptures, all in glowing stone, largely from quarries at Taynton, Cornbury and Burford. From the house the view leads to the column of Victory surmounted by the statue of John Churchill. Inside, the palace is remote, with great state rooms such as the classical great hall, in which people are dwarfed by the enormous scale of the Corinthian columns; the library, originally designed as a picture gallery, runs the whole length of the west front. The saloon is dominated by the immense dining-table, with murals painted by Louis Laguerre showing people looking in from behind painted pillars. The state rooms are resplendent with gold, the walls covered with tapestries illustrating Marlborough's campaigns and family portraits. His tomb in the chapel, designed by Rysbrack, is particularly magnificent. Winston Churchill, perhaps the most famous of John Churchill's descendants, is not neglected—the room in which he was born is shown, together with relics such as locks of hair and an exhibition devoted to him. He is buried simply in the churchyard at Bladon. Seeing the style and size of the rooms, one can sympathize with Sarah Churchill's wish for a "clean sweet house and gardens be it ever so small" and understand Alexander Pope's comment:

> See, sir, here's the grand approach;
> This way for his Grace's coach.
> There lies the bridge, and here's the clock,
> Observe the lion and the cock,
> The spacious court, the colonnade,
> And mark how wide the hall is made!
> The chimneys are so well design'd
> They never smoke in any wind.
> This gallery's contrived for walking,
> The windows to retire and talk in;

The council chamber for debate,
And all the rest are rooms of state.
Thanks sir, cried I, 'tis very fine,
But where d'ye sleep, or where d'ye dine?
I find, by all you have been telling
That 'tis a house, but not a dwelling.[12]

Perhaps Sarah took a little more pleasure in the grounds, as she wrote in 1725:

I have had a letter lately from a very good judge who says he has been at Blenheim and that the Lake, Cascade, Slopes above the Bridge are all finish'd and as beautiful as can bee imagin'd, the Banks being covered with a most delightful Verdure: The canals are allso finish'd the whole length of the Meadow under the Wood, and there are a hundred Men at work sloping the Hill near Rosamond's Well; and when all the Banks are don in the same manner and the whole Design compleat'd it will certainly bee a wonderfull fine Palace and I believe will be liked by every Body and I am glad it will bee so because it was the dear Duke of Marlborough's Passion to have it don.[13]

Vanbrugh and Henry Wise devised gardens to enhance the palace, with its military flavour:

The Gardens consist of 77 acres encompassed by a stone wall and laid out in the form of a Hexagon, having a round Bastion at each angle of 200 feet diameter. There is in this Garden a Wilderness of a vast extent with vistas cut through it. The Grand Gravel Walk which runs from the house southward is 2,200 feet long and there is another which crosses it in the middle 1850 feet in length. Noble Terraces (from whence we have an extensive view of the country) run from Bastion to Bastion, which in a fortified town would have been denominated the Curtains. There are also beautiful green walks planted with evergreens—summer houses, Alcoves, Fountains and everything that can render the place agreeable abound.[14].

Vanbrugh desired to make a feature of Woodstock Manor ruins, but Sarah insisted on their demolition, and some of the stone was used as rubble for the bridge, which contains many rooms and should have been surmounted by towers and arcading, which Sarah vetoed because of the extravagance. In the 1720s a formal canal system was laid underneath the bridge, then, as garden fashions changed, George, fourth Duke of Marlborough, in 1764–74 employed Lancelot 'Capability' Brown, who changed the symmetry and formality of the original garden, with its great parterre, topiary and lime walks, to show his worship of Nature, with her curved lines, grassing over the Great Court, ripping out the bastioned walls, damming the river to form two lakes and a grand cascade. He replanted his newly created rolling landscape with clumps of beeches, chestnuts, sycamores and limes by the lake, and Gothicized buildings, such as High Lodge and Park Farm. A temple dedicated to Diana was built facing the lake, and it was here that Winston Churchill proposed to his future wife, Clementine Hozier, in 1908. The ninth Duke restored some of Vanbrugh's formal gardens, replanting the great northern avenue in its 'battle order' and having a parterre designed in 1908 by Achille Duchêne to reconstruct Sarah Churchill's flower-garden and a water-garden.

Heythrop House was begun in about 1706, designed by Thomas Archer, a pupil of Vanbrugh, for Charles Talbot, twelfth Earl and first Duke of Shrewsbury, who had lived for some time in Italy. The exterior resembles an Italian Baroque palace, with a vivid sculptural effect achieved by pilasters and columns. A fire gutted the interior in 1831, destroying sumptuous decorations, which have been replaced by more classical ones, designed by Alfred Waterhouse for Albert Brassey, son of a railway magnate. Further alterations were made in 1923 when it was a Jesuit college, and more recently by National Westminster Bank architects. The clerestory windows have stained glass by Morris & Company depicting Faith, Hope and Charity.

Ditchley Park was designed in about 1720 by James Gibbs, with interior decoration by William Kent and Italian stuccoists. Sir Henry Lee purchased a house and land there in 1583. The family were favourites of Elizabeth I and the Stuarts and built up a magnificent collection of paintings, including one of Elizabeth herself standing on a map of Oxfordshire. Elizabeth and James I both hunted from there. Sir Edward Henry Lee, Earl of Litchfield, in 1677 married Charlotte Fitzroy, daughter of Charles II and Barbara Villiers, who bore him eighteen children. Their epitaph in Spelsbury church reads: "Though they were both framed for the honours and graces of the Court, they chose very young to retire from the splendour of it, and disengaged from pomp and magnificence to obtain more leisure for charity and religion." Their sixth son, George Henry, demolished the old house to build a new one. He was Member of Parliament for the county, Chancellor of Oxford University and first President of the Board of Governors of the Radcliffe Infirmary, Oxford. The third Earl, George Henry Lee, Privy Councillor and Member of Parliament, great-grandson of Charles I, married Diana Frankland, a great-granddaughter of Oliver Cromwell! As they had no children, the estate passed to his sister Charlotte, wife of Henry, eleventh Viscount Dillon. In 1933 Mr Ronald Tree purchased the house. It is now the headquarters of the Ditchley Foundation to promote joint study of matters of common interest to the British and American peoples.

Ditchley, designed by Gibbs, has an eleven-bay centre connected by curved corridors to pavilions surmounted by cupolas with lead statues of Loyalty and Fame decorating the roof. The east wing was for services—kitchens, laundry, dairy, brewhouse and bake-house, while the west wing had stables, servants' accommodation and the chapel. William Kent painted mythological scenes in the Hall, designing the décor and the furniture. The interior retains much of its eighteenth-century decoration and was obviously considered good by Horace Walpole who visited in 1760: "We went to Ditchley, which is a good house, well furnished, has good portraits, a wretched salon, and one handsome scene behind the house. There are portraits of the Litchfield-Hunt, in *true-blue* frocks, with ermine capes . . . " ("true blue" indicating Jacobite tendencies). He added in his journals: ". . . very good house except Salon, which too small, bad carved figures, painted olive; chimney and buffet, each in a corner. Fine hall, bas reliefs in marble, ornaments by Kent, cieling [sic] and side pieces by him, not so bad as is his common".[15]

'Capability' Brown landscaped the grounds in the 1770s, creating a lake close to the house, and his son-in-law Henry Holland may have designed the Rotunda. Ronald Tree moved the little temple in the 1920s and added a terrace and Italian garden, with lions and statuary.

Kirtlington Park was built for Sir James Dashwood, in 1742–6, designed by William Smith and John Sanderson, who took many ideas from designs submitted by James Gibbs, such as the

Palladian centre and wings, with its first-floor entrance approached by a double staircase. The ambitious interior decorations are incomplete, due to lack of money. The Monkey Room was painted in 1745 by J. F. Clermont, a rare example showing the four seasons with monkeys as huntsmen in a landscape background. The park was landscaped by Brown, who circled the house with a ha-ha and created a sweeping lawn.

Brown's work at Nuneham Courtenay was on a far grander scale. Sir Simon Harcourt, Solicitor General and Lord Chancellor, purchased Newnham from Sir John Robinson in 1712 for £17,000. The Harcourt family already owned Stanton Harcourt and Cokethorpe Park, which Sir Simon had built in 1709. Newnham, however, offered the chance of a fashionable house and a grand landscape. Sir Simon's grandson, the first Earl Harcourt, took full advantage of this opportunity—he had a classical education, including a 'Grand Tour', and in 1734 became a founder member of the Dilettante Society to promote interest in antiquity. He was a very correct, courteous man and became Lord of the Bedchamber to the Prince of Wales and proxy for George III in making arrangements to marry Princess Charlotte of Mecklenburg, later serving as Ambassador to Paris and Lord Lieutenant of Ireland. He intended to retire to Nuneham to indulge his cultural and sporting interests but died shortly after his retirement, being found standing on his head in a well after an unsuccessful attempt to rescue a dog.

Lord Harcourt was much influenced by the Italian idea of a villa in its own landscape, and at Nuneham he had an excellent view without the necessity of moving mountains of earth. His villa was designed as a small country house. Lady Harcourt wrote to her son about the

> design we have of building a villa at Nuneham, and not a seat, as was talk'd of; for besides the immense sum such a thing would cost, there is absolutely not a spot upon the whole estate, as my Ld, Mr Fanquier and several others think, so proper for a house, as near the clump of elms, which you are sensible cannot contain a large building. However, I think the situation will make amends for the smallness of the building.[16]

The ground floor provided offices with state apartments above, entered by a large staircase to take advantage of the delightful view over the River Thames. The architect was Stiff Leadbetter,

Charney Bassett water-mill.

The ruins of Minster Lovell Hall.

Stonor Park.

Rousham House.

William Kent's garden at
Rousham.

Church in the grounds of
Nuneham Courtenay.

White Lion Yard, Banbury, designed by Michael Gotch Associates.

Bun-throwing from Abingdon Country Hall.

Banbury Cross.

The bridge across the River Thames at Henley.

The statue of King Alfred in Wantage market-place.

The site of William Morris's garage in Longwall Street, Oxford.

The Botanical Gardens, Oxford.

Iffley church.   Blenheim Palace.

whose design was plain, with its seven-bay pedimented front
with double staircase flanked by two wings. Stone was brought
by barge from the ruins at Stanton Harcourt. The interior decoration was by 'Athenian' Stuart, who with the Earl designed a
Greek temple for a classical garden vista with a copper dome,
a pedimented Ionic portico, an apsidal east end with three
transepts—sanctioned by the Archbishop as the parish church
but more a classical monument. It is half hidden by trees to
provide a 'surprise vista'. The garden was designed to the classical formula of clearings and aligned vistas.

The second Earl Harcourt was a very different character: as a
young man he had a great antipathy to wealth and position: "I
think I could not wish my great enemy worse, than that he
might possess a title, a large acquaintance and a place in the
country celebrated for its beauty, that in other words he might
be flattered and cheated and be at the mercy of every fool and
idler."[17] He admired Rousseau, entertaining him at Nuneham
during his exile. So strong were his republican views that on his
father's death he removed the coronets from the carriages, dis-
posed of royal portraits and placed a statue of Rousseau in the
garden. These extreme views mellowed—Lady Harcourt enjoyed Court life and became Woman of the Bedchamber in 1784,
and he accepted the position of Master of the Horse in 1790. He
had copies made of the royal portraits he had discarded, and
entertained the royal family at Nuneham. The Earl retained
some of his early beliefs, including a love of nature, gardening,
landscape-painting and paternalism. He desired a very different house from his father's; although scruples about spending
money during the American War of Independence caused him to
cancel his contract with Carr of York, he retained 'Capability'
Brown to redesign his landscape, and he subsequently assisted
with the house, which was turned upside down—the ground
floor was brought into family use, with offices extending beyond
the south wing, leaving behind a rabbit warren of confusing
rooms and passages in which unwary visitors such as Fanny
Burney became hopelessly lost, leading to her cross comment
that it was "straggling, half-new, half-old, half-comfortable,
half-forlorn, begun in one generation and finished in another".[18]
Archbishop Harcourt built a new wing with state rooms and
extended the entrance hall in 1832.

The second Earl Harcourt was a keen gardener, and even

before his father's death he persuaded his friend the Reverend
William Mason to design a flower-garden for him. This venture
led to an amusing poem by Mr Whitehead:

> We laundry maids at Nuneham
> Are the happiest maids in the nation
> With a rub, rub, rub and a frothing tub,
> And a charming situation.
>
> No more shall our caps and aprons
> Be torn by gooseberry bushes
> Or our ruffles be rent by the thistle and bent,
> Or our sheets be soil'd with rushes.
>
> Our lines shall grace laburnams,
> Since such our master's will is,
> And our smaller things shall dangle on strings
> From tuberose tops and lilies.
>
> No more in our chests of linen
> Shall lavender reign despotic.
> We'll cull our flowers from yonder bowers
> And our smocks shall smell exotic.[19]

His father disapproved of such romanticism and built the
laundry next to the garden. 'Capability' Brown tidied up the
deer-park, adding clumps of trees and creating a vista towards
the Carfax conduit. Further romanticism was added by the wild
flowers whose seeds Rousseau is said to have planted by the
bower, with its wallpaper of roses, and the now ruined grotto.
Lady Harcourt wrote poems, which were hung around the busts
by the Temple of Flora. In the 1830s a pinetum was laid out by
William Sawrey Gilpin which is now part of the Oxford Botanical Gardens.

However, to create this idyllic scene an entire village of fifty
or so families had to be moved and their cottages demolished.
The new village straddles the Oxford-Henley road—neat
chequer-pattern semi-detached brick cottages, with an inn,
curate's house and forge (now a garage). The villagers accepted
their fate and moved to their new home without a demur, except
for Babs Wyatt, an old lady who begged to be allowed to stay in
the cottage where her husband had died: her request was con-

ceded, and her cottage was not pulled down until after her death.

Glympton Park was built in the mid eighteenth century by Sir Thomas Wheate, who may have financed it with money he made from supplying stone for the building of Blenheim Palace. Brown probably dammed the River Glyme to form its serpentine lake.

Pusey House, built in 1748, was the birthplace in 1800 of Edward Bouverie Pusey, a leader of the Oxford Movement. A circular temple stands in the grounds, erected to the memory of Elizabeth Pusey, wife of William Brotherton. The gardens have recently been restored by Michael Hornby and G. Jellicoe to include a water-garden, a lake with a Chinese bridge and water-lilies, and a walled garden resplendent with roses and clematis.

Hinton Manor has early seventeenth-century details, but the main part of the house is eighteenth century, with a seventeenth-century box garden and fountain. Buckland House was built in 1757 for Sir Robert Throckmorton, a prime example of its period and size, and in the grounds are a thatched ice-house resembling a grotto, with a rustic boat-house by the lake, a derelict apsidal building and a rotunda. In contrast to the stone of Buckland, Watlington Park in south Oxfordshire is of brick, built by John Tilson in about 1755 after he purchased the park from the Stonor Estate.

Chiselhampton House also uses locally made red brick with stone quoins, featuring Ionic pillars and the Peers' arms in a cartouche. It was built in about 1766–8 by Samuel Dowbiggin, a London builder, for Charles Peers, son of a Lord Mayor of London, Sir Charles Peers, who had been British Consul in Spain and had refused the baronetcy offered for his role in suppressing Jacobite riots. The house resembles a London building transported to the countryside, together with its contemporary church. He had plans for laying out the park with a fashionable lake and serpentine walks, but these were never realized. An orangery was built in about 1790—a magnificent five-sided glass affair with an umbrella-shaped roof.

A new house was built by the Fermor family of Tusmore in about 1770, from local stone and bricks. The gardens were landscaped complete with lake and a temple of peace dedicated to the ubiquitous Alexander Pope—Arabella Fermor was the heroine of Pope's poem 'The Rape of the Lock'. The Fermors were a Catholic family, and there is a tradition that Mrs Fitzherbert secretly married the Prince of Wales at Tusmore. This gem of a house was demolished in 1960, and a neo-Georgian house replaces it.

Buscot was purchased from the Stonor family by Walter Loveden in 1557. His great-nephew Edward Loveden Townsend, noted for his farming improvements, inherited the estate in 1757 and built Buscot Park, a nine-bay mansion, set in a landscape with a lake. The house was altered in the mid-nineteenth century when the enterprising Australian Robert Tertius Campbell purchased the estate, making it a highly industrialized complex, much in advance of its time, with a new irrigation system, a distillery and a narrow-gauge railway to collect sugar-beet for processing, a gas-works, a telegraph system and an artificial-fertilizer plant. His new farm buildings were concrete, steam-power replaced animals, and his sugar-beet pulp was used for feeding his stock. Unfortunately not all his projects proved successful; the distillery was closed after ten years, and the estate became heavily mortgaged. Buscot retained its reputation as an innovative farm when taken over by Alexander Henderson in 1889, as he concentrated on improving the quality of his stock, specializing in Shire horses. In recognition of his work as a Unionist member of Parliament, President of the Shire Horse Society and art connoisseur, he was made Baron Faringdon of Buscot in 1916. The third Lord Faringdon lives at Buscot although he has transferred the house and its contents to the National Trust. Henderson purchased Burne Jones's Briar Rose series of paintings which grace the saloon. The house is superbly furnished and decorated, forming a graceful setting for the Faringdon collection of paintings, which includes masterpieces by such notable artists as Rembrandt, Rubens, Sir Joshua Reynolds, Thomas Gainsborough, Landseer, Millais, Dante Gabriel Rossetti and Angelica Kauffman. Harold Peto remodelled the garden in the early 1960s linking the great lake and the house with a water-garden, Italianate in character with paths, stairways, basins and canals, box hedges, architectural features, statuary and cascades.

Barton Abbey, Steeple Barton, although its core was built by Sir John Dormer in the sixteenth century after the dissolution of the monastries, is now largely Victorian in appearance and has one of the last parks created in England, with a boating-lake and views through landscaped trees.

Kiddington Hall was so drastically remodelled in about 1850 that no visible traces of the seventeenth-century house can be seen. The present house is Italian in style, complete with terraces and formal gardens. The glazed orangery, with its flower-decorated arcade, is now a loggia.

Stratton Audley House was built for the wealthy banking family of Glen, to the designs of Robert Smith, who devised a Gothic-style house of blue limestone with an ornamental tower. The park was laid out with pleasure-grounds.

Perhaps the most fascinating and bizarre nineteenth-century house is Friar Park, Henley, built as a folly in 1896 by Sir Frank Crisp, a wealthy solicitor. The red brick is highlighted with yellow stone dressings and decorated in French Flamboyant Gothic, replete with towers and pinnacles. The grounds lived up to the eccentricity of the house, with mountain peaks and passes decorated with China chamois deer, a maze, caves and underground lakes, lit by electricity which showed the gruesome decorations of spiders, monsters and artificial grapes. More down to earth features were an alpine garden, Japanese topiary and herbaceous plants and glasshouses.

Middleton Park was built in 1938, designed by Sir Edwin and Robert Lutyens for the ninth Earl of Jersey, in neo-Georgian style replacing a Georgian house.

8

Towns

The pattern of towns in Oxfordshire, and their relationship to the communities around them, is constantly shifting and changing. Their layout, particularly that of market-places, is revealing. Domesday Book records markets at Oxford, Wallingford, Abingdon and Bampton, which was then a wealthy town. Market towns were a good commercial proposition, a fact of which lords of the manor and ecclesiastical landlords were not slow to take advantage. Banbury and Thame were created by the bishop of Lincoln, and Eynsham and Abingdon Abbeys exercised strong control over their respective towns. In some cases the market predated the market charter, which merely condoned an existing situation. Bampton's market function was its main urban feature—this is reflected in its unsophisticated plan with streets focusing on the market-place. Thame's main street was widened to a cigar shape to make room for the market-place. The wide open spaces created for markets were frequently encroached, as at Thame, Wantage, Banbury and Woodstock, where large portions have now disappeared under buildings. Charlbury's market took place in Church Street, which was deliberately built wide for this purpose. Banbury's rectangular market-place was situated outside the castle gate, typifying the town plan of a defended *burh*. Wallingford was built as a defensive walled Saxon *burh*, and the later market-place intrudes on the early grid pattern.

Some markets failed, perhaps because of inadequate communications or proximity to larger markets—Stratton Audley and Middleton Stoney suffered from being too near Bicester. Bignell, near Great Chesterton, is no longer even a village, although in 1377 it had a market and fair.

The medieval topography is still discernible in many cases. Wallingford's grid pattern reflects that of the ninth-century

burh, burned by the Danes in 1006 but recovered sufficiently by
Domesday to have a market, mint and guild merchant. Eynsham's plan reveals the stages of its growth; Acre End was
probably the original focus, superseded by the market square
set up in the twelfth century outside the abbey gates, after
which the burgage tenements west of Mill Street were developed; then in 1215 Newland was created to the north.

Earlier settlements were altered to suit their new functions
as towns—at Witney a new bridge was built across the Windrush, and the town realigned on a north-south axis, with a
wedge-shaped market-place north of the church, which was,
significantly, enlarged as Witney acquired urban status. Newland was laid out in 1212 by Robert Arsic, but it never acquired
urban characteristics.

The plan of Thame illustrates the burgage tenements so important in medieval town layouts. They consist of long strips of
land laid out by the owner of the town to raise rent, set at right
angles to the street with a house or shop along the frontage. At
Thame the frontages are about 60 feet wide and 600–700 feet
long, their gentle curve revealing that they were cut out of open
fields. Most towns still have traces of burgage plots—in Chipping Norton they are east of the market-place, in Woodstock
clustered around the triangular market-place.

The relative size and importance of towns has changed—
Deddington is now little more than a large village, although its
large market-place and castle site reveal its past; Chipping
Norton rose from ninth to third in the league of Oxfordshire
towns in the nineteenth century (excluding the Vale) and has
since declined. Changes in communications have affected towns
—Burford was bypassed by the realignment of the Oxford-to-
Gloucester road in the nineteenth century and consequently
stagnated, and most flourishing towns ensured their place on
the network of railways, sometimes, as in the case of Chipping
Norton, fighting long and hard for the privilege.

Towns are economically dependent on their hinterland, and it
is interesting to note that many are situated at the junction of
two geological zones and so served areas of contrasting
economies—Chipping Norton and Banbury straddling the lias
and oolite, Bicester and Witney the clay and cornbrash, while
Wantage and Watlington share chalk and clay. The market
function of towns was valuable, and charters usually grant

rights to markets and fairs. One of the most important annual fairs in most towns was the Statute or Hiring Fair, held around Michaelmas, to which many of the agricultural labourers and maidservants from the surrounding areas would come to find new jobs for the coming year, as many were employed on a yearly basis. The presence of so many young people encouraged the growth of the pleasure aspect of the fair, and the commercial aspect, as the labourers had just received their harvest money and were in a position to pay their bills, so many products were on sale that could not be obtained locally at other times of the year. Many towns had more than one fair, and both Bampton and Banbury had specialized horse-fairs. Buyers came to Bampton from South Wales, London and Liverpool, and the town seethed with activity for several days, as horses arrived by rail and road. The fair itself lasted for three days, the first day being the 'Show Day' when the best-quality horses were auctioned; the second was 'Big Fair Day', when buyers and sellers haggled over the remaining horses, and the third day was designated the 'Pleasure Day' after the serious business had been completed.

Banbury is now the second largest town in Oxfordshire. The area within a 10-mile radius of the town is nicknamed 'Banburyshire', as its people look towards Banbury as their local centre, even though they may live in Warwickshire or Northamptonshire. It is situated at the crossing-point of the roads from Oxford to Coventry, and across the Cotswolds to Northampton, at a ford over the River Cherwell, amidst some of the richest and most fertile land in Oxfordshire. The settlement around the church was the Saxon administrative centre for the bishop of Dorchester's estates in the area.

It was founded as a town by Alexander, Bishop of Lincoln, who built the castle, almost certainly built the church and laid out the market-place and burgage plots. The castle, situated to the north side of the market-place, dominated the town for over five hundred years, acting as the local administrative centre for the bishopric, as a 'hotel' for visiting monarchs and as a "terrible prison for convict men". Within the castle moat in the early seventeenth century were a twenty-three bay lead-roofed mansion house and a six-bay slate-roofed gatehouse, in addition to fish-ponds, an orchard and two water-mills. The castle was twice besieged during the Civil War, when it was owned by the

Parliamentarian Fiennes family but held by the Compton family for the Royalists.

The impact of the Civil War and a severe fire in 1628 combined to make the inhabitants of the town petition Parliament for permission to demolish the castle, so that they could use the castle stone to rebuild their houses. They were so thorough in their destruction that not a trace of the castle remains above ground.

Banbury people have acquired a reputation for demolition. Their Norman church was the largest in the county, nicknamed 'the cathedral of north Oxfordshire', being over 200 feet long, with additions and improvements made up to the fifteenth century when the tower and chancel were built. However, it was neglected and fell into decay, so it was decided to pull it down in 1790. The church actually began collapsing on the day before demolition commenced, but parts of the building were so stubborn that ten horses were unable to pull it down, and gunpowder had to be used. The new church was designed by Samuel Pepys Cockerell, but the town ran out of money, and the tower was not built until 1820. It is built of orange-brown local ironstone, which has weathered badly; the main rectangular shape has a semi-circular Tuscan portico, with a copper-covered half-dome topped by a cylindrical tower surmounted by a cupola.

Banbury is famous for its cross, as depicted in the nursery rhyme. There were once three crosses: the Market Cross, stepped, with a pillar and statues, situated in Cornmarket, near the entrance to the new shopping centre; the Bread Cross, stone-built with a slate roof large enough to protect the market stall-holders from the elements, stood in the Butchers' Shambles off the High Street; and the White Cross, a boundary-mark in West Bar. Banbury was notoriously Puritan, and one William Knight was horrified at the veneration given to the cross, so one day in 1600 he set about demolishing it. He and his accomplices were brought before Star Chamber and ordered to rebuild the cross but this was not done until 1858 when the people of Banbury erected the present cross in Horsefair to celebrate the marriage of the Princess Royal to the Prince of Prussia.

Banbury was the most industrialized town in Oxfordshire in the nineteenth century, with Grimsbury built up as an artisan area, partly for workers from Samuelson's Agricultural Engineering Works. The nineteenth century saw great changes—

its population exceeded that of Abingdon by 1821, and it grew more rapidly than all the other towns, being nine times the size of the smallest by 1900. Sir Bernhard Samuelson's Mechanics' Institute in Marlborough Road is now the library. The museum is now in the Horsefair, telling the story of Banbury and the Cherwell valley, illustrating the development of Banbury's textile and agricultural-engineering industries, as well as delving into the mysteries of Banbury cakes and ale, and Flora Thompson's way of life in the countryside.

The town has continued to expand, attracting new industries and becoming a London overspill town. The new shopping centre behind the market-place opened in 1976, and more shopping-areas are planned. The Spiceball Leisure Centre near the canal has been opened recently, and plans are afoot to turn Church House into a theatre. Banbury has not lost its original role as a market-town, having the largest cattle-market in Europe, and its twice weekly market-days bring many people into town from the surrounding villages. The medieval town plan remains largely unchanged—the street names Horsefair, Butchers' Shambles, Market-Place, revealing their former uses, but the increasing complexity of the circulation routes warrants the latest version of the Banbury Cross rhyme, heard on BBC Radio 4:

> Ride a cock horse to Banbury Cross,
> To see a fine lady on a white horse,
> With rings on her fingers and bells on her feet,
> Who can't find her way in a one-way street.

Deddington was twice as rich as Banbury at Domesday, although it is now little more than a large village, with its large market-place and town hall revealing its former role. It was soon outstripped in size by Banbury, which by 1225 had 247 burgage tenements to Deddington's maximum of thirty or forty, and by Adderbury and Bloxham. The most famous fair was the Pudding Pie Fair, held in November at Martinmas, where leggings and winter clothes were sold, together with Welsh sheep and ponies, Irish ponies and horses, cattle and local beasts. Pudding pies were traditional Deddington fare, consisting of a sort of bread pudding encased in a hard outer casing containing suet. From the sayings about it, it seems not to have been very palatable: "They say you could tie a label to one and send it through the post a hundred miles—so hard it was." "Deddington folk were supposed to save up all the scrapings from the candle drippings in the lanterns and put them in the pudding pies."[1]

Another tale alleges that a certain king was travelling from Woodstock to Banbury, via Deddington. As he passed through each place, he was presented with gifts—Woodstock gave gloves and Banbury cakes, and in Deddington his gift was a compromise between the two, rather like leather but intended to be eaten! This delicacy has not been made since the early 1930s.

The site of the polygonal bailey of Deddington Castle is now grass-covered, but the high quality of surviving late medieval building suggests some wealthy inhabitants—some thirty buildings date from before 1700, and another sixty were built shortly after. The most striking is Leadenporch House, on the main Banbury to Oxford road, built in about 1325. Its early features are a fourteenth-century doorway and two-light window and its medieval hall with arch-braced roof. Sir Thomas Pope, the founder of Trinity College, is said to have been born here in 1534.

Hudson Street commemorates the prosperous nineteenth-century grocer William Hudson who gave the church clock—perhaps to make up for the legend that the churchwardens once sold the church bells to buy drink, thus leading to the epithet 'Drunken Deddington'. All that remains of the museum, founded by Charles Duffel Faulkener, who died in 1871, are geological specimens and architectural fragments embedded in a wall.

Deddington had quite a range of employment in the nineteenth century, although it always remained primarily an agricultural community—J. S. Hiron's printing-press published *The North Oxfordshire Monthly Times and Agricultural Advertiser* in the 1850s; Joseph and Samuel Mason's axle-tree factory flourished from about 1820 but was overtaken by the petrol engine. About sixty to eighty men were employed at the foundry, and their axles were used for Queen Victoria's coach and by the crowned heads of Europe. Franklin's church-building and restoration firm did renovations on many Oxfordshire churches, such as St Giles and St Margaret's in Oxford, Magdalen College and Wroxton and Barton Abbeys and at Stratford-on-Avon and London. At nearby Clifton a beaver hat factory was run in conjunction with the 'Duke of Cumberland's Head' public house. Deddington had pretensions as a genteel social centre, with a thatched pavilion in the castle grounds, complete with spacious ballroom, musicians' gallery, chintz-covered walls and gas-lighting. Archery tournaments were held here, followed by balls. The Oxford band played, and the cream of the county disported themselves.

Bicester is the second largest town in the Cherwell district. Cassey's 1868 *Directory of Oxfordshire* delineated it:

> Bicester is a market town and parish, in the hundred of Ploughley, union of Bicester and diocese of Oxford, and includes the township of Market End and King's End; it is situated on the eastern border of the county and on the bank of a small stream called the Ray, falling into the Cherwell at Islip. The air is healthy and the water pure, and to the use of it is attributed the celebrity the town has obtained for its excellent ale . . .

Apparently even in the nineteenth century King's End and Market End, although linked by the Causeway, had distinct identities—the former being the older settlement, possibly with its minster founded in the seventh century by St Birinus. It had a Saxon minster church dedicated to St Eadburg, daughter of Edward the Elder, and formed part of the royal manor of Kirtlington in the eleventh century, whence its name. A manor-house, grange and cottages were built by the twelfth century for the Benedictine nuns of Markyate, Bedfordshire, who may have laid out the planned centre with a rectangular green or market-place. The main market-place is in Market End.

The town's prosperity increased, many houses being built in the sixteenth and seventeenth centuries, and some good half-timbered buildings survive in the market-place. Terrible fires in 1718, 1724 and 1730 necessitated further rebuilding, done in coursed rubble, sometimes faced with stucco in imitation of ashlar, and locally made brick. The town languished in the nineteenth century with agricultural depression, as it was still dependent on agriculture and related crafts, its eighteenth- and nineteenth-century trades including rope and sacking manufacture, basket making, leather trades, brewing, wool combing and the cottage industries, straw plaiting and lace making. Horse-racing was popular, and the Bicester and Warden Hill Hunt flourished.

An RAF station was built on the outskirts of the town in 1917, and the largest Ordnance Depot in southern England has been set up. This has brought many newcomers and necessitated much house-building, particularly since the Second World War. The population doubled between 1961 and 1971, to become twelve thousand and is still increasing.

Witney is the principal town in west Oxfordshire. Its Saxon settlement is linked by legend with Emma, granddaughter of Rolle, Viking founder of Normandy, and queen of both Aethelred the Unready and subsequently Canute, her sons by both marriages, Edward the Confessor and Hardicanute, becoming kings of England. It is said, although no documentary evidence supports the fact, that Witney was one of the manors she gave to the Bishop of Winchester in gratitude for being proved innocent in her trial by ordeal when charged with the murder of her son Alfred and an illicit relationship with the Bishop. She witnessed the grant of Witney to the Bishop of Winchester by Edward the Confessor. Emma's Dyke has no known connection with her—it is a canalized stream draining an abandoned river-meander west of the town and runs beneath Corn Street to join the Windrush below the church.

Witney remained part of the Winchester estates after the Conquest. The agricultural expansion of the area around the town in the twelfth and thirteenth centuries probably contributed to the foundation of the town by the Bishop of Winchester as it provided a need for a market centre. In 1279 the town housed 255 tenants and had a market and two fairs. It was drastically affected by the Black Death, which killed approximately two-thirds of the town's population. In the later Middle Ages the wool-trade flourished and with it the town, but few medieval buildings remain apart from the church. The Buttercross was built by William Blake of Manor Farm, Cogges, in the late seventeenth century. Blake also endowed a school in the High Street, but the Grammar School was founded by Henry Box in 1663, and the school still bears his name. The medieval timber buildings of the town have been replaced by stone ones, mostly of eighteenth- and nineteenth-century date, although some have earlier cores. The Blanket Hall was built in Baroque style in 1721 in the High Street, for measuring and weighing blankets. Some surviving blanket-factories date from the nineteenth century. The town is now an expansion area.

Surprisingly little is known about the development of Chipping Norton, although there was a settlement by Domesday. It may have been developed as a town by the fitzAlan family of Clun who were lords of the manor from the twelfth century. The town is, at 650 feet, one of the highest above sea level in southern England and is sometimes cut off by snow in the winter, the grey of its stone giving it a certain dourness and bleakness. Being situated on the main route from London to the West Midlands, it provided a good venue for markets and for coaching. 'Chipping' indicating the existence of a market, first appears attached to 'Norton' in 1224, and a fair is recorded in 1205. The Cotswold wool trade has been of great importance, and the wealth it brought is reflected in the church, which has, in addition to thirteenth- and fourteenth-century work, a particularly fine fifteenth-century interior, reputedly built at the expense of a local wool merchant, John Ashfield. The pillars are clustered together like the supports of a lantern, holding up the wooden roof. The town was first granted a charter in 1607, and it flourished during the eighteenth century, when many older houses were refronted, echoing the fashionable Baroque of nearby Heythrop House and Blenheim Palace.

Burford was an important Cotswold wool town in the Middle Ages. A Saxon battle fought here in 752 between Kings Cuthred of Wessex and Aethelbald of Mercia remains in the folk-memory of the town, in the Burford Dragon ceremony, recorded by Dr Plot who wrote in the seventeenth century that the people of Burford made a dragon each year and processed round town with it, and with a giant, on Midsummer Eve, "with great jollity". Perhaps the giant had a connection with the Guild of Merchant Taylors, as does the giant paraded at Salisbury. It appears to have died out in the eighteenth century, being revived by Burford School in 1971. Certainly it is delightful to watch—twenty children form the tail of the present dragon, which processes downhill with the giant to the church, accompanied by morris men, where a service is held, then the morris men dance.

Burford had had a long struggle over its corporate power. Throughout the Middle Ages it suffered from absentee landlords, and its charter having been acquired by one of them, Robert fitzHamon, between 1087 and 1107, the burgesses made little attempt to acquire additional rights, merely adding unofficially to their powers and neglecting to pay dues to their distant lords, believing themselves secure. However, in the sixteenth and seventeenth centuries they were rudely awakened, first by Edward VI's Act of Parliament which confiscated property given to provide Masses for the dead, which applied strongly to Burford property, and then by the purchase of the manor by Lord Tanfield, the first resident lord of the manor for many generations. The Corporation picked itself up after its first setback by transferring its activities to the Tolsey, as the Guildhall had been confiscated, and set about repurchasing the confiscated properties. Burford's more serious problem came from Sir Lawrence Tanfield who, from a humble background, became a lawyer, amassing enough wealth to buy Burford Priory and in 1617 the lordship of the manor. By that time he had become a judge and Chief Baron of the Exchequer, and in 1620 the Exchequer issued a writ against some of the burgesses, accusing them of usurping the privileges of the manor. The Exchequer won, and the town's privileges were seized. Lord Tanfield was, hardly surprisingly, a most unpopular figure in the town, as was his equally avaricious wife, who controlled his properties after his death. The terrible memory of this couple has persisted, as they have subsequently been seen in ghostly form; Lady Tanfield in particular menaced the town by flying over it in a burning coach, so terrorizing the people that they petitioned the priest to exorcize the ghost. Her spirit was trapped in a glass bottle, which was securely corked and thrown into the Windrush by Burford Bridge. However, if the bottle should ever rise above the water and the cork dry out, the spirit may be released, so it is said that, when the river runs low, the people top it up with buckets of water to avoid this calamity!

Burford, like most Oxfordshire towns, was affected by the Civil War, being the scene of conflict between the Levellers and the main body of Parliamentarians. Mutineers from Salisbury headed towards fellow rebels at Banbury and, crossing the Thames at Burford, were surprised by Colonel Fairfax, Oliver Cromwell and their troops, who rapidly put an end to the revolt, harshly disciplining the ringleaders. The rebels were imprisoned in Burford church for three nights, and three of the four leaders were shot; once that example had been made the remainder were pardoned. The inscription "Anthony Sedley prisner 1649" can still be seen on the lead font. The three soldiers executed are buried in Burford churchyard.

The town began to decline in size and importance in the late eighteenth century, partly because it was skirted by the new turnpike road and so lost its coaching-trade, and it never acquired a railway. The decline is to our advantage, as the layout of the town remains much as it was in the Middle Ages, and it has avoided the nineteenth-century and modern developments which have destroyed the appearance of many towns. Burford has a disproportionately large number of early houses, thirty of which date before the mid sixteenth century and many others before 1700. Some early ones are timber-framed, but the majority are of Cotswold stone.

The Tolsey appears much as it did in the sixteenth century, with its open ground floor, and the upper storey now houses Burford Museum, which has many items relating to borough history and social history, including a mug commemorating Wychwood Forest Fair and a gingerbread-mould used for making gingerbread sold at the races.

Woodstock was a royal borough, built at the gates of the royal park near a favourite royal hunting-lodge, and its early development is closely linked with royal patronage. Henry II needed accommodation and services for his retinue on his frequent visits to the palace, and in 1163–4, he "gave and granted divers parcels of land of the said waste place to divers men for the purpose of building hostelries therein, for the use of king's men".[2] He granted a market, and shortly afterwards it acquired a fair. As a royal borough it had slightly different status from other Oxfordshire towns, except Oxford itself, paying an annual payment—*firma burgi*—to the king, having collected his revenue from the town.

Most medieval kings came to stay and hunt at Woodstock. Henry II began the complex buildings at 'Everswell' near the palace, said to be where Fair Rosamund was hidden. A high wall surrounds an orchard, the chambers, a spring and pools. One pool was encircled by a cloister and a stone bench built by another, perhaps influenced by the design of Sicilian palaces, as Henry's daughter Joanna married William II of Sicily in 1177. The complex, it has been suggested, may recreate the part of the legend of Tristan and Isolde where the lovers had clandestine meetings in such an idyllic setting, away from King Mark—in this case the clandestine lovers being Henry II himself and Rosamund Clifford.

Henry III narrowly escaped being assassinated here in 1238 and the Black Prince was born here—probably at the palace rather than in Old Woodstock as legend tells. Chaucer's House near the Palace gate probably acquired its name from the poet Geoffrey Chaucer's son, Thomas, who received the manor of Woodstock in 1411. In 1438 Matilda Chaucer had a house called 'Hanwell' in Woodstock, which was renamed 'Chaucer's House' in the sixteenth century. The town's first charter was granted by Henry VI in 1453. Henry VIII added a tennis-court to the entertainments at Woodstock, often staying here with Catherine of Aragon. His daughter Elizabeth was imprisoned here during the reign of her sister Mary, engraving, it is said, the following words on a gatehouse window, with her diamond ring:

> Much suspected, of me
> Little proved can be,
> Quoth Elizabeth, Prisoner.

The people of Woodstock were sympathetic towards her, and, once Queen, Elizabeth remembered their loyalty, granting the town a new charter in 1558. Two of the properties she gave to the town have been identified as 'The Woodstock Arms' and 'The King's Arms' public houses.

James I was not popular with his Court when he came to stay at Woodstock, as the palace was in a ruinous state:

The king, regardless of the comfort of his courtiers, had it roughly fitted up for himself, while the household were obliged to camp even in tents, pitched near. Sir Robert Cecil speaks bitterly of the arrangements, so different from the pomp that always accompanied Elizabeth in her journeys. He writes: "The palace is unwholesome, all the house standing upon springs. It is unsavoury, for there is no savour but the cows and pigs. It is uneaseful, for only the king and queen, with the privy chamber ladies, and some three or four of the Scottish council, are lodged in the house, and neither chamberlain nor one English councillor have a room."[3]

Woodstock's appearance is dominated by eighteenth-century architecture, as the building of Blenheim increased the importance of the town. The buildings are largely of local stone, many featuring porches of stone slabs supported on wrought-iron brackets. It is recorded in the eighteenth-century *Acts of Council* "that Mr Dixon built a cockpit, and that the Common Council have liberty of going into the cockpit at any cock match to be fought gratis"—this has now disappeared, leaving only the name 'Cockpit Close'.

'Capability' Brown planned to link the appearance of the town and Blenheim Palace by battlementing the park wall and any houses which could be seen from the Palace, but this scheme was abandoned. The smart appearance of the stone-built houses has sometimes been compared with a French town (so much so that it was used as a French town in a recent film about the Second World War) and contrasts with the 'village' of Old Woodstock, which became part of the main borough only in the nineteenth century. It is older than the town and many have been founded by Henry I. A plaque on the wall of one house records it as the site where the first Blenheim Orange apple was grown. The old manor-house has portions dating from the late thirteenth or fourteenth century. Both Old and New Woodstock have new housing estates, as Woodstock has become a popular dormitory town for people working in Oxford. Its popularity as a tourist centre is shown by the number of hotels, notably the exclusive Bear Hotel, and the antique-shops.

Woodstock houses the headquarters of the Oxfordshire County Museum, in Fletcher's House, situated opposite the church and behind a pair of stocks. Here one can encompass the development of the whole county in a single display, with a reconstructed Neolithic barrow and a Roman pottery-kiln, an Elizabethan wall-painting and displays of local crafts, bringing the story up to the present day with Lord Nuffield and motorways. Behind the scenes the Museum Education Department is teaching and sending out hundreds of red boxes containing archaeological, historical, art, craft and natural historical items to schools round the county and collecting biological records; the Antiquities Department is collecting objects and doing research; the Field Department records sites and monuments and answers many enquiries, particularly on planning; the Workshop and Conservation Department restore and conserve objects and build displays, and the Administration holds the organization together. The informality of the museum is emphasized by the coffee-bar and bookstall, and in summer visitors can partake of tea on the lawn.

Bampton too has escaped many of the horrors of modern building. It was a Saxon 'royal vill', thus early assuming importance as an administrative centre. Its church is one of the largest and finest in west Oxfordshire, with some late-Saxon or early-Norman work in the tower, the main portion dating from 1270. Traces of medieval building are found in the Deanery, which has a fourteenth-century nucleus, with seventeenth-century alterations, and in Ham Court, which was once Bampton Castle, built by Aymer de Valence, Earl of Pembroke, about 1315. The castle gatehouse has been converted to a dwelling, and part of the battlemented curtain wall and polygonal turret are incorporated into the main building. Other buildings reflect the prosperity of the town in the seventeenth and eighteenth centuries, when it specialized in making gloves and sheepskin products—the grammar school was founded in 1635 by a woollen-merchant, Robert Vesey, and his original building is now the public library. The town formed a good base for sporting activities in the neighbouring countryside, and those who came to enjoy the sport attended the weekly assemblies and patronized the town's tradesmen, physicians and apothecaries. The remoteness of Bampton, surrounded by common land, with no metalled roads leading to it until the late eighteenth century, conspired to stifle the growth of the town. Its population decreased throughout the second half of the nineteenth century. The railway which reached Bampton in 1873 brought new middle-class and retired professional-class people who bought up the old farm-houses in the town and encouraged improvements such as cleaning and lighting. Now Bampton is perhaps most famous for its morris dancing. The dancers claim to have been dancing without a break (except during the First World War) for several hundred years. They perform on Whit Monday, which in the nineteenth century was also the village feast day, so the club members would march in procession to church, led by a fiddler, eight morris dancers, the 'Clown' or 'Fool' and a sword-bearer, who carried a cake in a round tin impaled on the sword blade, decorated with ribbons. The cake was divided up, and portions were sold to bystanders—it was thought to bring fertility to women. The morris dancers are particularly proud of their tradition, though this has brought dissension, and there are now rival teams in Bampton. The traditional dances are 'Green Garters', 'Constant Billy', 'Willow Tree', 'Maid of the Mill', 'Bob & Joan', 'Handsome John' and 'Highland Mary'. The New Inn public house has recently been renamed 'The Morris Clown' in honour of the morris men, whose fool traditionally wears a clown's outfit.

Eynsham was mentioned in the *Anglo-Saxon Chronicle* as being captured after the battle of Bedcanford (Bedford) in 571, but its history is then a blank until the foundation of the Benedictine abbey in 1005. Its first abbot was Aelfric, who played an important role in the late tenth-century monastic revival, leading the contemporary literary movement, and his writings in Anglo-Saxon include *Catholic Homilies, Lives of the Saints*, translations from the Scriptures, pastoral letters and the biography of his master, Aethelwold. He abridged the *Regularis Concordia* for his monks at Eynsham. The monastery was refounded after the Norman Conquest, gradually acquiring lands and wealth so that by 1447 it had land in seventy different parishes although housing only about thirty monks at any one time. The abbey's prosperity was aided by the proximity of Woodstock Manor, as when the king came to stay there, the clerics with him normally stayed at Eynsham. The abbey dominated the town and became prominent in the thirteenth century when it acquired the arm of St Andrew, which allegedly worked many miracles. Tensions existed between the townspeople and the abbey, culminating in a fight on Whit Tuesday 1296, in which some Oxford scholars were killed. The culprits escaped justice, so the whole town was excommunicated. The dissolution of the abbey greatly affected the town, but the sixteenth and seventeenth centuries were a period of change, during which the medieval timber buildings were replaced by stone ones, some of them built with abbey stone.

Charlbury was affected by the proximity of Eynsham Abbey, which had a courthouse there, but it has religious connections predating the abbey, as it is said to be the burial-place of St Diuma, first bishop of the Mercians, who died in 658, and in the late Saxon period it was the centre of a large episcopal estate. In 1094 Charlbury was transferred from the bishop of Lincoln to Eynsham Abbey, and a weekly market and a fair were granted to the abbot in 1256. Glove-making was the staple industry, but by the late nineteenth century Charlbury had declined to a small trading centre for the local agricultural community.

Thame in south Oxfordshire is also the focus for an agricultural area and is an ecclesiastical foundation—created in the mid-twelfth century by Alexander Bloet, Bishop of Lincoln. He gave Thame Park to the Cistercians and built a prebendal house in Thame, giving it supreme importance locally. Part of the house remains, including a thirteenth-century chapel and solar, and a fifteenth-century ground-floor hall. He may have been instrumental in founding New Thame, a deliberate creation which changed the important rural estate into a thriving market-town. New Thame rapidly eclipsed Old Thame, with its focus clustered round the church which dates mainly from the thirteenth century, being enlarged in the fourteenth and the tower heightened in the fifteenth.

Among the monuments is one to Lord Williams of Thame, a great benefactor to the town who died in 1559 having endowed the grammar school. His father was a cousin of Thomas Cromwell, and he married a wealthy furrier's daughter. As Master of the King's Jewels, one of his privileges was supplying cramprings blessed by the king. At the Dissolution he served as Visitor of the Monasteries and Treasurer of the Court of Augmentations, purchased Rycote House and served as Justice of the Peace, Sheriff of the County and Member of Parliament. His leniency in giving pensions to dispossessed monks without the permission of the Privy Council landed him in the Fleet Prison, but he was astute enough to change his views under Mary, witnessing the burning of Ridley, Latimer and Cranmer and becoming President of the Council of the Welsh Marches.

The original school building in Church Lane, with its diamond brickwork chimneys, mullioned windows and Lord Williams' coat-of-arms over the doorway, is now used as offices. A mock-Tudor school building on the Oxford road was designed in the 1870s by William Wilkinson, now forming part of the new comprehensive school. Lord Williams' School boasted some famous pupils in the seventeenth century: John Hampden, the Parliamentarian, Henry King of Worminghall, later Bishop of Chichester, Mr Speaker Lenthall of Latchford, the dramatist Shakerley Marmion, the orientalist Edward Pocock, the regicides Simon Mayne and Sir Richard Ingoldsby, John Fell,

Bishop of Oxford and Dean of Christchurch, Daniel Whistler, physician and founder member of the Royal Society, Anthony Wood, who wrote so much about his life in Oxford, the dramatist Sir George Etheridge and the Lord Chief Justice Sir John Holt.

There are several timber-framed and cruck buildings, the latter pre-1550, indicating the prosperity of the medieval town, and the quality of buildings the merchants were able to build. During the 'great rebuilding' of the sixteenth and seventeenth centuries, some half-timbered houses with elaborate barge-boarding were erected. The town had several brickworks, producing for local consumption and for the neighbouring area.

Today Thame has a population of about six thousand, but the county structure-plan envisages considerable development, and the new by-pass being built to decrease traffic in the town contrasts with the thirteenth-century diversion of the road to go through the town and take advantage of tolls.

The defensive role of Wallingford is emphasized by the Saxon rampart and the castle, both now decayed and covered by grassy mounds. The castle was built shortly after the Norman Conquest by order of William the Conqueror and played an important role in the medieval history of Wallingford. It was seized by Matilda in her war with Stephen, and she herself took refuge there in 1141 after escaping from besieged Oxford. According to tradition, she and her followers disguised themselves in white to cross the frozen Thames without being seen—or may have thought that they would be mistaken for ghosts. Wallingford Castle was central to activity during these wars, and Prince Henry, Matilda's son, and Stephen negotiated at Wallingford. In 1215 King John, fearing the revolt of his barons, ordered the strengthening of the castle, and further work was done later in the thirteenth century (probably under the ownership of Richard, Earl of Cornwall, Henry III's brother, who chose the castle as his principal residence), when a third moat was constructed. Perhaps he later regretted strengthening the castle when it was seized by Simon de Montfort, who threatened to place his captured nephew Edward (later Edward I) in a mangonal and shoot him out of the castle instead of shooting large stones!

Piers Gaveston, the favourite of Edward II, was granted the castle in 1307 and entertained lavishly there, giving a magnificent tournament, but his arrogance in insulting his noble guests only increased his unpopularity and in 1313 led to his downfall and execution. Queen Isabella gave the castle to her lover, Roger Mortimer, and it became a centre for their conspiracy against Edward II. His grandson the Black Prince lived at Wallingford Castle. It acted as a refuge for another Queen Isabella, when her husband Richard II was attacked by Henry Bolingbroke, and for Queen Katherine, wife of Henry V, and her son Henry, who was educated there. Henry VI's widow, Margaret, was imprisoned in the castle for three years in the care of the Constable, Alice de la Pole.

Henry VIII broke the royal connection with the castle, separating it from the Duchy of Cornwall. It was refortified as a Royalist stronghold during the Civil War and was besieged for sixteen weeks in 1646 until Charles ordered its surrender to Colonel Fairfax. Like Banbury Castle, it was demolished after the Civil War. It must have been an impressive sight in its heyday, with the keep on top of the 60-foot-high motte, its three moats and triple wall enclosing various buildings.

Wallingford has several pre-1700, mostly timber-framed buildings, but St Lucian's, to the south of the town, is of brick with decorative plasterwork, and 52 High Street is of flint with stone windows. The town hall, built in 1670, is particularly fine and still retains its original open ground floor and a Palladian window in the upper storey. Later buildings are mainly of locally made red brick.

> The moderate distance of Henley from the metropolis, combined with its other advantages, justly entitle it to the large share of public patronage it now enjoys, and which it is hoped, will be still further increased. To those persons who do not wish to enter the gay and extensive circles of fashionable watering places, this delightful spot will afford all the enjoyments of retirement, and tranquillity; while equestrian, the pedestrian, the artist and the angler, may here follow their respective amusements, and be equally delighted with the romantic and picturesque forms of nature, aided by the pleasing embellishments of art.[4]

As this eulogy of Henley indicates, in many ways the town has more links with London than the rest of Oxfordshire. The earliest clear reference to Henley is in 1179, making it likely that it is a twelfth-century 'new town', with the complete town being laid out within a short period. Its character has been influenced by its position on the bank of the River Thames and its bridge, which is first mentioned about 1225, although it existed before then. The two Bridgemen were among the most important officials. The present bridge, which replaces the old one destroyed by floods in 1774, is the focus of the town, with the main street extending from it, and St Mary's Church close by. River trade was always important, Henley acting as the gathering-point for grain from the Upper Thames Valley, which was shipped to London, and building stone, from the west of the county. Fishing was profitable, and in Henley's later history the Regatta and its concomitant riverside activities have played vital roles in the prosperity of the town.

Trade developed during the Middle Ages, a merchant guild formed in 1269; in the seventeenth century, the glass-maker George Ravenscroft was working in Bell Street making glass with a lead flux, and perhaps Mr Vidler's mailcoach-building business of the eighteenth century was encouraged by the town's coaching-trade. Victorian villas were built on the out-skirts of the town, and this exclusivity persists in Henley today. Its shops have acquired a reputation for high quality, and its appearance, with a preponderance of fine buildings, adds to the feeling of quality. Several medieval and sixteenth-century buildings survive, plus many of half timber and more recent brick buildings.

Watlington is a remote Chiltern town, not helped by the fact that in bad weather the road to Oxford was often impassable. At Domesday it was an agricultural community and, as part of the honour of Wallingford, may have acquired its market privileges through Richard, Earl of Cornwall, in 1252. It had no further urban privileges, and all market tolls went to the lord of the manor. Despite links with the wool trade and London mer-chants, the town was half the size of Henley in the seventeenth century, and consequently the medieval street pattern has been maintained. The remains of a moated manor lie near the church, although there was probably a Saxon church, the earliest portions of the present church date from the twelfth century.

Perhaps the most interesting building is the town hall built by Sir Thomas Stonor in 1664-5 to provide accommodation for the grammar school and a covered area for market stalls. The moulded brickwork on the hoods and the toothed decoration on the arches gives it a striking appearance. The mellow brick buildings and a preponderance of pre-1840 architecture in the town centre give it a slightly old-fashioned appearance as though unconnected with the present age.

Abingdon, the largest town in the Vale and third largest in Oxfordshire, had an important Saxon settlement, and its medieval history was dominated by Abingdon Abbey, first founded in the late seventh century. Little of the monastic buildings remain apart from the gatehouse, next to St Nicholas's Church, and a range of buildings by the mill stream, consisting of the twelfth century bakehouse, granaries, the 'Checker' or Exchequer and a long gallery—a strange assortment. The sixteenth-century long gallery has a plan similar to that of medieval inns, so it may have been used by abbey guests or have provided working-space for the Checker clerks. In the twelfth century the number of monks in the abbey increased from twenty-eight to eighty, so more accommodation was built, and the Abbot Faritius acquired more property for the abbey, becoming an important feudal lord. The abbey's increasing control over the town irritated and angered the townsmen, and mismanagement by a fourteenth-century abbot encouraged them to revolt, breaking into the abbey, burning and looting and causing the monks to flee for their lives. More troubles broke out in 1368, but the abbey maintained its strange control, and some of the ringleaders of the riot were hanged.

Abingdon had its own saint, Edmund Rich, who was born there in 1170. His mother, Matilda, encouraged him in his asceticism and his wearing of horsehair and rope as penance. He became a member of the Austin canons of Merton, rising in 1222 to become Treasurer of Salisbury Cathedral and prebend of Calne, and in 1233 he became Archbishop of Canterbury. He retired into exile at Soisy and Pontigny, dying in 1240. After performing a number of miracles, he was duly canonized. In 1288 the Earl of Cornwall built a chapel dedicated to him near his reputed birthplace in Abingdon, probably between St Edmund's Lane and West St Helen's Street.

St Helen's Church is a particularly fine example of Perpendicular architecture, with a thirteenth-century steeple and five gabled aisles, making the building broader than it is long. It was enlarged after the destruction of the abbey church in 1539. Much of its finery has survived the nineteenth-century restoration, including the early eighteenth-century Mayor's Seat, which has a carved lion and unicorn and a sword-rest. The roof of the north aisle was painted in about 1390, originally as a Tree of Jesse with prophets and kings alternating, some of which have been preserved.

After the dissolution of the abbey the town acquired its first charter, in 1556, for the first time having control over fairs and markets, previously controlled by the abbey. A market hall was erected in 1569, to be replaced in 1678 by the present 'County Hall', built to show Abingdon's pride in being the county borough of Berkshire, a distinction it retained until the 1860s, when that role was acquired by Reading. Celia Fiennes commented on the hall twice on different visits to Abingdon.

> Abington town seemes a very well built town and the Market Cross is the finest in England, its all of free stone and very lofty, even the Isles or Walk below it is a lofty arch on severall pillars of square stone and four square pillars, over it are large Roomes with handsome windows, above which is some Roomes with windows a little like the Theatre att Oxford, only this is a square building and that round, it makes a very fine appearance . . .

> . . . Abington where is a fine Town Hall for the Judges two barrs and all seates aboute set on stone pillars, the staires to the top is about 100, the leads fine and gives a large prospect all about; there is halfe way the staires a place to go in and in gallerys round company may stand to hear causes all above the Judges heads.[5]

The town councillors go up to the roof of the County Hall for the 'Bun-throwing Ceremony' on special occasions such as coronations (the first occasion seems to have been the accession of George III on 19th November 1760), Victory Day 1946, the Fourth Centenary of the Borough in 1956 and more recently Elizabeth II's Silver Jubilee in 1977 and the Queen Mother's eightieth Birthday in 1980. Buns are thrown by the councillors to the crowds massed in the market-place below, usually following a civic ceremony.

The County Hall now houses Abingdon Museum, which has a fascinating collection, including some of the archaeological remains discovered and excavated in and around the town: Saxon jewellery and a fragment of the earliest-known lyre in western Europe, from a Saxon cemetery in Saxton Road. Other treasures include the Borough pewter, a smock made in Abingdon for the Great Exhibition, a charming dolls' house and a wealth of other items reflecting the character of the town.

Ock Street stood outside the borough boundary and was known for its riotous inhabitants. The regalia of the morris men echoes this—they proudly carry the 'Ock Street Horns' said to have been won in a fight between the men of Ock Street and the rest of the town in 1700, when a local farmer, John Morris, presented a large black ox to be roasted. The applewood mace they carry is thought to have been carved from a club carried in the fight by one of the Hemmings family, famous in the annals of the Abingdon morris. The morris men dance each June at the election of the Mock Mayor of Ock Street. 'Mock Mayors' were elected in Banbury, Woodstock and Abingdon by parts of the town not entitled to vote for the proper Mayor and Corporation. In Woodstock, he was Mayor of 'Old Woodstock', outside the borough boundary until the late nineteenth century, and in Banbury he was Mayor of 'Newland', a twelfth-century attempt to establish a new town on the then outskirts of Banbury. The only Mock Mayor now elected regularly is that of Ock Street. Mock-mayoral candidates were traditionally from the lower orders of society, figures of fun or drunkards, but latterly the Abingdon Mayor has been chosen by ballot from among the ranks of the morris men and chaired up and down Ock Street, accompanied by morris men, visiting all the public houses.

Abingdon is the third largest town in Oxfordshire. Its position on the Thames was augmented by the building of the Wilts and Berks Canal in about 1820, and the railway which was opened in 1856 improved local communications. The County Gaol, built in 1805–11, has an octagonal central tower with radiating wings and is now used as an Arts Centre, and the Abingdon Abbey buildings are used each autumn for the Abingdon Crafts Fair.

There has been a settlement at Wantage at least since Roman times. In the late-Saxon era Wantage had a royal residence, King Alfred being born here, and it remained a royal manor until 1199. It did not prosper during the Middle Ages, and the only medieval building remaining is the church, which is basically thirteenth century, restored by G. E. Smith in 1857. It became more industrialized in the nineteenth century as communications improved with the building of the Wilts and Berks canal, the opening of the railway and the Wantage Tramway. A new town hall was built in 1865, shortly after King Alfred's Grammar School (1849–50). By this time the town had over-come its unfortunate image of 'Black Wantage', held in the early nineteenth century. It had a large number of public houses, and even before the advent of the navvies building the canal, the town had a reputation for drunkenness and blood-sports such as bull-baiting and cock-fighting. Drunken brawls were common occurrences, but fortunately there were few murders as senseless as that of Ann Pullin, a maid at the 'Red Lion'. In 1833 a customer threw her a coin, and when she refused to pick it up off the floor, this man, one Gregory King, a hedger, chopped off her head with one swift stroke of his beanhook. 'Lord' George Sanger was in Wantage with a travelling circus, and he and his father worked through the night preparing a peep-show of the gruesome murder.

Most houses appear to be of eighteenth-or nineteenth-century date, mainly of brick, but these façades in some cases conceal earlier buildings. Some timber-framing can be found at the rear of houses in Wallingford Street. The Stiles Almhouses dating from 1690 are an interesting example of early brick building in the town, one storey high with a hipped roof.

Wantage has a small museum in the modern Civil Hall, illustrating the way of life in the Vale, with a fascinating sec-tion on agriculture with splendid wooden cheese-moulds used for making Vale cheeses. A Vale and Downland Museum is planned, which will further illustrate aspects of social history in the Vale.

Faringdon occupied a strategic position—a castle was built here during the wars of Stephen and Matilda, though it was shortly ordered to be demolished. In 1387 in the reign of Richard II the Battle of Radcot Bridge was fought, and the Duke of Ireland, commanding the King's forces, was compelled to swim across the river to escape. Faringdon staunchly supported the Royalist cause during the Civil War—Faringdon House was a royal garrison commanded by Sir Marmaduke Rawdon, and Radcot Bridge was strengthened for the Royalists, though it fell to the Parliamentarians in 1646. The house, however, remained firm, and when in 1645 Cromwell himself attacked with six hundred men, the Governor, Roger Burgess, successfully re-pulsed him. The following year a further attack was led by Sir

Robert Pye, who actually owned the house, but not even he was successful. These military operations inflicted grievous damage on the town, destroying the church spire and many houses.

Sir Henry Pye, Poet Laureate of no great fame at the end of the eighteenth century, built the present Faringdon House, in typical neo-Classical style with a Tuscan porch and pedimented doorways. It has been suggested that the nursery rhyme "Sing a song of sixpence" refers to him, as his first ode written in honour of George III abounds in birds, but the rhyme pre-dates him. His poetry was so poor that he had the unfortunate distinction of being pilloried by Byron, in his 'Vision of Judgment':

> The monarch, mute till then, exclaimed, What, What,
> Pye come again! No more, no more of that.[6]

The town has many Georgian buildings and is overwhelmingly eighteenth century in character.

Several other villages in the Vale once had urban pretensions —in the thirteenth-century Stanford-in-the-Vale, Baulking and Shrivenham had markets. Stanford's former market-place is indicated by its two village greens and the double nucleus of the village. Baulking's wide green has traces of house foundations and burgage plots. East Hendred tried to take advantage of the wool-trade, and the prior of Sheen established a market and a wool-fair. All these markets declined by the seventeenth century. The pattern of towns and population and industry continues to change, but it is unlikely that Oxfordshire will ever become much more urban in character, although the accretions of mushrooming housing-estates sometimes threaten to swamp the old towns, entirely changing the balance of buildings.

9

Oxford

Duns Scotus's Oxford:

> Towery city and branchy between towers;
> Cuckoo-echoing, bell-swarmèd, lark charmèd, rook racked,
>   river-rounded;
> The dapple-eared lily below thee; that country and town did
> Once encounter in, here coped and posed powers.
>
> Gerard Manley Hopkins

To most people the image conjured up by the name Oxford is that of towers and spires, which dominate the view, epitomizing the strength of the university and the dominant role it has played in Oxford's history. However, Oxford was in existence for centuries before the university, has always stubbornly maintained its separate existence and has bestowed its name on a strange assortment of objects, including Oxford sausages, Oxford marmalade, Oxford finger biscuits, Oxford ragweed, Oxford bags (trousers), Oxford shirting, Oxford grey, Oxford frames (with cross-shaped corners), Oxford brogues, Oxford chairs, Oxford bath (a hip-bath advertised by the Army and Navy Stores in 1907 varying in price from 13s.9d to 22s.2d), Oxford vaporizer, Oxford accent, Morris Oxford cars and other disparate subjects. It has also become the headquarters for such world-wide organizations as the Oxford Committee for Famine Relief.

Yet Oxford is not as old as one might expect. It is situated at a crossing-point of the River Thames, a major navigable river, commanding the easily defended Sandford gap in the ridge of the Corallian Hills, but there was no major settlement here until mid-Saxon times. Man has settled here since at least Neolithic times, and the Romans made pottery in the Cowley-Headington area. According to legend, which is to some extent supported by the archaeological evidence showing intensive occupation beginning in the eighth century, Oxford received its minster in AD 727 from St Frideswide, its patron saint. Frideswide was allegedly the daughter of Prince Didanus, and her hand was sought in marriage by Prince Algar of Leicester. Frideswide rejected him, preferring to become a nun, but Algar was insistent and pursued his lady-love as she fled across the marsh outside the city walls. Just as he was about to recapture her, providence stepped in, and he was struck by lightning and blinded. Frideswide interceded with God, his sight was restored, and in his gratitude he ceased his unwelcome attentions. Frideswide is said to have founded a double priory for monks and nuns in Oxford, possibly at Binsey, at the site of the holy well which she is said to have created. (This well is Lewis Carroll's treacle well, 'treacle' in medieval usage meaning a healing fluid.)

When King Aethelred the Unready ordered a masscre of the Danes in 1002, the Danes in Oxford were burned to death inside St Frideswide's Church. Oxford had become a town in the ninth century, probably as part of King Alfred's Wessex defences against the depredations of the Viking raids. The *Anglo-Saxon Chronicle* tells us that in 912 King Edward took possession of London and Oxford. The town probably had defensive walls enclosing the houses and shops of merchants and townsmen— the rectangular street pattern today may reflect this Saxon town, although this was burned by Thorkell the Tall in 1009 in retribution for the earlier massacre of the Danes. In 1018 the town had been sufficiently re-established to be the venue of one of King Canute's Parliaments and of his son Harold Harefoot's coronation in 1037 and funeral three years later. Traces of Saxon Oxford can be seen in the tower of St Michael at the Northgate.

Domesday Book recorded almost half the houses as being 'waste', but the town regained its prosperity and once again became a thriving centre, with six parishes—St Frideswide, St Peter in the East, St Ebbe, St Michael at the Northgate, St Mary the Virgin and St Martin. It was defended by its massive castle and a stone wall; inside were crammed timber-framed buildings with a shopping-area centred around Cornmarket Street and High Street where merchants and craftsmen plied their respective trades.

Robert d'Oilly was granted Oxford by William the Conqueror and proceeded to build a large motte-and-bailey castle to reinforce his control. The mound, 80 feet high, and one stone tower survive, and the castle-remains now house an overcrowded prison, echoing the role it must have played since its inception—certainly 'rebellious scholars' were incarcerated there in 1236, and in 1239 it became a county gaol.

Another important group of people was that of the religious communities—such as Godstow Abbey, Oseney Abbey (founded in 1129), Rewley Abbey (founded in 1281), the Canons of St George, who had the crypt below the castle, the refounded priory of St Frideswide, and the friars. The Franciscans, or Grey friars, were the first to arrive in 1224, soon followed by Dominican and Carmelite friars and Austin canons. It was partly the influence of such organizations (which laid great emphasis on teaching and study, especially geared towards providing high-class churchmen) which encouraged the establishment of the university. One of the lecturers at St Frideswide's school was the Frenchman Theobald of Étampes, who gave himself the title 'Master of Oxenforde' and taught scripture. Oxford, although by no means in the forefront of European education at that time, was clearly able to attract foreign teachers, though conversely many of the more able students headed for the universities of Paris and Bologna.

By this time Oxford was the ninth largest town in the kingdom, boasted the royal palace of Beaumont and was much frequented by royalty. Although the precise reasons for the choice of Oxford as a major university town are now obscure, it seems to have been a royal political decision which gave it the impetus. Henry II, that tempestuous monarch, quarrelled with Louis VII of France in 1167 and imperiously ordered all scholars at Continental universities back to England, Louis also harried all Englishmen from Paris. English scholars no longer had the option of studying abroad, and some two thousand teachers and scholars were suddenly searching for somewhere to teach and study. Many came to Oxford, swamping the unsuspecting town and causing temporary chaos. The problems of providing such basics as lodgings, food and clothing were enormous, and the inhabitants of Oxford were not averse to taking advantage of the situation and making what profit they could and may thus have nurtured the growing alienation and distrust between town and gown, which formed a major feature of Oxford life until the nineteenth century.

The university took time to become established and nearly disappeared from the town once or twice, as in 1209, when King John sided with the townspeople instead of the university in one of their perennial disputes, during which several students were hanged for alleged murder. The dispute was not settled until 1214, giving the town time to realize how much it had come to depend on the university for its livelihood. In 1334 a riot between two sections of the university led to a mass migration to Stamford, but this was soon settled—the memory of such incidents died hard, as up to 1827 an oath not to give or attend lectures at Stamford was made by all candidates for an Oxford degree!

Once the university got a toehold, it spread over the town, especially the eastern area within the defensive walls. The large plots owned by some colleges may indicate encroachment over earlier streets and buildings. The colleges themselves are later innovations—Merton was the first to be created on a substantial scale, with statutes written in 1274 by Walter de Merton, who held the post of Chancellor and Regent. The college soon contained twenty-five Fellows and allowed scholars to work for Master of Arts and higher degrees, with the eventual aim of encouraging the secular priesthood and providing senior and well-qualified public servants. University and Balliol colleges were founded at about the same time, and the number of colleges has now risen to thirty-four—several having been added in the twentieth century. The magnificent college buildings which physically dominate the town provide some of the finest and most imposing architecture testifying to the power and influence of the university.

An important effect of the constant tussles between town and gown in the Middle Ages was the stranglehold the university gained and maintained jealously. The town had received its first charter from Henry II in about 1155, confirming its gild merchants, but future royal favour tended towards Gown rather than Town—Henry III warned the Mayor in 1231 that, if his fellow townsmen continued to overcharge and exploit scholars, they ran the risk of losing the university. The privileges of the town were gradually eroded, culminating in humiliation after the St Scholastica's Day riot which lasted three days, in the course of which three scholars and several townsmen were killed—mobs of countrymen augmented the townsmen in their struggle, and the town was overwhelmed by riot, fire and despoliation. The Mayor and Chancellor themselves risked death. The results were dire—an enquiry lasting a year tried to sort out what had happened, during which time the town was placed under interdict, which closed all the churches. The King pardoned the university but imprisoned the Mayor and bailiffs in the Marshalsea Prison and fined the town 500 marks plus an annual payment of 100 marks, with orders to compensate for all damage to property. The Chancellor took over many functions of town government, such as checking weights and measures, punishing those selling adulterated food, punishing miscreants at university courts and assessing the taxes of those who directly served the university. For the next five centuries, until 1825, the humiliation continued, as annually on St Scholastica's Day the Mayor, accompanied by his bailiffs and burgesses, walked in procession from the Guildhall to St Mary's Church for Mass, where they had publicly to kneel and pray for the souls of the victims and each offer a silver penny. Any who refused to participate were fined. The Mayor also had to swear to uphold the privileges of the university.

The university acquired rich and valuable collections. A visit to the Bodleian Library is a great privilege and a fascinating experience, in one sense taking one back into the world of the medieval university as one enters the massive School Quadrangle, built in about 1613–24, which had emblazoned in gold above the doorways 'Schola medecinae', 'Schola naturalis philosophiae' and so on, denoting the subjects taught by the university—medicine, natural philosophy, arithmetic, geometry, metaphysics, logics, astronomy, grammar, languages, history, law and music. The university has acquired books at least since the thirteenth century, and Bishop Cobham of Worcester built a library to house his gift in 1320. Duke Humphrey gave a vast and valuable collection in the fifteenth century, which was alas dispersed during the Reformation. His memory is preserved in the magnificent chamber bearing his name, which houses the Department of Western Manuscripts, in the library built by Sir Thomas Bodley, which opened in 1602 with a total of two thousand books. Library users swear to study in modesty and silence, to preserve all contents of the library and not to damage the books in any way. Bodley made an agreement with the Stationers' Company that his library should receive one copy of each of their publications. Several copyright acts have augmented this agreement, and the Bodleian now has a right to a copy of every book published in Britain, plus a manuscript collection of inestimable value.

Another famous collection—a cabinet of curiosities—was collected by John Tradescant the Elder and his son John and presented to the university by Elias Ashmole, and forms the nucleus of the Ashmolean Museum. The collection came to Oxford in twelve cart-loads on 20th March 1683 and was housed in a specially designed building in Broad Street, now between the Sheldonian and Exeter College—the cost of £4,000 was so great that for a while the Bodleian could buy no new books. The Ashmolean building also housed the Professor of Chemistry, a chemical laboratory and library. It is the oldest public museum in the country and was opened by James, Duke of York, on 21st May 1683, its first keeper being Dr Robert Plot, also Professor of Chemistry, who wrote *The Natural History of Oxfordshire*. Elias Ashmole wanted this bequest to be his monument to posterity and deliberately refrained from any mention of the Tradescants in his gift.

Among the items in the Tradescant Room, recently redisplayed to commemorate the museum's tercentenary, are 'the robe of the King of Virginia', the deerskin mantle decorated with white shells, which belonged to Powhattan, the father of Pocahontas, and a very early Canadian Indian hunting-shirt, decorated with porcupine quills—two of the earliest pieces of Indian clothing surviving. The miscellany was gathered from all parts of the then known globe—paper lanterns from China, a saddle from Central Asia and a marble Buddha from Burma, and added to it are historical relics, such as the 'dark' lantern carried by Guy Fawkes, which could be shaded when required, a pair of gloves presented to Queen Elizabeth I on one of her visits to Oxford, and the iron-reinforced hat worn by John Bradshaw while he presided over the trial of Charles I.

The Ashmolean is one of the richest museums in the country. in the scope of its treasures. In the 1840s C. R. Cockerell designed the imposing neo-Classical building in Beaumont Street. With the additional space, more material could be displayed and new collections acquired. The Arundel Marbles, an early collection, were given pride of place, and fine art became an element of the museum with the acquisition of Michelangelo and Raphael drawings. There are so many wonderful things in the museum that it is almost invidious to mention a few—however, perhaps the most famous item in the collections is the Anglo-Saxon 'Alfred Jewel', inscribed 'Alfred had me made' (in Anglo-Saxon), which has an enamelled man's portrait encased in gold and rock-crystal and was probably part of an elaborate bookmark sent by Alfred to one of his favourite monasteries. The Department of Antiquities has items varying from exquisitely chipped flint tools and plaster-covered skulls from Jericho, with cowrie shells for eyes, to gold laurel-wreaths and delicate gold jewellery from Greece.

The Department of Western Art is particularly proud of its Uccello painting, *A Hunt in the Forest*, with its quivering, rangy staghounds pursuing frightened deer zig-zagging through the trees, plus its sculptures, glass, pottery and porcelain, gold and silver works of art, musical instruments, tapestries and embroideries.

The Heberden coin room has a collection bettered in Britain only by that of the British Museum, containing approximately a quarter of a million items. The Department of Eastern Art was founded in 1962 and has one of the best collections in Britain, with a wealth of pottery and porcelain, the exquisite Japanese netsuke (minute and charming carvings of animals, fish and figures) and art objects from India, Tibet, Siam, Cambodia, Java and Burma, Persia and Arabia.

The Pitt Rivers and University Museums, which also contain some items from the Tradescant collection were designed by Benjamin Woodward, with splendid wrought-iron columns supporting the glass roof, walls resplendent in buff and red stone, whimsical carvings by the O'Shea brothers and their nephew, of monkeys, cats, foliage and—their downfall—caricatures of local notables, which led to their being sacked. Ruskin is said to have had a hand in the carving. The museum was founded with the serious scientific purpose of assembling "all the materials explanatory of the organic beings placed upon the globe" and played a role in the Darwinian controversy, with displays following his revolutionary principles—very forward-looking and much criticized by conservatives. The museum was the first stage in establishing science as a worthwhile subject in Oxford.

The museum hall today is dominated by skeletons of dinosaurs, towering above the visitors, and tucked away among other fascinating exhibits are the beak and foot of one of the two dodos from the Tradescant collection—these almost unique specimens mouldered away to such an extent that, to the eternal shame of the museum, they were burned in 1775.

The Pitt Rivers Museum of Ethnology is named after Lieutenant-General Henry Lane-Fox Pitt Rivers who in 1883 donated fifteen thousand specimens. The number now exceed a million. Pitt Rivers insisted that the displays should illustrate the evolution and development of objects. The variety of material is enormous—from a 40-foot totem-pole from the Queen Charlotte Islands, British Columbia, to lace-bobbins used in the neighbouring counties, with shrunken heads jostling for position with shadow puppets.

The Museum of the History of Science, founded in 1925, lives in the Old Ashmolean building, stimulated by the magnificent gift by Lewis Evans (Sir Arthur's brother) of early scientific instruments. It now houses many other collections, such as the Beeson Room of clocks and watches, fascinating and valuable orreries and astrolabes and Einstein's blackboard with his formula chalked on by the master himself.

The university's Botanical Garden by Magdalen Bridge, the oldest one in England, was founded as a physic garden in 1621 by Henry Danvers, Earl of Danby. He had intended to appoint John Tradescant the Elder as keeper, but for some reason he never took up the post, which was given to the German Jacob Bobart. Bobart's son had a sense of fun—he once converted a dead rat into a 'dragon', making alterations to its head and tail and distending the skin with tiny sticks to resemble wings, then letting the creature dry hard. His masterpiece was at first pronounced genuine, and, after the fraud was discovered, it was deposited in the Anatomy School. The garden was founded as a physic garden for growing medicinal herbs—in 1675 over three thousand species were cultivated. It was enclosed by high walls, and the beds were laid out in a formal pattern. In the eighteenth century the garden was divided into four square plots by yew hedges. The statues of Charles I and Charles II in niches were paid for out of a fine extorted from Anthony Wood for his libel on the Earl of Clarendon. The garden deteriorated and was revived by Charles Daubeny, Professor of Botany, who rebuilt the glasshouse, erected a laboratory and improved the collection. It has a wide variety of flowers and plants including hardy ones, a pinetum, herbaceous plants, a salicetum, an experimental garden, greenhouse and stove plants, dried collections and, of course, a medical garden.

In 1975 the County Council opened the Museum of Oxford in St Aldate's, as a branch of the Oxfordshire County Museum, illustrating the history of the town and the university, in a way not done in the university museums, which have far wider canvases. Now, for the first time, the visitor can glean an overall view of the town's development from its geological structure to its Roman kilns and on to Morris Motors, or compare a nineteenth-century Jericho kitchen with a more highbrow North Oxford drawing-room and see the sort of accommodation a student would have had in the eighteenth century. Children flock in to enjoy educational activities, and changing exhibitions reflect aspects of Oxfordshire not permanently on display.

The university provided a living for many townsmen—during the Middle Ages particularly, the making of paper and parchment flourished locally, and Oxford still has a paper-mill at Wolvercote. The students and their masters needed to eat, they required academic gowns and, when the number outgrew the college accommodation, they required lodgings. *The Adventures of Mr Verdant Green* written by 'Cuthbert Bede' (Edward Bradley) in 1854 satirically described how an unsuspecting young scholar was taken advantage of by such people. His scout, Mr Robert Filcher, knew exactly how to use his students: "There was cunning enough in his face to fill even a century of wily years; and there was a depth of expression in his look as he asked our hero if *he* was Mr Verdant Green, that proclaimed his custom of reading a freshman at a glance."[1] A scout's duties were arduous during term time—at 6 a.m. he raked out and lit the fires in the eight or so sets of rooms under his control, laid the tables for breakfast, brought hot water for washing and shaving, washed the breakfast things, emptied the slops and took orders for lunch. He might have time to go home for an hour or so before laying the tables for lunch at 12.30; then, when the students had eaten, their lunches required clearing. After that, the afternoon was his own until 5 p.m. when he cleared the tea-things (the students collected their own teas), replenished the coal-scuttles and waited at table in Hall at dinner, after which he could go home. The vacation was a financially bleak period, as he was paid only during term time, so many scouts left their families during the long vacations to seek work as waiters in holiday resorts. Some augmented their meagre earnings by keeping lodging-houses.

Mr Verdant Green was accompanied to his tailor's by his proud but inexperienced father:

> There were so many persons purporting to be 'Academical robe-makers', that Mr Green was some little time in deciding who should be the tradesman favoured with the order for his son's adornment. At last he fixed upon a shop, the window of which contained a more imposing display than its neighbours of gowns, hoods, surplices, and robes of all shapes and colours, from the black velvet-sleeved proctor's to the blushing gorgeousness of the scarlet robe and crimson sleeves of the DCL.
>
> "I wish you," said Mr Green, advancing towards a smirking individual, who was in his shirt-sleeves and slippers, but in all other respects was attired with great magnificence—"I wish you to measure this gentlemen for his academical robes, and also allow him the use of some to be matriculated in."
>
> "Certainly, sir," said the robe-maker, who said bowing and smirking before them—as Hood expressively says,
>
> "Washing his hands with invisible soap, In imperceptible water:"
>
> "Certainly sir, if you wish it; but it will scarcely be necessary, sir; as our custom is so extensive, that we keep a large ready-made stock constantly on hand."[2]

The tailor subtly humiliated his customers by letting Verdant Green try on a scholar's robe, which his father was about to purchase when it was discovered that he had not won a scholarship and was thus a commoner not a scholar—an important distinction—as he was entitled only to a short commoner's gown.

Tailoring still flourishes, and many current firms such as Shepherd & Woodward, Castell & Son and until recently G. E. Taylor's have a long history. Castells began trading in 1846 and specialize in club colours and academic robes. Shepherd & Woodward have operated under several variants of the names, and the Woodward side of the business used to make academic caps. Many people were unable to afford such high-quality items and instead relied on such businesses as Jackson & Company who ran 'The People's Cash Clothing and Boot Stores' in Castle Street in the 1880s and 1890s. Undergraduates' dress has changed according to the fashions of the day—blue jeans provide a modern 'uniform', but academic gowns are still obligatory on formal occasions and for examinations.

Retailers geared their wares to attract the undergraduates—our naïve Verdant Green was an easy prey. He visited Spier's, a noted nineteenth-century manufacturer of fancy goods, whose wares were exhibited in the Great Exhibition of 1851:

> Mr Verdant Green was soon deeply engaged in an inspection of those *papier-maché* 'remembrances of Oxford' for which the Messrs Spiers are so justly famed; but after turning over tables, trays, screens, desks, albums, portfolios, and other things—all of which displayed views of Oxford from every variety of aspect . . . Charles Larkyns . . . proposed to Verdant that he should astonish and delight his governor by having the Green arms emblazoned on a fire-screen . . . [3]

Nineteenth-century advertisements reveal the large number of victuallers. Undergraduates and townsmen regaled themselves with delicacies from Alfred Boffin, the University and City Baker, cook, confectioner, bread and biscuit maker, or procured their Royal Oxford Sausages from John Wiblin of St Giles Street, and their tea, coffee and chocolate from C. Shillingford of Cornmarket Street, Drink was not neglected—one wine and spirit merchant, William Mayo, in the 1870s sold 'family ales' brewed at the City Brewery, as well as such brands as Guinness, Dublin Stout, Scotch Ales from William Younger & Co, and wines and spirits. Tobacconists too plied an extensive trade—in the 1880s Joseph Carter of Cornmarket Street proudly proclaimed himself as an importer of Havannah cigars, tobaccos, foreign fancy snuffs etc, while J. Ambler of Turl Street combined tobacco-selling with being a sports outfitter.

Booksellers, too, were vitally important to the university—in the nineteenth century Henry Slatter in the High Street combined book selling with stationery and printing. Booksellers such as Blackwell's and Parker's are now concentrated around the area of the Bodleian Library.

Despite the importance of university custom, the loss of which during the vacations was much lamented, the shops also catered for the town. Medieval shops tended to congregate in groups largely around Cornmarket Street and the High Street—the fishmongers in Fish Street, the butchers in Slaying Lane, the drapers in Drapery Lane and so on.

A row of much-altered late fourteenth-century shops remains in Cornmarket Street on the corner of Ship Street, with jettied upper storeys and timber framing. The covered market was constructed in 1772–4, with space inside it for forty butchers' shops, separated by an avenue from a smaller block containing poultry-shops. A roofed area covered fishboards, a butter-bench, a market house and a couple of other shops. A further avenue was added in 1838–9. The Victorian period witnessed growth and diversification in retail trading. Oxford was still a town of individual shops. The department store Elliston & Cavell's (now part of the Debenham Group), which opened in 1823, began as a draper's, extending its range to clothes and furniture. Minty's, the cabinet-makers, was founded in 1886, with stores in the High Street and St Clements. By 1939 they were one of the larger employers, with 150 staff, comprising a quarter of all Oxford cabinet-makers. The Minty factory was moved to Horspath in 1965.

The poorer area of St Ebbes was served by a wide variety of shops with names indicating the type of customer— Co-operative Stores and The People's Cash Clothing and Boot Stores. Many people still remember Webber's and the neighbouring City Drapers' Stores, sporting the initials 'SPQR'— 'Small Profits, Quick Returns'. Perhaps the most well-known shop of this type was F. Cape & Co, founded as a small shop by Faithful Cape in the late 1860s; he enlarged it into a thriving department store. After 1914 business expanded to include ready-made clothes, household goods and furniture, wholesale as well as retail business. An important side of the trade was that conducted with the local carriers, which continued until the 1930s. Cape's network thus stretched as far as Kingston Bagpuize, Fifield, Ickford and Woodstock. 120 people were employed in 1907, sixty-three at the main St Ebbes shop, twenty-four in Cowley Road and ten in Walton Street, plus carpenters, domestic servants, porters, drivers and bicycle messengers. Forty-seven of the more experienced and better-paid employees lived on the premises. They led quite a restricted life, having to obtain written permission to sleep a night away. The young men living in started at 7.45 a.m., when they uncovered the counters, put display goods in the doorways and dusted and swept the shop. At 8.30 the senior male assistants came down, followed at 9 a.m. by the females. The shop closed at 8 p.m., or 10 p.m. on Saturdays. If an assistant failed to induce a customer to buy, the shopwalker had to be called to make a further attempt. Until the Second World War the female assistants wore black dresses, stockings and shoes, the more senior wearing silk or satin. The men had dark suits with black jackets and pin-stripe trousers, the more senior of them morning dress. All were expected to provide their own clothes. The management was concerned for staff welfare, providing swimming, football and cricket clubs and organizing annual outings, stocktaking parties, dances and recitals.

The loss of Cape's, which closed in 1972, epitomizes the changes that have taken place in Oxford shops. Queen Street was almost entirely rebuilt in the ninetenth century to become a shopping-street, and Marks & Spencers established a branch in Oxford in the 1930s, but the major changes have come since the 1950s, when chain stores began to take over the smaller establishments, particularly in Cornmarket Street and Queen Street. In 1963 Grimbly Hughes, the high-class grocery store, was replaced by a branch of Littlewood's, and now the shopping is dominated by chain stores—Selfridge's, Debenham's, Fenwick's, Peter Robinson, C & A, Freeman Hardy & Willis, Sainsbury and so on. Major banks dominate Carfax, and the smaller individual shops have disappeared, and with them the individual flavour of Oxford shopping. Areas such as Little Clarendon Street have shops with slightly more flavour, selling trendy clothes for students, with a more 'crafty' atmosphere, while the better-heeled buy their dresses at Campus in the High Street, for designer labels, or Anna Belinda for an individual and exclusive style.

Fairs provided a further outlet for selling as well as a favourite recreation for the working classes. The most famous Oxford fair is St Giles, surprisingly the most recent, originating in a local wake, which in the early nineteenth century became a small pleasure fair, with bustling stalls selling gingerbread and toys, and plenty of drinking-booths. It took place in September, after the harvest, so many agricultural labourers flocked to Oxford to enjoy themselves. *Jackson's Oxford Journal* described the showy tinsel toys and the "baskets, glass and china ornaments, cheap tools, sweets, gingerbreads, cakes, etc, while there were scores of barrows on which were fruit, mostly apparently of a wholesome description, coconuts, hedge nuts, cheap jewellery, photographs, ices, canaries, and other cage birds, braces, gilding fluid, potato peelers, name stamps and other things too numerous to mention".[4] The Great Western Railway ran special excursion trains from Birmingham to see the mermaids, boa constrictors, African lions, menageries, roundabouts, flying-boats, switchbacks and shooting-galleries. Local manufacturers such as Cape's took the opportunity to display their wares, and new mechanical inventions, such as Norton's Patent Incubator, were displayed. The fair still takes over St Giles each September.

It is ironic that the Playhouse Theatre in Beaumont Street now often has undergraduate drama productions and has a theatre workshop, whereas in the sixteenth century the university prohibited common players within the town, as being a bad influence on undergraduates. The present Playhouse Theatre opened in 1938 and has recently received considerable financial help from Richard Burton and Elizabeth Taylor. It still maintains its own repertory company and has pre-London runs and visiting companies. Many visiting companies acted in Oxford, but it was not until 1823 that the New Theatre opened—previously plays were acted in tennis-courts, the town hall and inn yards. Four theatres have stood on the site of the New Theatre, which in its fourth metamorphosis became a large provincial theatre capable of showing opera and ballet.

The town has changed drastically in character—in 1771 the Paving Commissioners were set up and transformed the town by paving roads and so on. They, and the Board of Guardians set up at the same time, began the trend of shifting power away from the university towards the town. Town life was controlled by an élite of prosperous townsmen—brewers, bankers, lawyers, clothiers, newspaper-proprietors and so on. The town's population doubled twice during the nineteenth century, and new buildings sprang up everywhere—a new County Hall was built in 1841. The Town Hall opened in 1851, and Sir Gilbert Scott designed the Martyrs' Memorial for St Giles. The Ashmolean and Taylorian dominated the newly laid-out Beaumont Street, and much of the High Street and Queen Street was rebuilt. The pressure of population was so great that areas outside the central parishes of Oxford and the villages around were caught in the web of the town, losing their separate identities. The 1869 boundary-changes brought Cowley, Headington, Marston, Iffley, Wolvercote and North and South Hinksey within the city. Suburbs grew around new sources of work such as the Friars' area of St Ebbes round the gas-works, Jericho around the new site of the University Press. It is ironic that the red-and-blue-brick workers' cottages in Jericho are now trendy homes beyond the reach of the working classes. Colleges such as St John's released much land in North Oxford for building, so St John's Street was built in the 1840s, and speculators built Park Town a decade later. Earlier houses were built in isolated positions as 'country houses' for professors (who were exempt from university celibacy regulations), for rich tradesmen, municipal worthies and wealthy teaching clergy. The layout and several buildings were designed by William Wilkinson in an enthusiastic Gothic style. Speculative builders also built homes for labourers, as in the Kingston Road area, where printers, tailors, municipal workers, college servants, masons and victuallers lived. After the university dons were permitted to marry in 1887, North Oxford became a popular residential area, but it had already been substantially developed.

The development of Summertown began in 1820 with the sale of some freehold land, bought by George Kimber and Crews Dudley, speculative builders. In the next twelve years 125 houses were built to house 562 people. Some were low-quality tenements, on the east side of the Woodstock Road, and many Summertown inhabitants were labourers, including chairmakers Stephen Hazell, Thomas Slater and William Wardell, clay-pipe makers, laundry workers, small craftsmen and agricultural labourers. Better-quality houses were built for wealthy men such as Mr Grimbly of Grimbly Hughes. Summertown established itself as a community, with a parish church, built in 1830, and a Dissenters' meeting-house. St Edward's School moved from New Inn Hall Street, catering for five hundred boys, and numbers among its past pupils author Kenneth Grahame, the pilot Douglas Bader and the actor Laurence Olivier. Oliver and Gurden, chefs from Keble College, in 1919 took over a disused bakery in Middle Way, where they made Oxford cakes until 1975, the products being sold under the brand names of Scribona, Kunzle, Kemp and Fuller's. Radio Oxford broadcasts to the county from Summertown, providing a valuable service in involving the community, and Oxfam has its headquarters there.

The villages adjoining Oxford have now become suburbs. Headington was gradually infiltrated by wealthy families who wanted to live near, but not in, Oxford, so it had patrons to finance local clubs and organizations, and in 1929 Headington became part of Oxford City. Tucked away one can still find the old seventeenth century stone cottages which formed the nucleus of the original village.

Headington Quarry was an illegal settlement on the fringes of Shotover Forest until disafforestation in 1662, and this formed the keynote of its character—as an open village, with no landowner exercising a controlling influence. Many inhabitants were stone-quarriers, brickmakers and agricultural labourers, and a number of them built their own cottages. Women took in college laundry to augment the family incomes, as quarrying and brickmaking particularly depended on good weather and were seasonal occupations. Headington stone was used to build New College, Merton College, Oriel, Magdalen and many others. Headington Quarry morris team has existed almost without a break for hundreds of years and was the first team seen by Cecil Sharp, which gave him such enthusiasm for morris dancing that he spent many years studying it and writing about it.

Nearby Iffley is more sedate, with its exquisite Norman church, with elaborate late twelfth-century sculptured doorways. The village still retains its rural character, with its school in a thatched barn, despite the proximity of the Oxford ring road. Mrs Graham Greene has her charming dolls' house museum here, in a specially built rotunda—it is not a museum for children but offers endless fascination for adults and illustrates domestic history in miniature.

Cowley was once two villages—Temple Cowley and Cowley St John, and amidst the modern housing estates one can find the occasional thatched cottage. The Knights Templar had a medieval hospital in Temple Cowley in the Middle Ages, and it was in Temple Cowley that William Morris established Morris Motors. Cowley is now dominated by and synonymous with BL and built up with housing-estates for those working there.

Marston is clearly divided into 'Old' and 'New', the older village retaining its mellow stone buildings and its bell-ringers, the new section overlooked by the new John Radcliffe Hospital which dominates the skyline.

Wolvercote is a mixture of industry, with its paper-mill, and rural charm, with the Trout Inn by the river bank, where one can sit and drink on a summer's evening, listening to the raucous cries of the peacocks. Nearby are the ruins of Godstow Abbey.

The university has not stood still—it, as well as the town, has adapted to suit the modern world. Dons can now marry; women have penetrated many colleges—and men have been allowed to infiltrate women's colleges. Recent trends have favoured the foundation of graduate colleges—William Morris's Nuffield College for the social services, St Antony's for recent history, St Cross and Linacre. Sir Isaac Wolfson founded the college named after him (originally Iffley College) again for graduates, which in 1968 moved into its present fine buildings on the river bank in North Oxford, designed by Powell and Moya. St Catherine's College, which opened in 1964, is a masterpiece of modern architecture, designed by the Dane Arne Jacobsen as a complete entity—Jacobsen even created the furniture and cutlery. Undergraduate colleges created this century are, in addition to St Catherine's, St Edmund Hall and St Peter's. St Anne's became a college in 1952, having started as the Society of Oxford Home Students in 1879, and St Hugh's Hall, founded in 1886, achieved full college status in 1959. The most recent is Green College, specializing in medicine.

A slight question-mark hangs over the future of Oxford—with petrol increasingly rare and expensive (although the congested traffic clogging Oxford's streets seems to belie this), the future of the motor-industry is in doubt, and Oxford's prosperity depends to a frighteningly large extent on the fate of British Leyland. Perhaps the university will once again reign supreme.

References

CHAPTER 1

1. Quoted in James Dyer, *Southern England. An Archaeological Guide* (Faber, 1973), p.17.
2. Quoted in L. V. Grinsell, *Folklore of Prehistoric Sites in Britain* (David & Charles, 1971) pp.146–8.

CHAPTER 2

1. Flora Thompson, *Lark Rise to Candleford* (Penguin edition, 1973), p.79.
2. Thomas Banting, *Notes of Thomas Banting of Filkins* (Bodleian Library MS Top. Oxon, c.220, pos. 65r 96r, 1887).
3. Thomas Hughes quoted in Nancy Stebbing, *Vale of White Horse; Land and People* (Oxfordshire County Museum, 1977), p.26.
4. Alfred Beesley, *History of Banbury* (London, 1841), p.568.
5. Clare Sewell Read, *On the Farming of Oxfordshire* (London, 1854), p.289.
6. J. B. Spearing, 'On the Agriculture of Berkshire' (*Journal of the Royal Agricultural Society of England,* volume XXI, part i, no. lxiv, 1860), p.17.

CHAPTER 3

1. R. Plot, *The Natural History of Oxfordshire* (2nd edition, Oxford, 1705) pp.283–4.
2. *Op. cit.,* p.284.
3. Alfred Plummer and Richard E. Early, *The Blanket Makers* (Routledge and Kegan Paul, 1969) p.25.
4. J. S. Burn, *History of Henley* (1861) p.64.
5. R. Plot, *Natural History of Oxfordshire* (1677) p.265.
6. Ben Jonson, *Bartholomew Fair,* 1614.
7. William Potts, *A History of Banbury* (Gulliver Press, 1978) p.160.
8. H. Taunt, *Oxford and Its Historical Traditions* (1905) p.13.
9. H. Carter, *Wolvercote Mill* (Clarendon Press, 1957) p.9; quotation from memorandum by J. H. Lacey, manager 10th July 1876.

CHAPTER 4

1. Lewis Carroll, *Alice in Wonderland* (Macmillan edition, 1975), p.9.
2. H. R. Robertson, *Life on the Upper Thames* (London, 1875), pp.2–3.
3. Charles Dickens, *Dickens's Dictionary of the Thames* (Macmillan, 1888), p.18.
4. Mary Prior, *Fisher Row: Fishermen, Bargemen and Canal Boatmen in Oxford, 1500–1900* (Oxford University Press, forthcoming).
5. Red Quill (James Englefield), *The Delightful Life of Pleasure on the Thames* (Horace Cox, London, 1912), p.4.
6. H. R. Robertson, *op. cit.*, p.24.
7. Rev. W. E. Sherwood, *Oxford Rowing* (Henry Froude, Oxford, 1900), p.2.
8. *Ibid.*, pp. 60–61.
9. George Bernard Shaw, *Saturday Review* (1898) quoted in Jan Morris, ed., *The Oxford Book of Oxford* (Oxford University Press, 1978), p.268.
10. Max Beerbohm, *Zuleika Dobson* (Penguin edition, 1967), p.78.
11. *Punch*, quoted in R. R. Bolland, *Victorians on the Thames* (Midas Books, 1974), p.6.
12. *Lock to Lock Times* (1888), quoted in R. R. Bolland, *op. cit.*, p.74.
13. Charles Dickens, *op. cit.*, p.237
14. Jerome K. Jerome, *Three Men in a Boat* (Penguin edition, 1978), p.173.
15. H. R. Robertson, *op. cit.*, pp.110–11.
16. L. T. C. Rolt, *Narrow Boat* (Eyre & Spottiswoode, 1945), p.25.
17. Thomas Ward Boss, *Reminiscences of Old Banbury* (William Potts, Banbury, 1903), p.8.
18. *Ibid.*, p.4.
19. William Tucknell, *Reminiscences of Oxford* (1900) quoted in Jan Morris, *op. cit.*, pp.20–21.
20. Edward Thomas, *Collected Poems* (Faber & Faber, 1979), p.66.
21. Richard Lingard, *Princes Risborough, Thame-Oxford Railway* (Oxford Publishing Company, 1978), pp.9–10.

CHAPTER 5

1. John Kibble, *Historical & Other Notes on Wychwood Forest* (Charlbury, 1928), p.7.
2. Quoted in J. Charles Cox, *The Royal Forests of England* (London, 1905), p.257.
3. C. Belcher, 'On the Reclaiming of Waste Lands as Instanced by Wichwood Forest' (*Journal of the Royal Agricultural Society of England*, volume XXIV, part ii, no li, 1863), pp.274–5.
4. Lewis Carroll, *Alice Through the Looking-Glass* (Macmillan edition, 1918), p.165.

5. C. E. Prior, 'Otmoor' (*Transaction of Oxford Archaeological Society*, Banbury, 1900), p.7.
6. Alexander Croke, *The Case of Otmoor* (Oxford, 1831), p.21.
7. C. E. Prior, *op. cit.*, p.7.
8. PRO HO/52/9, Rev. T. L. Cooke's account of the disturbances.
9. *Jackson's Oxford Journal* (11th September 1830).
10. Oxfordshire Archaeological Society Reports for 1903 (Banbury, 1904), pp.22–3.

CHAPTER 6

1. Flora Thompson, *op. cit.*, pp.47–8.
2. Penelope Jessel and Edith Stedman, *These Notable Things: 800 Years of Dorchester Abbey* (Dorchester, n.d.), p.7, quotation from the Visitation of 1445.
3. Nigel Hammond, *The White Horse Country* (Reading, 1972), p.70.
4. 'Arcadia Realised', *Daily News* (25th September 1891).

CHAPTER 7

1. Celia Fiennes quoted in J. S. W. Gibson, 'Travellers' Tales (*Cake and Cockhorse*, volume V, no. 7, autumn 1973), p.131.
2. John Byng quoted in J. S. W. Gibson, *op. cit.* (no. 8, spring 1974), p.152.
3. Leland quoted in T. Camoys, *Stonor—The Stonor Family House for at least 8 Centuries* (1979), p.13.
4. Mary Russell Mitford, *Recollections of a Literary Life* (1851) quoted in *Greys Court* (National Trust, 1980), p.5.
5. Robert Gittings, *This Tower My Prison* quoted in Greys Court, *op. cit.*, p.14.
6. R. Plot, *National History of Oxfordshire* (London, 1705) pp.271–2.
7. Alexander Pope quoted in Jennifer Sherwood and Nikolaus Pevsner, *The Buildings of England: Oxfordshire* (Penguin Books, 1974), p.783.
8. William Morris quoted in A. R. Dufty, 'William Morris and the Kelmscott Estate' (*The Antiquaries' Journal*, volume XLIII, part i, 1963), p.105.
9. Celia Fiennes quoted in J. S. W. Gibson, *op. cit.* (1973), p.133.
10. Horace Walpole quoted in J. S. W. Gibson, *op. cit.* (1974), pp. 143–4.
11. Quoted in J. S. W. Gibson, *op. cit.*, (1974), p.148.
12. Alexander Pope in Margaret Tims (ed.), *Poet's England, I, Buckinghamshire, Berkshire & Oxfordshire* (Brentham Press, London, n.d.).
13. Sarah Churchill quoted in David Green, *Blenheim Palace* (Country Life, 1951), p.163.

14. Salmon's *County and University of Oxford 1748* quoted in David Green, *op. cit.*, p.241.
15. Horace Walpole quoted in J. S. W. Gibson, *op. cit.* (1974), p.148.
16. Lady Harcourt quoted in Dorothy Stroud, *Capability Brown* (Faber & Faber, 1975), p.190.
17. Quoted in Mavis L. Batey, *Nuneham Courtenay, Oxfordshire* (University of Oxford, 1979), p.6.
18. *Ibid.*, p.11.
19. Quoted in Mavis L. Batey, *Four Aspects of Nuneham* (CPRE, 1975), p.5.

CHAPTER 8
1. Mary Vane Turner, *The Story of Deddington* (Brackley, 1937), p.63.
2. A. Ballard, *Chronicles of the Royal Borough of Woodstock* (1896), p.8.
3. Cooper's *Life and Letters of Ar. Stuart* (London, 1866), volume I, p.87, quoted in Edward Marshall, *The Early History of Woodstock Manor and its Environs* (Oxford, 1873), p.169.
4. *A Guide to Henley upon Thames and its Vicinity* (Hickman & Kinch, London, 1838).
5. Celia Fiennes. *The Journal of Celia Fiennes* (Cresset Press edition), pp.38–9, p.337.
6. Quoted in Rev. P. J. Goodrich, *Great Faringdon Past and Present* (Oxford, 1928), p.49.

CHAPTER 9
1. Edward Bradley (Cuthbert Bede), *The Adventures of Mr Verdant Green* (London, 1854), p.30.
2. *Ibid.*, p.38.
3. *Ibid.*, p.91.
4. *Jackson's Oxford Journal* (10th September 1887).

Select Bibliography

Sally Alexander, *St Giles' Fair 1830–1914* (1970).

K. J. Allison, M. W. Beresford and J. G. Hurst, *The Deserted Villages of Oxfordshire* (1965).

J. R. L. Anderson, *The Upper Thames* (1970).

W. J. Arkell, *Oxford Stone* (1947).

Michael Aston and James Bond, *The Landscape of Towns* (1976).

J. H. Baker, *The Story of the Chiltern Heathlands* (1932).

Dacre Balsdon, *Oxford Now and Then* (1970).

Mavis Batey, *Nuneham Courtenay, Oxon.* (1970).

R. P. Beckinsale, *Companion into Berkshire* (1951).

Don Benson, D. Miles, C. J. Balkiwell and N. Clayton, *The Upper Thames Valley: An Archaeological Survey of the River Gravels* (1974).

Christine Bloxham, *The Book of Banbury* (1975).

R. R. Bolland, *Victorians on the Thames* (1974).

Edward Bradley (Cuthbert Bede), *The Adventures of Mr Verdant Green* (1854).

Cake and Cockhorse—the magazine of the Banbury Historical Society

John Campbell, *The Bones of the Region: Some Oxfordshire Rocks and their Uses* (1979).

John Campbell, *The Making of the Rocks: An Introduction to Oxfordshire Geology* (1979).

John Campbell, *The Ice Age in Oxfordshire: The Quaternary Period* (1979).

Ethel Carleton Williams, *Companion into Oxfordshire* (1944).

Hal Cheetham, *Portrait of Oxford* (1971).

Gerald Clarke, *The Book of Thame* (1978).

Alan Clutton-Brock, *Chastleton House* (n.d.).

H. M. Colvin, *A History of Deddington* (1963).

Elsie Corbett, *History of Spelsbury* (1962).

Mieneke Cox, *Abingdon: Abbey to Borough* (1974).

Judy and Stuart Dewey, *The Book of Wallingford* (1977).
Charles Dickens, *Dickens's Dictionary of the Thames* (1888).
P. H. Ditchfield, *Byways in Berkshire and the Cotswolds* (1921).
Alan Diwell and Bob Smith, *Real Ale in Oxfordshire* (1979).
A. R. Dufty, *Kelmscott—an illustrated guide* (1969).
James Dyer, *Southern England: An Archaeological Guide* (1973).

Frank Emery, *The Oxfordshire Landscape* (1974).

Ruth Fasnacht, *Summertown since 1820* (1977).
Edward Llewelyn French, *Goring* (1978).
Josceline Finberg, *The Cotswolds* (1977).
Richard Foster, *F. Cape & Co* (1973).

Rev. P. J. Goodrich, *Great Faringdon Past and Present* (1928).
Sarah Gosling, *Banbury and the Cherwell Valley* (1978).
David Green, *Blenheim Palace* (1951).

Charles Hadfield, *The Canals of the East Midlands* (1966).
Charles Hadfield, *The Canals of South and South-Eastern England*
    (1967).
Nigel Hammond, *The Book of Abingdon* (1979).
Nigel Hammond, *White Horse Country* (1972).
Nigel Hammond, *Rural Life in the Vale of the White Horse* (1974).
M. A. Havinden, *Estate Villages* (1966).
M. G. Hobson and K. L. H. Price, *Otmoor and its Seven Towns* (1961).

Mary Jessup, A History of Oxfordshire (1975).

John Kibble, *Historical and Other Notes on Wychwood Forest* (1928).
John Kibble, *Charming Charlbury* (1930).

Keith Lawrence, *Drove Roads in Oxfordshire* (1977).
Keith Lawrence, *Milestones of Oxfordshire* (1977).
Keith Lawrence, *Tollhouses of Oxfordshire* (1977).

Felix Markham, *Oxford* (1967).
Edward Marshall, *The Early History of Woodstock Manor and its
    Environs* (1873).
H. J. Massingham, *Chiltern Country* (1943).
Jan Morris, *Oxford* (1965).
Jan Morris, ed., *The Oxford Book of Oxford* (1978).

Peter Northeast, *This Venerable Village* (1975).

John Orr, *Agriculture in Oxfordshire* (1916).

Harold Peake, *The Archaeology of Berkshire* (1976).

Nikolaus Pevsner, *The Buildings of England: Berkshire* (1966).

David Piper, *The Treasures of Oxford* (1977).

Robert Plot, *The Natural History of Oxfordshire* (1677).

Alfred Plummer and Richard E. Early, *The Blanket-Makers* (1969).

William Potts, *A History of Banbury* (1978).

Mary Prior, *Fisher Row: Fishermen, Bargemen and Canal Boatmen in Oxford, 1500–1600* (forthcoming).

M. Prister-Crudwell, *Ewelme: Its History and its People* (1976).

Mari Pritchard and Humphrey Carpenter, *A Thames Companion* (1975).

Bernard Reaney, *The Class Struggle in 19th-Century Oxfordshire* (1970).

John Rhodes, *Oxfordshire—A County and its People* (1980).

Julia C. Richards, *The Archaeology of the Berkshire Downs* (1978).

H. R. Robertson, *Life on the Upper Thames* (1875).

Kirsty Rodwell, ed., *Historic Towns in Oxfordshire* (1975).

R. P. P. Rowe, C. M. Pitman and P. W. Squire, *The Badminton Library: Rowing/Punting* (1898).

Raphael Samuel, *Village Life and Labour* (1975).

Jennifer Sherwood and Nikolaus Pevsner, *The Buildings of England: Oxfordshire* (1974).

Rev. W. E. Sherwood, *Oxford Rowing* (1900).

John M. Steane, ed., *Cogges* (1980).

Nancy Stebbing, *The Vale of White Horse: Land and People* (1979).

Dorothy Stroud, *Capability Brown* (1950).

M. Sturge Gretton, *Burford Past and Present* (1920).

Flora Thompson, *Lark Rise to Candleford* (1939).

Margaret Tims, *Poets' England I: Berks, Bucks and Oxon* (n.d.).

G. H. J. Tomalin, *The Book of Henley-on-Thames* (1975).

Mary Vane Turner, *The Story of Deddington* (1933).

Michael Turner and David Vaisey, *Oxford Shops and Shopping* (1972).

Victoria County History of Berkshire.

Victoria County History of Oxfordshire.

Martin Welch, *The Tradescants and the Foundation of the Ashmolean Museum* (1978).

R. B. Wood-Jones, *Traditional Domestic Architecture in the Banbury Region* (1963).

Diane Woolner, *The White Horse, Uffington,* (Newbury and District Field Club, volume XI, no.3), (1965).

Arthur Young, *A General View of the Agriculture of Oxfordshire* (1813).

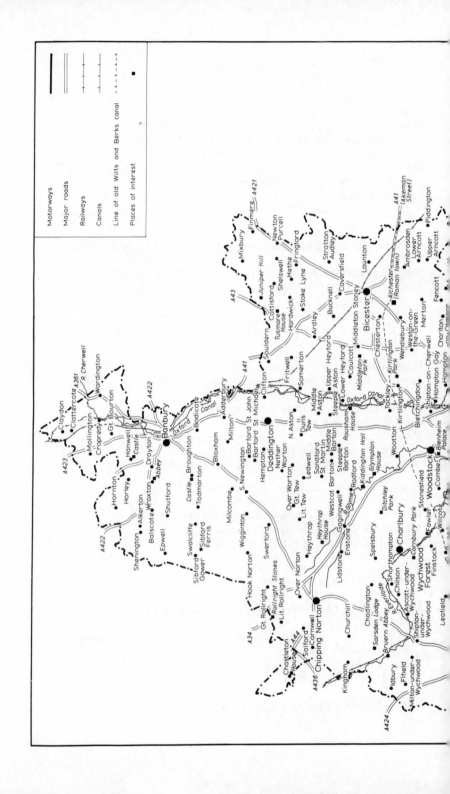

Motorways

Major roads

Railways

Canals

Line of old Wilts and Berks canal

Places of interest

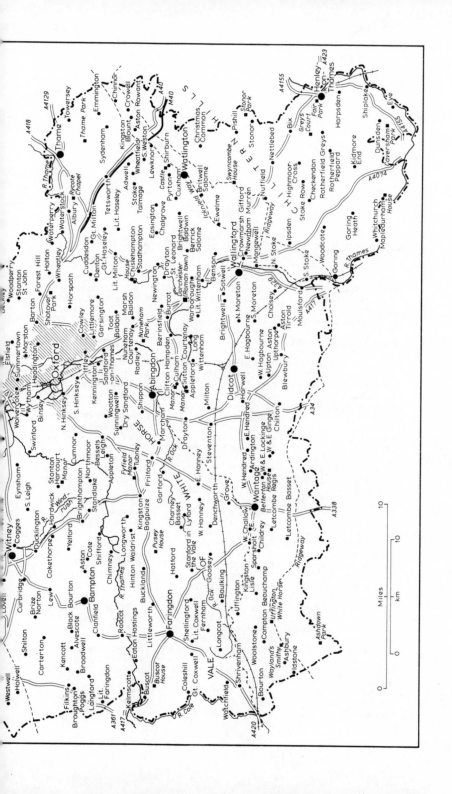

Index